Alone in West Africa

Mary Gaunt

Alpha Editions

This edition published in 2024

ISBN : 9789366388564

Design and Setting By
Alpha Editions
www.alphaedis.com
Email - info@alphaedis.com

As per information held with us this book is in Public Domain.
This book is a reproduction of an important historical work. Alpha Editions uses the best technology to reproduce historical work in the same manner it was first published to preserve its original nature. Any marks or number seen are left intentionally to preserve its true form.

CHAPTER I
SONS OF THE SEA WIFE

Hereditary taste for wandering—A first adventure—"Little girls you must not be tired"—How Carlo was captured by savages in West Africa—Life in Ballarat—Nothing for a woman to do but marry—Marriage—Plans for wandering twenty years hence—Life in Warrnambool—Widowhood—May as well travel now there is nothing left—London for an aspirant in literature—Stony streets and drizzling rain—Scanty purse—Visit to the home of a rich African trader—Small successes—At last, at last on board s.s. Gando bound for the Gambia.

"There dwells a wife by the Northern Gate,

And a wealthy wife is she;

She breeds a breed o' rovin' men,

And casts them over sea."

Sometimes when people ask me with wonder why I went to West Africa, why I wanted to go, I feel as if that wife must have grown old and feeble and will bear no more men to send across the sea. I hope not. I trust not. More than ninety years ago she sent my mother's father into the Honourable East India Co.'s service, and then, in later years with his ten children to colonise Van Diemen's Land. Nearly sixty years ago she sent my father, a slim young lad, out to the goldfields in Australia, and she breathed her spirit over the five boys and two girls who grew up in the new land. I cannot remember when any one of us would not have gone anywhere in the world at a moment's notice. It would not have been any good pointing out the dangers, because dangers at a distance are only an incentive. There is something in the thought of danger that must be overcome, that you yourself can help to overcome, that quickens the blood and gives an added zest to life.

I can remember as a small girl going with my sister to stay with an uncle who had a station, Mannerim, behind Geelong. The house had been built in the old days of slabs with a bark roof, very inflammable material. I loved the place then because it spoke of the strenuous old days of the Colony. I love the memory of it now for old times' sake, and because there happened the first really exciting incident in my life.

It was a January morning, the sky overcast with smoke and a furious hot wind blowing from the north. The men of the household looked out anxiously, but I sat and read a story-book. It was the tale of a boy named Carlo who was wrecked on the coast of West Africa—nice vague location; he climbed a cocoa-nut tree—I can see him now with a rope round his waist and his legs dangling in an impossible attitude—and he was taken by savages. His further adventures I do not know, because a man came riding in shouting that the calf paddock was on fire and everyone must turn out. Everyone did turn out except my aunt who stayed behind to prepare cool drinks, and those drinks my little sister and I, as being useless for beating out the flames, were sent to carry to the workers in jugs and "billies."

"Now little girls," said my aunt who was tenderness and kindness itself, "remember you are not to get tired."

It was the first lesson I really remember in the stern realities of life. We had hailed the bushfire as something new and exciting; now we were to be taught that much excitement brings its strenuous hard labour. The fire did not reach the house, and the men and women got their drink, but it was two very weary, dirty, smoke-grimed and triumphant little girls who bathed and went to bed that night. I never finished the story of Carlo. Where he went to I can't imagine, but I can't think the savages ate him else his story would never have been written; and from that moment dated my deep interest in West Africa.

We grew up and the boys of the family went a-roving to other lands. One was a soldier, two were sailors, and the two youngest were going to be lawyers, whereby they might make money and go to the other ends of the world if they liked. When we were young we generally regarded money as a means of locomotion. We have hardly got over the habit yet. Only for us two girls was there no prospect. Our world was bounded by our father's lawns and the young men who came to see us and made up picnic parties to the wildest bush round Ballarat for our amusement. It was not bad. Even now I acknowledge to something of delight to be found in a box-seat of a four-in-hand, a glorious moonlight night, and four horses going at full speed; something delightful in scrambles over the ranges and a luncheon in the shade by a waterhole, with romantic stories for a seasoning, and the right man with a certain admiration in his eyes to listen. It was not bad, but it was not as good a life as the boys of the family were having, and it was giving me no chance of visiting the land Carlo had gone to that had been in my mind at intervals ever since the days of my childish bushfire.

There was really nothing for a woman but to marry, and accordingly we both married and I forgot in my entrance into that world, which is so old and yet always so new, my vague longings after savage lands.

I wonder sometimes would I have been contented to lead the ordinary woman's life, the life of the woman who looks after her husband and children. I think so, because it grew to be the life I ardently yearned for. The wander desire was just pushed a little into the back-ground and was to come off twenty years hence when we had made our fortune. And twenty years looked such a long long while then. It even looks a long time now, for it has not passed, and I seem to have lived a hundred years and many lives since the days in the little Victorian town of Warrnambool when my handsome young husband and I planned out our future life. But I was nearer to Carlo's land than I thought even then, and if I could have peeped into the future I would only have shrunk with unspeakable dread from the path I must walk, the path that was to lead me to the consummation of my childish hopes. In a very few years the home life I had entered into with such gladness was over, my husband was dead, and I was penniless, homeless, and alone. Of course I might have gone back to my father's house, my parents would have welcomed me, but can any woman go back and take a subordinate position when she has ruled? I think not; besides it would only have been putting off the evil day. When my father died, and in the course of nature he must die before me, there would be but a pittance, and I should have to start out once more handicapped with the added years. Again, and I think this thought was latent beneath all the misery and hopelessness that made me say I did not care what became of me, was I not free, free to wander where I pleased, to seek those adventures that had held such a glamour for me in my girlhood. True, I had not much money with which to seek them. When everything was settled up I found if I stayed quietly in Australia I had exactly thirty pounds a year to call my own. Thirty pounds a year, and I reckoned I could make perhaps fifty pounds by my pen. My mother pointed out to me that if I lived with my parents it would not be so bad. But it was not to be thought of for a moment. The chance had come, through seas of trouble, but still it had come, and I would go and see the great world for myself. I thought I had lived my life, that no sorrow or gladness could ever touch me keenly again; but I knew, it was in my blood, that I should like to see strange places and visit unknown lands. But on thirty pounds a year one can do nothing, so I took a hundred pounds out of my capital and came to London determined to make money by my pen in the heart of the world.

Oh, the hopes of the aspirant for literary fame, and oh, the dreariness and the weariness of life for a woman poor and unknown in London! I lodged in two rooms in a dull and stony street. I had no one to speak to from morning to night, and I wrote and wrote and wrote stories that all came back to me, and I am bound to say the editors who sent them back were quite right. They were poor stuff, but how could anyone do good work who was sick and miserable, cold and lonely, with all the life crushed out of her by the grey skies and the drizzling rain? I found London a terrible place in those days; I longed with all my heart for my own country, my own little home in Warrnambool where the sun shone always, the roses yellow and pink climbed over the wall, the white pittosporum blossoms filled the air with their fragrance, and the great trees stood up tall and straight against the dark-blue sky. I did not go back to my father, because my pride would not allow me to own myself a failure and because all the traditions of my family were against giving in. But I was very near it, very near it indeed.

Then after six months of hopelessness there came to see me from Liverpool a friend of one of my sailor brothers, and she, good Samaritan, suggested I should spend my Christmas with her.

I went. She and her daughters were rich people and the husband and father had been an African trader. So here it was again presented to me, the land to which I had resolved to go when I was a little child, and everything in the house spoke to me of it. In the garden under a cedar tree was the great figurehead of an old sailing ship; in the corridor upstairs was the model of a factory, trees, boats, people, houses all complete; in the rooms were pictures of the rivers and swamps and the hulks where trade was carried on. To their owners these possessions were familiar as household words that meant nothing; to me they reopened a new world of desire or rather an old desire in a new setting—the vague was taking concrete form. I determined quite definitely that I would go to West Africa. The thing that amazed me was that everybody with money in their pockets was not equally desirous of going there.

About this time, too, I discovered that it was simply hopeless for me to think of writing stories about English life. The regular, conventional life did not appeal to me; I could only write adventure stories, and the scene of adventure stories was best laid in savage lands. West Africa was not at all a bad place in which to set them. Its savagery called me. There and then I started to write stories about it. Looking back, I smile when I think of the difficulties that lay in my path. Even after I had carefully read every book of travel I could lay my hands on, I was still in deepest ignorance, because every traveller left so much undescribed and told nothing of the thousand and one little trifles that make ignorant eyes see the life that is so different from that in a civilised land. But if you will only look for a thing it is astonishing how you will find it often in the most unlikely places; if you set your heart on something it is astonishing how often you will get your heart's desire. I sought for information about West Africa and I found it, not easily; every story I wrote cost me a world of trouble and research and anxiety, and I fear me the friends I was beginning to make a world of trouble too. But they were kind and long-suffering; this man gave me a little information here, that one there, and I can laugh now when I think of the scenes that had to be written and rewritten before a hammock could be taken a couple of miles, before a man could sit down to his early-morning tea in the bush. It took years to do it, but at last it was done to some purpose; the book I had written with great effort caught on, and I had the money for the trip I had planned many years before when I was a small girl reading about those distant lands. I hesitated not a moment. The day I had sufficient money to make such a thing possible I went up to the City to see about a passage to West Africa.

And now a wonderful thing happened. Such a piece of good luck as I had not in my wildest dreams contemplated. Elder Dempster, instigated by the kind offices of Sir Charles Lucas, the permanent head of the Colonial Office, who knew how keen was my desire, offered me a ticket along the Coast, so that I actually had all the money I had earned to put into land travel, and Mr Laurie, my publisher, fired by my enthusiasm, commissioned a book about the wonderful old forts that I knew lay neglected and crumbling to decay all along the shores of the Gold Coast.

As I look back it seems as if surely the fairy godmother who had omitted to take my youth in charge was now showering me with good gifts, or maybe, most probably, the good gifts had been offered all along and I had never recognised them. We, some of us, drive in a gorgeous coach and never see anything but the pumpkin.

At least I was not making that mistake now. I was wild with delight and excitement when, on a cold November day, when London was wrapped in fog, I started from Euston for Liverpool. One of the brothers who I had envied in my youth, a post captain in the Navy now (how the years fly), happened to be in London and came down to the station to see me and my heaped impedimenta off.

He understood my delight in the realisation of my dream.

"Have you any directions for the disposal of your remains?" he asked chaffingly, as we groped our way through the London fog.

"Oh, that will all be settled," said I, "long before you hear anything about it"; and we both laughed. We did not think, either of us, my adventure was going to end disastrously. It would have been against all the traditions of the family to think any such thing.

He told me how once he had gone into action with interest because he wanted to see what it would be like to be under fire, and whether he would be frightened. He didn't have much time to contemplate the situation, for presently he was so badly wounded that it took him six months to crawl off his bed, but it brought him a cross of honour from Italy. "And now," says he, with a certain satisfaction, "I know." So he sympathised. He felt that whatever happened I would have the satisfaction of knowing.

It is hardly necessary to describe to an English reader Liverpool on a cold, grey morning in November. There is the grey sky and the grey streets and the grey houses, and the well-to-do shivering in their wraps, and the poor shivering in their rags, all the colourless English world, that is not really colourless for those who know how to look at it, but which had driven me to sunnier lands; and there was the ship with her wet decks, her busy officers in comforters and sea-boots, her bare-footed sailors, and her gangways crowded with cargo, baggage, and numbers of bewildered passengers themselves.

And I think as we crowded into the smoking-room for warmth I was the only enthusiastic person among them. The majority of the passengers on board s.s. *Gando* actually didn't want to go to West Africa.

It seems strange, but so it was; the greater part of them, if they could have afforded to stay at home, would actually have stayed. I was inclined to be impatient with them. Now I forgive them. They know not what they do. It is a pity, but it can be remedied.

The *Gando* was not a mail boat. I had chosen her because she called at Dakar, and I thought I would like to go if possible to the first settlement on the Coast, and I wanted to see how the French did things. I may say here I never got to Dakar—still it is something to be looked forward to in the future, to be done when next I write a book that pays—for on board the *Gando* was Sir George Denton, the Governor of the Gambia, surely the nicest governor ever lucky colony had, and for such an important person the ship went a little out of her way and called first at Bathurst, port and capital of the Gambia colony.

Now, I had a letter of introduction to Sir George and I presented it, and he promptly asked me to come ashore with him. I had never thought of staying in the Gambia beyond the day or two the ship would take to discharge her cargo—"a potty little colony," as I had heard it called, and it hardly seemed worth while to waste my time in a miniature Thames. How the Governor laughed when he found out my appalling ignorance, and how ashamed I was when I found it out!

"The Thames," said he; "well, we only hold the mouth of the river about four hundred miles up, but the Gambia is at least a thousand miles in extent, and may be longer for all I know."

I apologised to the Gambia.

"But could I see the river?"

"Why, of course; we'll send you up in the *Mansikillah*, the Government steamer"; and I accepted his invitation with alacrity and with gratitude.

Truly, my fairy godmother was more than waving her wand. I hadn't left English shores a week, and here was an invitation to go four hundred miles into the interior of the continent of my dreams.

We went first to the Canary Islands, the islands of the blest of the ancients, but the Canaries were as nothing to me; they have been civilised too long. They were only a stepping-stone to that other land, the land of romance, that I was nearing at last.

And now I have an apology to make, an apology which very few people will understand, but those few will, and to them it is a matter of such importance that I must make it. I went to see a savage land. I went to seek material for the only sort of story I can write, and to tell of the prowess of the men who had gone before and left their traces in great stone forts all along three hundred miles of coast. I found a savage land, in some parts a very wild land indeed, but I found what I had never expected, a land of immense possibilities, a land overflowing with wealth, a land of corn and wine and oil. I expected swamp and miasma, heat, fever, and mosquitoes. I found these truly, but I found, too, a lovely land, an entrancingly lovely land in places; I found gorgeous nights and divine mornings, and I found that the great interest of West Africa lay not in the opportunity it gave for vivid descriptions of heroes who fought and suffered and conquered, or fought and suffered and died, but in showing its immense value to the English crown in describing a land where every tropical product may be grown, a land with a teeming population and a generous soil, a land in fact that, properly managed, should supply raw material for half the workshops in England, a land that may be made to give some of its sunlight to keep alight the fires on English hearths in December, a land that as yet only the wiser heads amongst us realise the value of.

"A man comes to West Africa," said a Swiss to me once, "because he can make in ten years as much as he could make in thirty in England."

That is the land I found, and I apologise if I have ever written or thought of it in any other way.

"The White Man's Grave," say many still. But even the all-powerful white man must have a grave in the end. Live wisely and discreetly and it is, I think with wise old Zachary Macauley who ruled Sierra Leone at the end of the eighteenth century, no more likely to be in West Africa than in any other place.

And the ship sailed on, and one morning early, before daylight, we heard the bell buoy that marks the mouth of the Gambia before lazy eyes can see there is a river, and knew that we had arrived at our destination. At last, at last I was on the very threshold of the land I had dreamed of years before.

CHAPTER II
THE GROUNDNUT COLONY

Rejoicing-, half-eastern and wholly tropical, on arrival of the Governor—Colonies governed and held as the Romans held their colonies of Britain—Great g-ulf between the black and the white—The barrier of sex—Received as a brother but declined as a brother-in-law—Lonely Fort St James—The strenuous lives led by the men of the past—Crinted walls—The pilot's wife—Up the river in the Mungo Park—The river devil's toll—"Pass friend and all's well."

When I was a little girl the Queen held something the same place in my mind as the Almighty. The ruler of the nation hardly had any personality. She was there, of course, and people talked about her as conferring great benefits upon us; but so we also talked about God in church and when we said our prayers at night. As a family, we objected to saying prayers in the morning. They were not supposed to be necessary till you had arrived at mature years, say, five, and by then, I suppose, we had imbibed the idea that we could really take care of ourselves very well during the day-time. So the Queen, too, was in the same category as God and Heaven, that distinctly dull place, which was to be the reward of good works on earth, and His Excellency the Governor took her place in the minds of all young colonials. Of course, as I grew older, I realised that the Governor was a man like unto other men, that he could be talked to like an ordinary man, could ask you to dinner, and even take a polite interest in your future; but, still, some of the rags of the childish vagueness and glory clung round him, and so I was quite pleased to find myself on board a steamer with a real live Governor. More, I sat next him at table; we discussed the simple commonplace doings of ship-board life together, and as we arrived at the buoy I shared in the little fuss and bustle which the landing of such an exalted personage always makes. And he wasn't really such a very exalted personage in his own opinion. There was a merry twinkle in his nice brown eyes as he admitted that his gold-laced coat, made to be worn on state occasions such as this, was a great deal too hot for the Tropics, and that its donning must be left to the very last moment; and so I stood on the flag-dressed deck by myself and watched the land of my dreams come into view.

A long, low shore is the Gambia—a jutting point, with palms upon it, running out into a glassy sea, from which is reflected the glare of the tropical sun. There was a little denser clump of greenery that marked the site of Bathurst, the capital; and, as we drew closer, we could see the roofs of the houses peeping out, bright specks of colour that were the flags, and the long line of red on the wharf, the soldiers turned out to welcome the returning Governor.

This is the only place along that line of surf-bound coast where a ship may come up to the wharf and land her passengers dry-shod; but, to-day, because the captain was in a hurry, he dropped us over the side in boats, and we landed to all the glory of a welcome that was half-eastern and wholly and emotionally tropical. The principal street of Bathurst, the only street worth mentioning, runs all along the river-side, with houses on one side and the wharfs and piers on the other; and the whole place was thronged with the black inhabitants. The men shouted and tossed their hats and caps when they had any; and the women, the mammies, as I learned to call them later, flung their gaily coloured cloths from their shoulders for their dearly loved Governor to walk over; and the handful of whites—there are twenty-five English and some French and Swiss—came forward and solemnly shook hands. He had come back to them, the man who had ruled over them for the last ten years, and white and black loved him, and were glad to do him honour.

In the midst of great rejoicing, a good omen for me, I set my foot on African shore. I began my journeying, and I looked round to try and realise what manner of country was this I had come to—what manner of life I was to be part and parcel of.

These colonies on the West-African coast are as unlike as possible to the colony in which I first saw the light, that my people have helped to build up. I fancy, perhaps, the Roman proconsul and the officials in his train, who came out to rule over Britain in the first century before Christ, must have led lives somewhat resembling those of the Britons who nowadays go out to West Africa. One thing is certain, those Italians must have grumbled perpetually about the inclemency and unhealthiness of the climate of these northern isles; they probably had a great deal to say about the fever and ague that was rife. They were accustomed to certain luxuries that civilisation had made into necessities, and they came to a land where all the people were traders and agriculturists of a most primitive sort. They were exiles in a cold, grey land, and they felt it bitterly. They came to replenish their purses, and when those purses were fairly full they returned to their own land gladly. The position describes three-quarters of the Englishmen in West Africa to-day; but between the Roman and the savage Piet of Caledonia was never the gulf, the great gulf, which is fixed between even the educated African and the white man of whatever nationality. It is no good trying to hide the fact; between the white man and the black lies not only the culture and the knowledge of the west—that gulf might, and sometimes is bridged—but that other great bar, the barrier of sex. Tall, stalwart, handsome as is many a negro, no white woman may take a black man for her husband and be respected by her own people; no white man may take a black girl, though her dark eyes be soft and tender, though her skin be as satin and her figure like that of the

Venus of Milo, and hope to introduce her among his friends as his wife. Even the missionaries who preach that the black man is a brother decline emphatically to receive him as a brother-in-law. And so we get, beginning here in the little colony of the Gambia, the handful of the ruling race set among a subject people; so the white man has always ruled the black; so, I think, he must always rule. It will be a bad day for the white when the black man rules. That there should be any mingling of the races is unthinkable; so I hope that the white man will always rule Africa with a strong hand.

The Gambia is the beginning of the English colonies on the Coast, and, the pity of it, a very small beginning.

In the old days, when Charles the Second was king, the English held none of the banks of the river at all, but contented themselves with a barren little island about seventeen miles from where Bathurst now stands. One bank was held by the French, the other by the Portuguese; and the English built on the island Fort St James to protect their interest in the great trade in palm oil, slaves, and ivory that came down the river. Even then the Gambia was rich. It is richer far to-day, but the French hold the greater part of it. The colony of the Gambia is at the mouth of the river, twelve miles broad by four hundred long, a narrow strip of land bordering the mouth of a river set in the heart of the great French colony of Senegal—a veritable Naboth's vineyard that our friends the other side of the Channel may well envy us. It brings us in about £80,000 annually, but to them it would be of incalculable value as an outlet for the majority of their rich trade.

At first I hardly thought about these things. I was absorbed in the wonder of the new life. I stayed at Government House with the Governor, and was caught up in the little whirl of gaieties that greeted his return. The house was tropical, with big, lofty, airy rooms and great wide verandahs that as a rule serve also as passageways to pass from one room to another; for Government House, Bathurst, is built as a tropical house should be—must be—built, if the builder have any regard for the health of its inmates. There were no rooms that the prevailing breeze could not sweep right through. There was a drawingroom and a dining-room on the ground floor, but I do not think either Sir George or I, or his private secretary, ever used the drawing-room unless there were guests to be entertained. The verandahs were so much more inviting, and my bedroom was a delightful place. It ran right across the house. There was no carpet, and, as was only right, only just such furniture as I absolutely needed. The bed was enclosed in another small mosquito-proof room of wirenetting, and it was the only thing I did not like about the house. There, and at that season, perhaps it did not very much matter, for a strong Harmattan wind, the cool wind of the cold, dry season, was blowing, and it kept the air behind the stout wire-netting fresh and clean; but I must here put on record my firm belief that no inconsiderable number of lives in Africa must be lost owing to some doctor's prejudice in favour of mosquito-proof netting. A mosquito-proof netting is very stout indeed, and not only excludes the mosquito, but, and this far more effectually, the fresh air as well. The man who has plenty of fresh air, day and night, will be in better health, and far more likely to resist infection if he does happen to get bitten by a fever-bearing mosquito, than he who must perforce spend at least a third of his time in the vitiated air of a mosquito-proof room. This I did not realise at Government House, Bathurst, or if I did, but dimly, for there in December the strong Harmattan would have forced its way through anything. I spent most of my time on the verandah outside my own room, where I had a view not only of the road that ran to to the centre of the town but right away across the river. Here I had my breakfast and my afternoon tea, and here I did all my writing.

In Africa your own servant takes charge of your room, gets your bath, and brings you your early-morning tea; and here in Bathurst in this womanless house my servant was to get my breakfast and my afternoon tea as well, so the first thing to be done was to look out for a boy. He appeared in the shape of Ansumanah Grant, a Mohammedan boy of three-and-twenty, a Vai tribesman, who had been brought up by the Wesleyan missionaries at Cape Mount in Liberia. When I engaged him he wore a pink pyjama coat, a pair of moleskin breeches, and red carpet slippers; and, when this was rectified—at my expense—he appeared in a white shirt, khaki knicker-bockers, a red cummerbund, and bare feet, and made a very respectable member of society and a very good servant to me during the whole of my stay in Africa.

PILOT'S WIFE AGAINST PRINTED WALL.

I always made it a practice to rise early in West Africa, because the early morning is the most delightful time, and he who stays in bed till halfpast seven or eight is missing one of the pure delights of life. When I had had my early breakfast, I went to inspect the town. The market lies but a stone's throw from Government House, and here all the natives were to be found, and the white men's servants buying provisions for the day. To me, before I went to Africa, a negro was a negro, and I imagined them all of one race. My mind was speedily disabused of that error. The negro has quite as many nationalities, is quite as distinct as the European. Here in this little colony was a most cosmopolitan gathering, for the south and north meet, and Yorubas from Lagos, Gas from Accra, mongrel Creoles from Sierra Leone meet the Senegalese from the north, the Hausas from away farther east; and the natives themselves are the Mohammedan Jolloff, who is an expert riverman, the Mandingo, and the heathen Jolah, who as yet is low down in the scale of civilisation, and wears but scanty rags. And all these people were to be found in the market in the early morning. It is enclosed with a high wall, the interior is cemented, and gutters made to carry off moisture, and it is all divided into stalls, and really not at all unlike the alfresco markets you may see on Saturdays in the poorer quarters of London. Here they sell meat, most uninviting looking, but few butchers' shops look inviting; fish—very strange denizens come out of the sea in the Gambia; native peppers, red and green; any amount of rice, which is the staple food of the people, and all the tropical fruits, paws-paws, pine-apples, and dark-green Coast oranges, which are very sweet; bananas, yellow and pink, and great bunches of green plantains. They are supposed to sell only on the stalls, for which they pay a small, a very small rental; but, like true natives, they overflow on to the ground, and as you walk you must be careful not to tread on neat little piles of peppers, enamelled iron-ware basins full of native rice, or little heaps of purple kola-nuts—that great sustaining stimulant of Africa.

There were about half a dozen white women in Bathurst when I was there, including one who had ostracised herself by marrying a black man; but none ever came to the market, therefore my arrival created great excitement, and one good lady, in a are held, half the houses are owned by rich negroes, Africans they very naturally prefer to be called, but the poorer people live all crowded together in Jolloff town, whither my guide led me, and introduced me to her yard. A Jolloff never speaks about his house, but about his "yard." Even Government House he knows as "Governor's Yard."

Jolloff town looks as if if were made of basket-work; they call it here "crinting," and all the walls of the houses and of the compounds are made of this split bamboo neatly woven together. For Bathurst is but a strip of sand-bank just rescued from the mangrove swamp round, and these crinted walls serve excellently to keep it together when the strong Harmattan threatens to blow the whole place bodily into the swamp behind. My friend's home was a very nice specimen of its class, the first barbaric home I had ever seen. The compound was surrounded by the crinted walls, and inside again were two or three huts, also built of crinting, with a thatched roof. As a rule I am afraid the Jolloff is not clean, but my pilot's wife had a neat little home. There were no windows in it, but the strong sunlight came through the crinted walls, and made a subdued light and a pattern of the basket-work on the white, sanded floor; there were three long seats of wood, neatly covered with white napkins edged with red, a table, a looking-glass, and a basket of bread, for it appeared she was a trader in a small way. It was all very suitable and charming. Outside in the compound ran about chickens, goats, a dog or two, and some small children, another woman's children, alas, for she told me mournfully she had none.

It is easy enough to make a friend; the difficulty is to know where to stop. I am afraid I had soon exhausted all my interest in my Jolloff woman, while to her I was a great source of pride, and she wanted me to come and see her every day. At first she told me she "fear too much" to come to "Governor's Yard," but latterly, I regret to state, that wholesome fear wore off, and she called to see me every day, and I found suitable conversation a most difficult thing to provide, so that I grew to look very anxiously indeed for the steamer that was to take me up the river.

"ANOTHER WOMAN'S CHILDREN IN HER YARD."

The Government steamer, the *Mansikillah*, had broken down. She was old, and it was, I was told, her chronic state, but I was bitterly disappointed till the Governor told me he had made arrangements for me to go in the French Company's steamer, the *Mungo Park*. She was going up the river with general cargo; she was coming down again with some of the groundnut crop, little nuts that grow on the root of a trefoil plant, nuts the Americans call peanuts, and the English monkey-nuts.

I had to wait a little till there came a messenger one day to say that the steamer was ready at last, and would start that afternoon. So I went down to the little wharf with my servant, my baggage, and the travelling Commissioner, who was also going up the river.

The *Mungo Park* was a stern-wheeler of 150 tons, drawing six feet of water, and when first I saw her you could hardly tell steamer from wharf, so alive were they both with crowded, shrieking people, all either wanting to get on, or to get off, which was apparently not quite clear. After a little wait, out of chaos came a courteous French trader and a gangway. The gangway took us on board, and the trader, whose English was as good as mine, explained that he, too, was going up the river to look after the houses belonging to his company along the banks. Then he showed me my quarters, and I was initiated into the mysteries of travelling in the interior of Africa. There was but one cabin on board the *Mungo Park*, a place about eighteen feet square amidship; in it were two bunks, a table, a couple of long seats, a cupboard, and washing arrangements. The sides were all of Venetian shutters, which could be taken away when not wanted. It was all right in a way, but I must confess for a moment I wondered how on earth two men and a woman were to stow away there. Then the trader explained. I should have the cabin to sleep in, and we all three would have our meals there together, while arrangements might be made by which we could all in turn bathe and wash. I learned my first lesson: you accept extraordinary and unconventional situations, if you are wise, with a smile and without a blush in Africa. The Commissioner and the trader, I found on further inquiry, would sleep on the top of the cabin, which was also what one might call the promenade deck. I arranged my simple belongings, and went up on deck to look, and I found that it was reached by way of the boiler, across which some steps and a little, coaly hand-rail led. It would have been nice in the Arctic regions, but on a tropical afternoon it had its drawbacks. On the deck I was met by a vociferous black man, who was much too busy to do more than give an obsequious welcome, for it appeared he was the captain. I shall always regret I did not take his photograph as he leaned over the railing, shouting and gesticulating to his men, and to the would-be passengers, and to the men who were struggling to get the cargo on board. He cursed them, I should think, all impartially. The French trader said he was an excellent captain, and he remains in my mind as the most unique specimen of the genus I have ever seen. He wore a khaki coat and very elderly tweed trousers, split behind; his feet were bare; he did not pander to that vitiated taste which demands underlinen, or at least a shirt, but, seeing it was the cold weather, he adorned his black skull with a woolly cap with ear-flaps, such as Nansen probably took on his North-Pole expedition.

There was a great deal of cargo—cotton goods, sugar, salt, coffee, dates; things that the French company were taking up to supply their factories on the river, and long before it was stowed the deck passengers began crowding on board. Apparently there was no provision whatever made for them; they stowed on top of the cargo, just wherever they could find a place, and every passenger—there were over ninety of them—had apparently something to say as to the accommodation, or the want of accommodation, and he or she said it at the very top of his or her voice in Jolloff or Mandingo or that bastard English which is a *lingua franca* all along the Coast. Not that it mattered much what language they said it in, because no one paid the least attention; such a babel have I never before heard. And such a crowd as they were. The steamer provided water carriage only for the deck passengers, so that they had their cooking apparatus, their bedding, their food, their babies, their chickens (unfortunate wretches tied by one leg), and, if they could evade the eagle eye of the French trader, their goats. The scene was bedlam let loose to my unaccustomed eyes. We were to tow six lighters as well, and each of them also had a certain number of passengers. As we started it seemed likely we should sweep away a few dozen who were hanging on in the most dangerous places to the frailest supports. Possibly they wouldn't have been missed. I began to understand why the old slaver was callous. It was impossible to feel humane in the midst of such a shrieking, howling mob. The siren gave wild and ear-piercing shrieks; there were yells from the wharf, more heartrending yells from the steamer, a minor accompaniment from the lighters, bleating of goats, cackling of protesting fowls, crying of children, and we were off without casualty, and things began to settle down.

I had thought my quarters cramped, but looking at the deck passengers, crowding fore and aft over the coals and on top of the boiler, I realised that everything goes by comparison, and that they were simply palatial. I had eighteen feet square of room all to myself to sleep in. It had one drawback. There was £5000 worth of silver stowed under the seats, and therefore the trader requested me to lock the doors and fasten the shutters lest some of the passengers should take a fancy to it. His view was that plenty of air would come through the laths of the shutters. I did not agree with the French trader, and watched with keen interest those boxes of silver depart all too slowly. I would gladly have changed places and let him and the Commissioner have my cabin if only I might have taken their place on the deck above. But on the deck was the wheel, presided over by the black captain, or the equally black and more ragged mate, so it was not to be thought of.

And that deck was something to remember. There were the large water-bottles there and the filter, the trader's bed in a neat little roll, the Commissioner's bed, draped with blue mosquito curtains, the hencoops with the unhappy fowls that served us for food, the Commissioner's washing apparatus on top of one of the coops, for he was a young man of resource, the rest of his kit, his rifle, his bath, his cartridge-belt, his dog, a few plates and cups and basins, a couple of sieves for rice, two or three stools, the elderly black kettle, out of the spout of which the skipper and the mate sucked refreshment as if they had been a couple of snipe, and last, but not least, there was the French company's mails for their employees up river. I was told the correspondence always arrived safely, and so it is evident that in some things we take too much trouble. The captain attended to the sorting of the mails when he had time to spare from his other duties. I have seen him with a much-troubled brow sorting letters at night by the light of a flickering candle, and, when the mails overflowed the deal box, parcels were stacked against the railing, newspapers leaned for support against the wheel, and letters collogued in friendly fashion on the deck with the black kettle.

For the first seventeen miles the little ship, towing her lighters behind and alongside, went up a river that was like a sea, so far away were the mangrove swamps that are on either side. Then we reached Fort St James, and the river narrows. Very pathetic are the ruins of Fort St James. No one lives there now; no one has lived there for many a long day, but you see as you pass and look at the crumbling stones of the old fort why West Africa gained in the minds of men so evil a reputation. The place is but a rocky islet, with but a few scanty trees upon it; above is the brazen sky, below the baked earth, on which the tropical sun pours down with all the added heat gathered from the glare of the river. They must have died shut up in Fort St James in those far-away days. Tradition, too, says that the gentlemen of the company of soldiers who were stationed there were for ever fighting duels, and that the many vacancies in the ranks were not always due to the climate. But the heat and the monotony would conduce to irritability, and when a hasty word had to be upheld at the sword's point, it is no wonder if they cursed the Coast with a bitterness that is only given to the land of regrets. But all honour to those dead-and-gone Englishmen. They upheld the might of Britain, and her rights in the trade in palm oil and slaves and ivory that even then came down the river. And if they died—now, now at last, after many weary years, their descendants are beginning dimly to realise, as they never did, the value of the land for which they gave their lives.

It is the custom to speak with contempt of a mangrove swamp, as if in it no beauty could lie, as if it were only waste land—dreary, depressing, ugly. Each of those epithets may be true—I cannot say—except the last, and that is most certainly a falsehood. What my impressions would be if I lived in the midst of it day after day I cannot say, but to a passer-by the mangrove swamp has a beauty of its own.

When first I saw the Gambia I was fascinated, and found no words too strong for its beauty; and, having gone farther, I would take back not one word of that admiration. But I am like the lover who is faithless to his first mistress—he acknowledges her charm, but he has seen someone else; so now, as I sit down to write, I am reminded that the Volta is more ravishingly lovely, and that if I use up all my adjectives on the Gambia I shall have no words to describe my new mistress. Therefore must I modify my transports, and so it seems to me I am unfair.

As we moved up the river we could plainly see the shore on either side, the dense mangrove swamp, doubled by its reflection, green and beautiful against its setting of blue sky and clear river. Crocodiles lay basking in the golden sunshine on the mud-banks, white egrets flew slowly from tree to tree, a brown jolah-king, an ibis debased for some sin in the youth of the world, sailed slowly across the water, a white fishing-eagle poised himself on high, looking for his prey, a slate-blue crane came across our bows, a young pelican just ahead was taking his first lesson in swimming, and closer to the bank we could see king-fishers, bright spots of colour against the dark green of the mangrove.

"The wonder of the Tropics"—the river seemed to be whispering at first, and then fairly shouted—"can you deny beauty to this river?" and I, with the cool Harmattan blowing across the water to put the touch of moisture in the air it needed, was constrained to answer that voice, which none of the others seemed to hear, "Truly I cannot."

It would be impossible to describe in detail all the little wharves at which we stopped; besides, they all bore a strong family resemblance to one another, differing only when they were in the upper or lower river. Long before I could see any signs of human habitation the steamer's skipper was wildly agitated over the mails, wrinkling up his brows and pawing them over with his dirty black hands—mine were dirtier, at least, they showed more, and the way to the deck was so coaly it was impossible to keep clean. Then he would hang on to a string, which resulted in the most heartrending wails from the steamer's siren; a corrugated-iron roof would show up among the surrounding greenery, and a little wharf, or "tenda," as they call them here, would jut out into the stream. These tendas are frail-looking structures built of the split poles of the rhon palm. There seem to be as many varieties of palm as there are of eucalyptus, all much alike to the uninitiated eye.

The tendas look as if they were only meant to be walked on by bare feet—certainly very few of the feet rise beyond a loose slipper; and whether it was blazing noonday or pitchy darkness only made visible by a couple of hurricane lanterns of one candle-power, the tenda was crowded with people come to see the arrival of the steamer, which is a White-Star liner or a Cunarder to them—people in cast-off European clothing and the ubiquitous tourist cap, Moslems in fez and flowing white or blue robes, mammies with gaily coloured handkerchiefs bound round their heads and still gayer skirts and cloths, little children clad in one garment or no garments at all, beautiful grey donkeys that carry the groundnuts or the trade goods, fawn-coloured country cattle, and goats and sheep, black, white, and brown—and every living creature upon that tenda did his little best towards the raising of a most unholy din. And the steamer was not to be beaten. Jolloff and Man-dingo too was shrieked; the captain took a point of vantage, shook his black fist at intervals, and added his quota of curses in Jolloff, Mandingo, Senegalese, and broken French and English, and the cargo was unloaded with a clatter, clatter, punctuated by earpiercing yells that made one wonder if the slaving days had not come back, and these lumpers were not shrieking in agony.

But, when I could understand, the remarks were harmless enough. What the black man says to his friends and acquaintances when he speaks in his own tongue I cannot say, but when he addresses them in English I can vouch for it his conversation is banal to the last degree. In the general din I catch some words I understand, and I listen.

"Ah, Mr Jonsing, dat you, sah? How you do, sah?" Mr Jonsing's health is quite satisfactory; and Mrs Jonsing, and Miss Mabel, and Miss Gladys, and Mr Edward were all apparently in perfect health, for they were inquired after one by one at the top of the interested friend's voice. Then there were many wishes for the continuance of the interesting family in this happy state, and afterwards there was an excursion into wider realms of thought.

"You 'member dat t'ing you deny las' mont', sah?" The question comes tentatively.

"I deny it dis mont', sah," Mr Jonsing answers promptly, which is, so far, satisfactory, as showing that Mr Jonsing has at least a mind of his own, and is not to be bounced into lightly changing it. I might have heard more, and so gleaned some information into the inner life of these people, but unfortunately Mr Jonsing now got in the way of the stalwart captain, and being assisted somewhat ungently by the collar of his ragged shirt to the tenda, he launched out into curses that were rude, to put it mildly, and my knowledge of his family affairs came to an abrupt conclusion.

In the breaks in the mangrove, Balanghar is one of them, there is, of course, a little hard earth—the great shady *ficus elasticus*, beautiful silk-cotton trees, and cocoa-nut palms grow; the traders' yards have white stone posts at the four corners marking the extent of their leaseholds, and in these enclosures are the trading-houses, the round huts of the native helpers, and the little crinted yards, in which are poured the groundnuts, which are the occasion of all this clatter.

One hundred and fifty miles up we came to McCarthy Island, five miles long by a mile wide, and markedly noticeable because here the great river changes its character entirely, the mangrove swamps are left behind, and open bush of mahogany, palm, and many another tree and creeper, to me nameless, takes its place. On McCarthy Island is a busy settlement, with the town marked into streets, lined with native shops and trading-houses. There are great groundnut stores along the river front, seven, or perhaps eight white people, a church, a hospital, obsolete guns, and an old powder magazine, that shows that in days gone by this island was only held by force of arms.

They tell me that McCarthy Island is one of the hottest places in the world, though that morning the river had been veiled in white mist, the thermometer was down to between 50 deg. and 60 deg., and my boy had brought in my early-morning tea with his head tied up in a pocket handkerchief like an old woman; and at midday it was but little over 90 deg., but this was December, the coolest season of the year. I discussed the question with a negro lady with her head bound up in a red-silk handkerchief. She was one of our passengers, and had come up trading in kola-nuts. Kola-nuts are hard, corner-shaped nuts that grow on a very handsome tree about the size of an oak, which means a small tree in Africa. They are much esteemed for their stimulating and sustaining properties. I have tried them, and I found them only bitter, so perhaps I do not want stimulating. A tremendous trade is done in them, and all along the coast you meet the traders, very often, as in this case, women. I had seen it in her eye for some time that she wanted to exchange ideas with me, and at last the opportunity came. She told me she came from Sierra Leone.

"You know Freetown?" That is the capital. I said I had heard it was the hottest place in the world.

"Pooh!" She tossed her head in scorn. "You wait two mont's; it be fool to M'Cart'y! You gat no rest, no sleep"; and she showed her white teeth and stretched out her black hands as if to say that no words of hers could do justice to this island.

Truly, I think the sun must pour down here in the hot season, judging by my experience in the cool. The hot season is not in June, as one might expect, for then come the rains, when no white man, and, indeed, I think no black man foreign to the place, stays up the river, but in March and April. I do not propose to visit McCarthy in the hot season. In the cool the blazing sun overhead, and the reflected glare from the water, played havoc with my complexion. I did not think about it till the District Commissioner brought the fact forcibly home to me. He was a nice young fellow, but the sort of man who is ruin to England as a colonising nation, because he makes it so patent to everyone that he bitterly resents colonising on his own account, and will allow no good in the country wherein lies his work.

I asked him if he did not think of bringing out his wife.

He looked at me a moment, seeking words to show his opinion of a woman who insisted upon going where he thought no white woman was needed.

"My wife," he said, with emphasis that marked his surprise; "my wife? Why, my wife has such a delicate complexion that she has to wash her face always in distilled water."

It was sufficient. I understood when I looked in the glass that night the reproof intended to be conveyed. In all probability the lady was not quite such a fool as her husband intimated; but one thing is quite certain, she was buying her complexion at a very heavy cost if she were going to allow it to deprive her of the joy of seeing new countries.

McCarthy was very busy; dainty cutters, frail canoes, and grimy steamers crowded the wharves, and to and fro across the great river, 500 yards wide here, the ferry, a great canoe, went backwards and forwards the livelong day, and I could just see gathered together herds of the pretty cattle of the country that looked not unlike Alderneys.

When we left the island the river was narrower, so that we seemed to glide along between green walls, where the birds were singing and the monkeys barking and crying and whimpering like children. Again and again we passed trees full of them, sometimes little grey monkeys, and sometimes great dog-faced fellows that rumour says would tear you to pieces if you offended them and had the misfortune to fall into their hands. Now and then a hippopotamus rose, a reminder of an age that has gone by, and always on the mud-banks were the great crocodiles. And the trading-stations were, I think, more solitary and more picturesque. The little tendas were even more frail, just rickety little structures covered with a mat of crinting, for the river rises here very high, and these wharves are sure to be carried away in the rainy season. And then come hills, iron-stone hills, and tall, dry grass ten and twelve feet high. Sometimes we stopped where there was not even the frailest of tendas, and one night, just as the swift darkness was falling, the steamer drew up at a little muddy landing-stage, where there was a break in the trees, and three dugouts were drawrn up. Here she became wildly hysterical, and I began to think something would give way, until all shrieks died down as a tall black man, draped in blue, and with a long Dane gun across his shoulder, stalked out of the bush. Savage Africa personified. We had stopped to land a passenger, a mammy with her head tied up in a handkerchief, and a motley array of boxes, bundles, calabashes, chairs, saucepans, and fowls that made a small boat-load. She waved a farewell to the French trader as her friends congregated upon the shore and examined her baggage.

"She is an important woman," said he; "the wife of a black trader in the town behind there. He's a Christian."

"He's got a dozen wives," said the Commissioner.

"His official wife, then. Oh, you know the sort. I guarantee she keeps order in the compound."

At Fatta Tenda, which is quite a busy centre, from which you may start for the Niger and Timbuctoo, we gave a dinner-party, a dinner-party under difficulties. Our cook was excellent. How he turned out such dainties in a tiny galley three feet by six, and most of that taken up by the stove, I do not pretend to understand, but he did, so our difficulties lay not there, but with the lamp. What was the matter with it I do not know, but it gave a shocking light, and the night before our dinner-party it went out, and left us to finish our dinner in darkness. Then, next day, word went round that the mate was going to trim the lamp, and when we, with two men from the French factory, went into dinner, an unwonted light shed its brilliancy over the scene. Unfortunately, there was also a strong scent of kerosene, which is not usually considered a very alluring fragrance. But we consoled ourselves; the mate had trimmed the lamp. He had. He had also distributed most of the oil over the dinner-table—the cloth was soaked in it, and, worse than that, the salt, pepper, and mustard were full of it; and then, as we sat down to soup, there came in through the open windows a flight, I should say several flights, of flying ants. They died in crowds in the soup, they filled up the glasses, they distributed themselves over the kerosene-soaked table, till at last we gave them best and fled to the deck. Finally the servants reduced things to a modified state of order, but whenever I smell a strong smell of kerosene I am irresistibly reminded of the day we tried to foregather with our kind, and be hospitable up the Gambia.

BALA, CHIEF OF KANTORA.

There were some Mandingo chiefs here. Bala, Chief of Kantora, and Jimbermang Jowlah, the local Chief, came to call. Bala dashed up on horseback, with a large following, to complain that there was trouble on the

Border, for the French had come in and said that his town should pay a poll tax of 500 dollars. He ranged all his horses, with their high cantled saddles and their heavy iron stirrups, on the steep, red bank, and he and his chief man came on board the little steamer to talk to the Commissioner. They made a quaint picture—the fair, good-looking Commissioner, with his boyish face grave, as suited the occasion, and the Chief, a warrior and a gentleman, as unlike Mr Jonsing in his tourist cap as the Gambia is unlike the Thames at Wapping. The Commissioner wore a blue-striped shirt and riding breeches, and the Chief was clad all in blue of different shades; there was a sort of underskirt to his knees of dark-blue cotton patterned in white, over that was a pale-blue tunic, through which came his bare arms, and over that again a voluminous dark-blue cotton garment, caught in at the waist with a girdle, from which depended a very handsome sporran of red leather picked out in yellow; on his bare feet were strapped spurs, a spur with a single point to it like a nail. He had a handsome, clean-cut face, his shaven head was bared out of courtesy, and at his feet lay his headgear, a blue-velvet cap, with a golden star and crescent embroidered upon it, and a great round straw hat adorned with red leather such as the Hausas farther east make. He was a chief, every inch of him. And his manners were those of a courtly gentleman too. He did not screech and howl like the men on the wharf, though he was manifestly troubled and desperately in earnest; but, sitting there on the deck of the little steamer, with the various odds and ends of life scattered around him, he stated his case, through an interpreter, to the young Commissioner seated on the hen-coop and taking down every word. When it was done he was assured that the Governor should be told all about it, and now rose with an air of intense relief. He had thrown his burden on responsible shoulders, and had time to think about the white woman who was looking on. He had seen white men before, quite a number, but never had he seen a white woman, and so he turned and looked at me gravely, with not half the rude curiosity with which I felt I had been steadily regarding him. I should like to have been a white woman worth looking at, instead of which I was horribly conscious that the coal dust was in my hair, that my hands had but recently grasped the greasy handrail of those steps across the boiler, and that my skirts had picked up most of the multifarious messes that were to be gathered there and on the unclean deck. There is no doubt skirts should not come much below the knees in the bush.

"He wishes to make his compliments to you," said the interpreter, and the grave and silent Chief, with a little, low murmur, took my hand in both his delicate, cold, black ones, held it for a moment with his head just a little bent, and then went his way, and I felt I had been complimented indeed.

The chief of Kantora, having done all he came to do, swam his horses across the river, trusting, I suppose, to the noise made by his numerous followers to scare away the crocodiles, and we went up the river to Kossun, which is within two miles of Yarba Tenda, where the British river ends. At Kossun there is a French factory only, and that managed by a black man, and here are the very beginnings of the groundnut trade. All around was vivid green— green on the bank, green reflected in the clear waters of the river; the sun was only just rising, the air was cool, and grey mists like a bridal veil rent with golden beams lay across the water; only by the factory was a patch of brown, enhancing the greenery that was all around it.

HEAP OF GROUNDNUTS.

The groundnut grows on a vine, and behind the factory this was all garnered into great heaps, and surrounded by crinted fences until time should be found to comb out the nuts. In the empty fields shy women, who dared not lift their faces to look at the strange, white woman, were gleaning, and the little, naked children were frankly afraid, and ran shrieking from the horrid sight. And just behind the factory were little enclosures of neatly plaited straw, and each of these contained a man's crop ready waiting to be valued and bought by the trader. Kossun was the only place where I saw the nuts as they belonged to the grower. All along the river there were heaps of them, looking like young mountains, but all these heaps were trader's property. At Nianimaroo, on the lower river, I saw a heap, which the pleased proprietor told me was worth £1000. He apparently had finished his heap, and was waiting to send it down the river, but everywhere else men, picturesque in fluttering rags or grotesque in cast-off European garments, were bringing calabashes and sacks of groundnuts to add to the heaps; and, since they cannot walk on the yielding nuts, which are like so many pebbles under their bare feet, little board ladders or steps of filled sacks were placed for them to run up. And no sooner were the heaps piled up than they had to be dug out again.

At Fatta Tenda, on the way down, having got rid of her cargo and her deck passengers, the *Mungo Park* began to load again with groundnuts; and men were busy through all the burning hot midday digging into the groundnut heap, filling up sacks, and as the sacks were filled stalwart, half-naked black men, like a line of ants, tramped laden down the steep bank and poured their loads into the steamer's hold in a cloud of gritty dust that penetrated everywhere. The trader told me that when he wanted labourers he appealed to one of the principal men who live in the town a mile or so behind the wharf, and he sent in his "family," who are paid at the rate of a shilling a day. It is very, very doubtful whether much of that shilling ever reaches the man who actually does the hard work. Things move slowly in the Gambia as in all Africa, and "family" is probably a euphonious term for household slave. After all, it is possibly only like the system of serfdom that existed in Europe in days gone by and will not exist very long here, for knowledge is coming, though it comes slowly, and with wealth pouring into the country and a Commissioner to appeal to in cases of oppression the black man will presently free himself. Even the women are already beginning to understand the difference. The morals of the country, be it remembered, are the primitive morals of a primitive people. A man may have four legal wives by Mohammedan law. He may have ever so many concubines, who add to his dignity; and then, if he is a big man—this was vouched for by the official native interpreter, who joined his Commissioner at M'Carthy—he has ever so many more women in his household, and these he expects to have children.

It is their business and he sees that they do it, and the children belong to him no matter who is the father. Children, it will be seen, are an asset, and the woman is now beginning to understand that the children are hers alone, and again and again a troubled woman, angry and tearful, walks miles to appeal to the travelling Commissioner, such and such a man, her master has taken away her children and she has heard that the great white master will restore them to her. And in most cases the great white master, who has probably a laughing, round, boyish face, fancies he has not a desire above good shooting, and speaks of the country as "poisonous," does all that is expected of him and often a good deal more also.

EACH MAN'S OWN LITTLE HEAP OF GROUNDNUTS.

And yet, only ten years ago, they were very doubtful still about the white man's protectorate in the Gambia, as graves in the Bathurst cemetery testify. Then was the last rising, when the district of San-nian Kunta was very disaffected, and two Commissioners, Mr Sitwell and Mr Silva, were sent with twelve native police to put matters straight. After the wont of the English, they despised their enemy and marched into a hostile village with the ammunition boxes screwed down, sat themselves down under a tree, and called on the Chief and village elders to come up before them. But the chief and elders did no such thing. Hidden in the surrounding bush, they replied with a volley from their long Danes, killing both the Commissioners and most of the policemen, but one escaping got away to the next Commissioner, a young fellow named Price. Now, Mr Price had only four policemen, but he was by no means sure of the death of his comrades, so promptly he sent off to headquarters for help, and without delay marched back to the disaffected village. The white men were dead and shockingly mutilated, but with his four faithful policemen he brought their remains back for decent burial. He did not know what moment he might not be attacked. He had before him as object lessons in savage warfare the dead bodies of his comrades. He had to march through thick bush, and they say at the end of that day's work young Mr Price's hair turned white. Punishment came, of course. Six months later the new Governor, Sir George Denton, with a company of W.A.F.F."s— West African Field Force—marched to that disaffected village; the chief was deposed and exiled, and peace has reigned ever since.

And now much farther away from Bathurst a woman may go through the country by herself in perfect safety. All the towns are still from one to four miles back from the tenda, away in the bush, from the old-time notion I suppose that there was danger to be dreaded by the great waterway, and early in the morning I used to take the narrow track through the long grass which was many feet above my head, and go and see primitive native life.

Up at the head of the river our steamer filled rapidly. When our holds were full the groundnuts were put in sacks and piled on the decks fore and aft, half-way up the masts, almost to the tops of the funnels, and the only place that was not groundnuts was the little cabin and the deck on top. There were £600 worth of groundnuts on board the *Mungo Park*, and we stowed on top of them passengers, men and women, and all their multifarious belongings, and then proceeded to pick up lighters also laden with groundnuts bound down the river.

Towards the evening of the second day of our homeward journey we came to a big creek down which was being poled by six men a red lighter, deep in the water and laden to the very brim with groundnuts. This the steamer was to tow behind. But it was not as simple as it sounds. The heavily laden lighter drifted first to one side and then to the other and threatened to fill, and the Commissioner's interpreter, sitting on deck, told me a long story of how here in the river there is a devil that will not allow a steamer or a cutter to go past unless the owner dances to placate him. If he do not care to dance himself he must pay someone else to dance for him. Unless someone dances, the engines may work, the sails may fill, but that vessel will not go ahead till the river devil has his toll. No one danced on board the *Mungo Park*, unless the black captain's prancing about and shaking his fist and shouting what sounded like blood-curdling threats at the skipper of the lighter might be construed into dancing. If so, it had not the desired effect, for the heavy lighter wouldn't steer, and presently the captain decided to tow it alongside. The darkness fell; all around us was the wide, weird, dark river, with the green starboard light just falling upon the mast of the lighter alongside, and for a few brief moments there was silence and peace, for the lighter was towing all right at last. Then the mast bent forward suddenly, there was a stifled, strangled cry, the captain gave a wild yell, the engines were stopped, and there was no more lighter, only the smooth dark water was rough with floating groundnuts and the river devil had taken his toll. Five of the crew had jumped for the *Mungo Park* and reached her, but the sixth, a tall Man-dingo, wrapped in a blue cloth, had gone down a prey for the wicked crocodiles or the cruel, strong undercurrents. They launched a boat and we felt our impotence and the vastness of the river, for they only had a hurricane lantern and it looked but a tiny speck on the waste of dark waters. The boat went up and down flashing its feeble light. Here was a patch of groundnuts, here a floating calabash, here a cloth, but the lighter and the man were gone, and we went on our way, easily enough now, because, of course, the steamer had paid toll.

There are the beginnings, it seems to me, in the groundnut trade of the Gambia, of what may be in the future a very great industry. True, the value of the groundnut is regulated by the price of cotton-seed oil, for which the oil pressed from the groundnut makes a very excellent substitute. Last year the Gambia's groundnuts, the harvest of the simplest, most ignorant peasants but one remove from savagery, was worth between £500,000 and £600,000, and not one-twentieth of the soil was cultivated, but the colony's existence was fairly justified. The greater part of this crop goes into French hands and is exported to Marseilles, where it is made into the finer sorts of soap. What wonder then if the French cast longing eyes upon the mighty river, for not only is the land around it rich, but they have spent large sums upon railways for their great colony of Senegal, and had they the Gambia as well they would have water carriage for both their imports and exports even in the dry season, and in the rains they could bring their heavy goods far far inland.

I realised all this as I came back to Bathurst with the dust from the groundnuts in my hair and eyes and nostrils, and dresses that had not been worn an hour before they were shrieking for the washtub. But what did a little discomfort matter?

I returned in time for the Christmas and New-Year festivities. On Christmas night all the English in the colony dined at Government House to celebrate the festival. Exiles all, they would have said. I have been told that I judge the English in West Africa a little hardly, and of course I realise all the bitterness of divided homes, especially at this season that should be one of family reunions. But after all the English make their life in West Africa far harder than they need. Dimly I saw this on my visit to the Gambia; slowly the feeling grew upon me till, when I left the Coast eight months later, I was fully convinced that if England is to hold her pride of place as a colonising nation with the French and Germans, she must make less of this exile theory and more of a home in these outlands. The doctors tell me this is impossible, and of course I must bow to the doctors' opinion, but it is saying in effect—which I will not allow for a moment—that the French and Germans—and especially the French and German women—are far better than the English.

Here in the Gambia I began to think it, and the fact was driven in more emphatically as I went down the Coast. The Englishman makes great moan, but after all he holds a position in West Africa the like of which he could not dream of in England. He is the superior, the ruler; men bow down before him and rush to do his bidding—he who would have a suburban house and two maid-servants in the old country, lives in barbaric splendour. Of course it is quite possible he prefers the suburban house and two maid-servants and his wife. And there, of course, the crux of the matter lies. Why, I know not, but English women are regarded as heroines and martyrs who go out to West Africa with their husbands. Possibly it is because I am an Australian and have had a harder bringing-up that I resent very much the supposition that a woman cannot go where a man can. From the time I was a little girl I have seen women go as a matter of course to the back-blocks with their husbands, and if, barring a few exceptions, they did not stay there, we all supposed not that it was the country that did not agree with them, but the husband. We all know there are husbands and wives who do not agree. And I can assure you, for I know both, life in the back-blocks in Australia, life in many of the towns of Australia, with its heat and its want of service, is far harder for a woman than it is in West Africa. Yet here in the Gambia and all along the Coast was the same eternal cry wherever there was a woman, "How long can she stay?"

The difference between the French and the English views on this vexed question was exemplified by the Commissioner's view and the French trader's. I have already given the former. Said the latter, "Of course my wife will come out. Why should she not. She is just waiting till the baby is a month old. What is the good of a wife to me in Paris? The rains? Of course she will stay the rains. It is only the English who are afraid of the rainy season." And I was sorry for the little contempt he put into his voice when he spoke of the English fear. I know this opinion of mine will bring down upon my devoted head a storm of wrath from West-Coast officials, but whether the Coast is healthy or not there is no denying the fact that the nation who takes its women is far more likely to hold a country, and in that the French and Germans are beating us hands down.

But this I only realised dimly during my stay in the Gambia. I was to leave on New Year's Day and on New Year's Eve we all went to the barracks of the W.A.F.F.'s to see the New Year in. And then in the soft, warm night the Governor and I went back to Government House. The stars were like points of gold, the sky was like dark-blue velvet, and against it the graceful palms stood out like splashes of ink, the water washed softly against the shore, there was the ceaseless hum of insects in the air, and from the native town behind came a beating of tom-toms subdued by the distance. The sentry started out of the shadow at the gate as the rickshaws arrived, and there came his guttural hail, "Who goes dere?"

"Friend," said the Governor's voice. It was commonplace, everyday to him.

"Pass friend and all's well," came the answer, and we went in and up the steps; but surely, I thought, it was a very good omen, a very good omen indeed. "Pass friend and all's well." I was leaving that day that had not yet dawned; I was going down the Coast and all should be well.

CHAPTER III
THE WHITE MAN'S GRAVE?

The origin of Sierra Leone—The difficulties of disposing of freed slaves—One of the beauty-spots of the earth—Is it possible that in the future, like Jamaica, it may be a health-resort?—Zachary Macauley's views—Few women in Freetown—Sanitary matters taken out of the hands of the Town Council and vested in a sanitary officer—Marked improvement in cleanliness and health of the town—A remarkable man of colour—Extraordinary language of the Creole—Want of taste in dress when they ape the European—Mrs Abraham Freeman at home.

I had no intention of going to Sierra Leone, but in West Africa as yet you make your way from one place to another along the sea-board, and not only did Sierra Leone lie directly on my way, but the steamer, the *Zaria*, in which I was travelling, stayed there for four days.

In the old days, a little over one hundred years ago, England, successfully policing the world, was putting down the iniquitous slave-trade all along the coasts of Africa, and found herself with numbers of black and helpless men, women, and children upon her hands. They had been collected from all parts of the Coast; they themselves often did not know where their homes lay, and the problem—quite a difficult one—was to know what to do with them. To land them promiscuously on the Coast was to seal their fate; either they would be killed or at the very best they would at once relapse into the condition from which they had been rescued. In this dilemma England did perhaps the only thing she could do. She bought from the chiefs a strip of land round the mouth of a river and landed there her somewhat troublesome charges to make for themselves, if they could, a home. Of course she did not leave them to their own devices; to do that would have been to insure their destruction at the hands of the Mendi and Timini war-boys, but she planted there a Governor and some soldiers, and made such provision as she could for the future of these forlorn people. Then the colony was but a little strip of land. It is but a small place still, but the British Protectorate now takes in those warlike Timinis and Mendis, and extends some hundreds of miles inland and as far south as the negro republic of Liberia, which I was on my way to visit.

CAPE SIERRA LEONE LIGHTHOUSE.

I don't know who chose Sierra Leone, but whoever he was the choice does him infinite credit. It is the most beautiful spot on all the west coast of Africa. I have seen many of the beautiful harbours of the world, Sydney, and Dunedin, and Hobart, which to my mind is the most beautiful of them all, Cape Town, and Naples, and Vigo, Genoa, Palermo, Messina, and lovely Taormina, which after all is not a harbour. I know them intimately, and with any of these Sierra Leone can hold her own. We entered the mouth of the river, passed the lighthouse, a tall, white building nestling among the palms, and all along the shore were entrancing little green bays, with green lawns. They looked like lawns from the ship, shaded by over-hanging trees. The blue sea met softly the golden sands, and the hills behind were veiled in a most alluring mist. It lifted and closed down and lifted again, like a bride longing yet fearing to disclose her loveliness to her lord. Here it seemed to me that a man might, when the feverish heat of youth is passed, build himself a home and pass the evening of his days resting from his labours; but I am bound to say I was the only person on board who did think so. One and all were determined to impress upon me the fact that Sierra Leone was known as the White Man's Grave, and that it deserved the name. And yet Zachary Macauley, who ruled over it in the end of the eighteenth century, staunchly upheld its advantages. I do not know that he exactly recommends it as a health-resort, but something very near to it, and he is very angry when anyone reviles the country. Zachary Macauley was probably right. If a man is not prepared to stand a certain amount of heat he must not go to the Coast at all; and if he does go he must be prepared so to guide his life that it is possible to conform to the rules of health demanded of the white man in the Tropics.

If he looks for the pleasures and delights of England and her temperate climate, he will find himself bitterly disappointed, but if he seeks for what Africa can give, and give with lavish hand, he will probably find that the country will treat him well.

We cast anchor opposite the town appropriately named Freetown, and I landed, presented my letter, and was asked by the kindly Governor to stay for a few days at Government House.

The majority of the Europeans, with the exception of the Governor, do not live in Freetown. They have wisely built their bungalows on the healthier hillsides, and I suppose as the colony increases in importance the Governor will go too; but I am glad when I was there he was still at Fort Thornton.

FREETOWN.

Of the history of the fort I know nothing. The bungalow is raised on thick stone walls, and you go up steps to the dwelling-house, past great rooms that are railed off with iron bars. There are ornamental plants there now, but there is no disguising the fact these are evidently relics of old slave days; I presume the barracoons of the slaves. But behind the one-time courtyard is filled up and sown with Bahama grass kept close-cropped and green, so that croquet and bowls may be played upon it. The bastions are now embowered in all manner of tropical greenery, and the great guns, the guns that Zachary Macauley used against the French privateers, peep out from a tangle of purple bougainvillea, scarlet hibiscus, fragrant frangipanni, and glorious white moon flowers.

There are white women in Freetown, not very many, but still fifteen or sixteen—the wives of the soldiers, of the political officers, medical officers, and the traders, and their number is growing, so that when the Governor gives a garden-party, the lawn that was once the courtyard of the fort is gay with bright muslin dresses, ribbons, and flowers. They seemed to like it too, those to whom I spoke, and there is no doubt that the place is improving from a health point of view. Until within the last two or three years the management of sanitary affairs was in the hands of the Town Council, of whom a large number were negroes, and the average negro is extremely careless about things sanitary; at last, so evil a reputation did the most beautiful town on the Coast get that it was found necessary to vest all power in the hands of a strong and capable medical officer, and make him responsible for the cleanliness of the town. The result, I believe, has more than justified all hopes. Perhaps some day the town may be as healthy as it is beautiful.

But I really know very little about Sierra Leone. I intended to come back and go up the railway that goes a couple of hundred miles up country, but as yet I have not had time, and all I can speak about with authority is its exceeding beauty. The streets are wide and rather grass-grown, for it is difficult to keep down vegetation in a moist and tropical climate, and I am glad to say there are, though the town is by no means well-planted, some beautiful trees to be seen. Government House is embowered in verdure, and the first station on the railway that runs up to the hill-top is "Cotton-tree."

And the dwellers in this earthly paradise? Knowing their pathetic and curious history I was anxious to see this people sprung from men and women gathered from all corners of Africa, unfortunate and unhappy.

Frankly, I share with the majority of Coasters a certain dislike to the educated negro. But many of the men I like best, the men whose opinion I have found well worth taking about things West-African, tell me I am wrong. You cannot expect to come up from savagery in a few decades, and the thing I dislike so in the negro clerk is but a phase that will pass. Here in Sierra Leone I met one man who made me feel that it would pass, that the time will come when the colour of the skin will make no difference, and that is the African known to all the world as Dr Blyden. He is an old man now and he was ill, so I went to see him; and as I sat and talked to him one still, hot evening, looking down the busy street where men and women in all stages of dress and undress were passing to and fro, carrying burdens on their heads, shrieking and shouting at one another in the unintelligible jargon they call English, had I not looked and seen for myself that his complexion was the shadowed livery of the burnished sun, I should have thought I was talking to some professor of one of the older Universities of England. His speech was measured and cultivated and there was no trace in it of that indescribable pompous intonation which seems peculiar to the educated black man. He gave me good advice, too.

COTTON TREE STATION.

"What shall I write about?" I asked, and halfexpected him to enter into a long dissertation upon the possibilities that lay latent in his race. But I might have known this man, who had conquered more difficulties on his way upwards than ever I had dreamed about, better than that.

"Write about what you see," said he. "And if you do not understand what you see then ask until you do."

So I have taken his advice and I write about what I have seen, and though afterwards I found reason to like much the peasant peoples of West Africa, I did not like the Creoles, as these descendants of freed slaves call themselves. Do I judge them hardly, I wonder? If so, I judge only as all the West Coast judges. They are a singularly arrogant people, blatant and self-satisfied, and much disliked along the Coast from the Gambia to San Paul de Loando. But they have taken advantage of the peace which England has ensured to them, and are prosperous. Traders and town-dwellers are they if they can manage it, and they pursue their avocations up and down the Coast. A curious thing about them is their language. If you ask them they would tell you it is English, and they would tell you they know no other; and English it is, as to the words,

- 34 -

but such an extraordinary jargon it is quite as difficult to understand as any unknown tongue. Yet it is the peculiar bastard tongue that is spoken all over the Coast. Many who speak it as the only means of communication between them and their boys must have wondered how such a jargon ever came into existence, and it was not till Mr Migeod wrote his book on the languages of West Africa that anyone in fact thought of classing it as a separate language. But once pointed out, the fact is undoubted. Sierra Leonese is simply English spoken with a negro construction.

Listening very carefully, it took a great deal of persuasion to make me believe the words were English. When I bought bananas from a woman sitting under the shade of a spreading cotton tree and the man behind her came forward and held out his hand, saying: "Make you gi'e me heen ooman coppa all," I grasped the fact that he intended to have the money long before I understood that he had said, in the only English, the only tongue he knew: "Give me her money," even though I did know that "coppa" stood for money. Some of the words, of course, become commonplaces of everyday life, and I am sure the next time I call on a friend, who is rich enough to have a man-servant, association of ideas will take me back, and I shall ask quite naturally, "Massa lib?" instead of the customary "Is Mrs Jones at home?" Of course, in the case of Mrs Jones it would be "Missus," but it was generally a master I was inquiring for in Africa.

Sunday or some high holiday is the day to see Freetown in its best clothes. Then the black gentleman appears in all the glory of a tall, black-silk hat, a frock coat, a highly starched waistcoat, the gayest of ties, scarlet or pink, the palest of dove-coloured trousers, and bright-yellow kid gloves; and the negro woman hides her fine figure with ill-fitting corsets, over which she wears an open-work muslin blouse, through which her dark skin shows a dull purple. Of all the places in Africa to transgress the laws of beauty and art Freetown is the very worst, and if ever a people tried their best to hide their own charms it is the Creoles of Sierra Leone. It would be comic if it were not pathetic. And yet, that these clothes are not part and parcel of the lives of these children near bred to the sun is promptly seen if a shower of rain comes on. In a lightning flash I saw a damsel, who might have come out of Fulham Road, or, at the very least, Edgeware Road, strip off the most perishable of her precious finery, do them up in a neat parcel that would carry easily under her umbrella, and serenely and unembarrassed march home in her white chemise and red petticoat. And she seemed to think as she passed me smiling she was doing the only right and proper thing to be done; as indeed she was.

I was a seeker after knowledge while I was in Freetown, and was always anxious to go anywhere and everywhere if a reason could be possibly contrived, so it happened that on one occasion I went to Lumley in search of fish. Lumley is a little village in the environ of Freetown, and the fish was to be bought from one Abraham Freeman, who dwelt at the side of the lagoon there. I went in a hammock, of course, and the way was lovely, up hill and down dale, through country that looked like a gigantic greenhouse run wild. The village was mostly built of mud with thatched roofs, but sometimes the houses were of wood, and the upper parts very wisely of trellis-work so as to insure a free current of air. When I arrived I looked round and told my hammock-boys to set me down at a cottage where a negro clad in a white shirt and trousers was lolling in a hammock. He did not scream at the scenery. He was rather suitably clad, I thought. It seemed he was the schoolmaster and a person of authority in the place.

"Can you tell me where Abraham Freeman lives?" I asked.

He corrected me gently but decidedly in his pompous English.

"Mr Freeman's abode is a little farther on by the lagoon. I believe Mr Freeman is absent in his boat, but Mrs Freeman is at home and will receive you."

So we went on a little farther through the tangle of greenery till the waters of the lagoon showed up. A dried mud-shack, thatched with palm leaves, stood between the row of cocoa-nut palms that fringed the lagoon and the roadway, and there my hammock-boys set me down.

"Dis Abraham Freeman's?" They were Timini and did not waste their breath on titles for a Creole, whom they would have eaten up save for the presence of the white man.

I got out and a tall, skinny black woman clad in a narrow strip of blue cloth round her hips came forward to meet me. Nothing was left to the imagination, and all her charms had long since departed. She hadn't even a handkerchief round her head, and the negro woman has lost all sense of vanity when she leaves her wool uncovered. Mrs Abraham Freeman was at home! My boys found a box for me to sit upon, and I contemplated Mrs Freeman and her family. Rebecca Freeman, about fifteen, was like a bronze statue so beautifully moulded was she; she really did not need anything beyond the narrow cloth at her hips, and being very justifiably vain she wore a gaily coloured silk turban. Elkanah Freeman, when he took off his coat to shin up a cocoa-nut palm, wore no shirt, was built like a Greek god; and "my little gran'-darter, Deborah," stark but for a string of green beads round her middle, was a delightful little cuddlesome thing, but "my sistah Esther an' Mistah Freeman's sistah Elizabeth" were hideous, skinny, and withered old hags, and the little strips of cloth they wore did not hide much. Each had a stone between her bony knees, and on it was breaking up some small sort of shell-fish like periwinkles. I got Mrs Freeman to show me the inside of her house. It was just four windowless rooms with openings under the eaves for air, with walls of dried clay, and for all furniture two wooden couches heaped up with rags. Outside on three stones a pot was boiling, and I asked her what was in it and could not make out her answer till she pointed out three skinny pigs rooting among the unsavoury refuse of the yard, then I grasped she was saying "hog," and I was thankful I was not going to have any of that dinner. She begged from me on the score of her poverty, and in pity I gave her a shilling, and then the little grand-daughter was so winsome, she had to have a penny, and then the two poor old souls, cracking shell-fish and apparently done with all that makes life good for a woman, begged so piteously that they had to have something; so, on the whole, it was rather an expensive visit, but it was well worth it to see Mrs Freeman "at home."

But I don't know Sierra Leone. I speak of all the West Coast as a passer-by speaks of it; but I know less of Sierra Leone than any other place I visited. Only it charmed me—I am going back some day soon if I can afford it—and I went on with regret to the negro republic.

CHAPTER IV
WHERE THE BLACK MAN RULES

America's experiment in the way of nation-making—Exiles in their mothers' land—The forlorn little company on Providence Island—Difficulties of landing and finding accommodation—British Consul to the rescue—The path to the British Consulate and the Liberian College—An outrageously ill-kept town—"Lovely little homes up the river"—A stickler for propriety—Dress and want of dress—The little ignorant missionary girl—At prayer in Lower Buchanan—The failure of a race.

No one on board the *Zaria* really believed I would land in Liberia. When I heard them talk I hardly believed it myself, and yet being there it seemed a pity not to see all I could see. The captain and officers were strongly of opinion there was absolutely nothing to see whatever. If it was madness for a woman to come alone to the Coast, it was stark-staring madness that almost needed restraining in a strait-waistcoat to think of landing in Liberia, for Liberia of all the countries along the Guinea Coast is the one most disliked by the sailors, most despised, and since I have been there I am inclined to say not without reason. For of course I did land; I should have been ashamed of myself if I had not, and I spent the best part of a fortnight there, and thanks to the kindness of His Britannic Majesty's Consul spent it very comfortably indeed.

Liberia is America's experiment in the way of nation-making even as Sierra Leone is Great Britain's, and if I cannot praise the Creole of Sierra Leone I have still less admiration for his American cousin.

In the second decade of the last century philanthropists began to consider the future of the freed slave in the United States, and it was decided that it would be wisdom to transport him back to the continent from which his forefathers came, and let him try there to put into practice the lessons he had learned in the art of civilisation. Bitter is the slur of black blood in the States; bitter, bitter was it ninety years ago when the forlorn little company who were to found a civilised negro state first set foot on their mothers' land. America was but young among the nations in 1822, so she took no responsibility, made no effort to launch these forlorn people in their new venture, or to help them once they were launched. Their leader was a quadroon with a fine face if one may judge from the picture in Executive Mansion, Monrovia, and he dreamed I suppose of wiping away the slur, the unmerited slur which lay across him and all like him with dark blood in their veins. With the chain and with the lash had America enforced the stern law that by the sweat of his brow shall man live, and she had seen to it that the personal toil of the negro and all with negro blood in their veins profited them only after their taskmasters had been satisfied. They belonged to a degraded subject race; no wonder they came back gladly, hopefully to the land from which certainly all their mothers had sprung. But it was no easy task they had before them. For a strong, hopeful, virile people it would have been difficult; to a people burdened with the degradation of centuries of servitude it has proved a task well-nigh beyond their capabilities. And before we condemn as do all the men along the Coast, as very often I do myself, it is only fair to remember the past.

PROVIDENCE ISLAND.

It must have been a very forlorn little company of people who landed on a small island at the mouth of that unknown river in 1822. They called the island Providence Island, and there they were cooped up for some weeks, for the people on the shore, warlike savages who brooked no master, objected to the newcomers, and it was some little time before they could set foot on the mainland and found their principal town of Monrovia. That was nearly ninety years ago, but very far inland they have never been able to go, for though Liberia takes up quite a large space on the map it is only Liberia in name. The hinterland is held by fighting tribes who resent any interference with their vested rights, and make the fact particularly clear.

The outlines of the history of Liberia I had known vaguely for many a long day even to the name of Monrovia their capital, so called after President Munro, and it seemed to give point to the story to sit on the deck of the ship that swung at her anchors just beyond the surf of the river mouth. At least they had chosen a very beautiful place. Blue sky, blue sea, snow-white surf breaking on the bar, and a hillside clothed in dense greenery with palms cutting the sky line and the roofs of houses peeping out from among the verdure, that is what I saw, and the captain was emphatic I had seen the best of it. I did not doubt his word then, and having been ashore I am bound to confess he was right.

But the difficulty was to get ashore. I had a letter to the British Consul, but I had not sampled the kindliness of British Consuls as I had that of the Governors, and I did not know exactly what he would say. "I wonder if there is an hotel," I said doubtfully to the captain, and he sniffed.

"You couldn't stay in a negro hotel."

I sent off my letter to the Consul and waited, and a little cloud came up out of the sea and spread over all the sky, and it rained, and it rained, and it rained, and it rained. The sky was dark and forbidding, the sea was leaden-coloured, the waves just tipped with angry, white foam, and the green hills were blotted out, the decks were awash, the awnings were sopping and wept coaly tears, and the captain said as if that settled it, "There, you can't possibly go ashore." But I was by no means sure. Still there was no letter from His Majesty's Consul. Morning passed on to afternoon, and afternoon waned towards evening and still there was no letter. A ship on a pouring wet day is just about as uncomfortable a place as one can be in, but still I was inclined to accept the captain's opinion that Monrovia without someone to act as guide, philosopher, and friend would be a worse place.

No letter, and the captain came along.

"I must get away before dark." He spoke as if that settled it, and he was right, but not the way he expected.

I felt I simply could not go without seeing this place, and I decided. "Then I'll go ashore."

"You can't possibly."

"Oh yes, I can. They won't eat me."

I don't know though that I was quite comfortable as I was dropped over the side in a mammy chair into a surf boat that was half-full of water. The rain had stopped at last but everything in that boat was wet, and my gear made a splash as it was dropped down.

My soldier brother had lent me his camp-kit for the expedition.

"Can't possibly hurt it," said he good-naturedly. "It's been through two campaigns. If you spoil it, it shall be my contribution; but you won't."

I accepted, but I thought as I sat on the bedding-roll at the bottom of that very wet boat, with my head not coming above the gunwale, that he did not know Africa. I hoped I should not have to sleep on that bed that night, because it was borne in on me it would be more than damp.

Luckily I didn't. We crossed the bar, and the ragged, half-naked Kroo boys, than whom there are surely no better boatmen in the world, begged a dash, "because we no splash you," as if a bucket or two of salt water would have made much difference, and I gave it and was so absorbed in the wonder as to what was to become of me that I gave hardly any heed to the shore that was approaching. When I did it was to notice that all the beauty I had seen from the deck was vanishing. Man's handiwork was tumble-down, dirty, dilapidated, unfinished. I stepped from the boat to a narrow causeway of stone; it is difficult to get out of a boat five feet deep with grace, more especially when your skirts are sopping, and I stepped from the causeway, it was not above a foot wide, into yellow mud, and saw I was surrounded by dilapidated buildings such as one might see in any poor, penniless little port. There were negroes in all stages of rags round me, and then out from amongst them stepped a white man, a neat and spick-and-span white man with soldier written all over him, the soldier of the new type, learned, thoughtful, well-read.

"Mrs Gaunt?"

I said "Yes" with a little gasp, because his immaculate spruceness made me feel I was too much in keeping with the buildings and the people around us.

"Did you get my note? I am sorry I only got yours a couple of hours ago."

Oh, I understood by now that in Africa it is impossible for a note to reach its destination quickly, and I said so, and he went on to arrange for my accommodation.

"If you will stay at the Consulate I will be delighted, but it is a mile and a half from the town, and I have no wife; or there is a boarding-house in the town, not too uncomfortable I am told."

There could be but one answer to that. Of course I accepted his invitation; there are but few conventions and no Mrs Grundy in out-of-the-way spots, thank heaven, and in the growing darkness we set off for the Consulate. It was broken to me regretfully that I would have to walk; there is no other means of progression in the negro republic.

Such a walk as it was. Never have I met such a road. It was steep, and it was rough, and it was stony as a mountain torrent; now after the rain it was wet and slippery and the branches of the overhanging trees showered us with water as we passed. It was lonely as a forest path in Ashanti, and the jungle was thick on either hand, the night birds cried, the birds that loved the sun made sleepy noises, the ceaseless insects roused to activity by the rain made the darkness shrill with their clamour, and there were mysterious rustlings as small animals forced their way through the bush or fled before us. My host offered me his stick to pull me over the steepest rocks, and also supplied the interesting information that round the Consulate the deer came down to lick the salt from the rocks, and the panthers, tigers they called them there, came down and killed the deer. I made a mental note not to walk in that path by night; indeed I made a note not to walk in it ever again, as drenched and dripping with perspiration we emerged into a clearing and saw looming up before us a tropical bungalow and beyond the sea. It is an exquisite situation but is desperately lonely.

ROAD TO LIBERIA COLLEGE.

My gear came on men's heads and the Consul's note was delivered to me in the bush. Neither he nor I understood why it had come by such a roundabout path. One of his servants also met us half-way with a lantern, and since I had heard by then about the "tigers" I confess to thinking it was a wise precaution.

The Consulate is a fine two-storied building with wide verandahs and a large hall where we generally sat, and that hall was very inadequately lighted by some excellent lamps. The Consul didn't understand them and the negro servants didn't understand them, and darkness was just visible and I determined as soon as I knew my host well enough to ask him to let me have a turn at his lamps. Such is the power of a little knowledge; when I left the Consulate it was lighted as it should be, but that first night we spent in a dim, religious light, and I felt I was going to enjoy myself hugely, for here at last was something new. The Gambia and Sierra Leone had been too much regulation Tropics; all that I had seen and done I had at least read of before, but this was something quite different. This had all the glamour of the unknown and the unexpected. I am bound to say that His Majesty's Consul did not look at things with the same eyes. He didn't like Liberia, and he said frankly that things might be unexpected in a measure but he always knew they would be unpleasant. But I went to bed that night with the feeling I was really entering into the land of romance.

Next morning I told my host I would go and see the town.

"But I shan't go by the short cut," I added emphatically.

"What short cut?"

"The way we came last night."

"That's not a short cut," said he, and he smiled pitifully at my ignorance of what was before me. "That's the main road."

And so it was. Afterwards I tried to photograph it, but in addition to the difficulty of getting an accurate picture of a steep slope, I had the misfortune to shake the camera, and so my most remarkable picture was spoiled. I give a picture of the road, but I always felt when I came to that part the worst was left behind. And yet on this road is the Liberian College where the youth of Liberia, male and female, are educated. It is a big building built of brick and corrugated iron, in a style that seems wholly unsuited to the Liberian climate, though viewed from a distance it looks imposing in its setting of greenery. They teach the children algebra and euclid, or profess to do so—evil-tongued rumour has it that the majority of the Liberian women can neither read nor write—but to attain that, to them a useless edge, they have to scramble over without exception the very worst road I have ever met.

But the road only matches the rest of the place. Monrovia is not only an ill-kept town, it is an outrageously ill-kept town.

BROAD STREET, MONROVIA

Many towns have I seen in the world, many, many towns along this west coast of Africa, so I am in a position to compare, and never have I seen such hopelessly miserable places as Monrovia and the other smaller Liberian towns along the Coast. The streets look pretty enough in a photograph; they are pretty enough in reality because of the kindly hand of Nature and the tropical climate which makes vegetation grow up everywhere. There is no wheeled traffic, no possibility of getting about except on your own feet, and in consequence the roadways are generally knee-deep in weeds, with just a track meandering through them here and there, and between the roadway and the side walk is a rough gutter, or at least waterway, about two feet deep, and of uncertain width, usually hidden by the veiling weeds. Occasionally they have little gimcrack bridges apparently built of gin cases across these chasms, but, as a rule, if I could not jump as the wandering goats did, I had to make my way round, even though it involved a detour of at least a quarter of a mile.

And the houses in the streets were unlike the houses to be seen anywhere else on the West Coast, and, to my mind at least, are quite unsuited to a tropical climate. They are built of wood, brick, or, and this is the most common, of corrugated iron, are three or four stories high, steep and narrow, with high-pitched roofs, and narrow balconies, and many windows which are made with sashes after the fashion of more temperate climes. The Executive Mansion, as they call the official residence of the President, is perhaps as good a specimen as any and is in as good repair, though even it is woefully shabby, and the day I called there, for of course I paid my respects, clothes were drying on the weeds and grass of the roadway just in front of the main entrance. Two doors farther down was a tall, rather pretentious redbrick house which must have cost money to build, but the windows were broken and boarded up, and one end of the balcony was just a ragged fringe of torn and rotting wood. So desolate was the place I thought it must be deserted, but no. On looking up I saw that on the other end of the balcony were contentedly lolling a couple of half-dressed women and a man, naked to the waist, who were watching with curiosity the white woman strolling down the street.

A great deal of the Liberian's life must be spent on his balcony, for the houses must be very stuffy in such a climate, and they are by no means furnished suitably; of course it is entirely a matter of taste, but for West Africa I infinitely preferred the sanded, earthen floor of my friend the Jolloff pilot's wife to the blue Brussels-carpet on the drawing-room floor of the wife of the President of the Liberian republic. But, as I have said, this is a matter of taste, and I may be wrong. I know many houses in London, the furniture of which appears to me anything but suitable.

It was quaint to me, me an Australian with strong feelings on the question of colour, to be entertained by the President's wife, a kindly black lady in a purple dress and with a strong American accent. She had never been out of Africa, she told me, and she had great faith in the future of Liberia. The President had been to England twice. And the President's sad eyes seemed to say, though he hinted no such thing, that he did not share his wife's optimism.

TYPICAL LIBERIAN HOUSE.

"We have lovely little homes up the river," she said as she shifted the array of bibles and hymn-books that covered the centre-table in the drawingroom to make room for the tray on which was ginger-beer for my refreshment, "and if you will go up, we will make you very welcome."

She would not let me take her photograph as I desired to do; possibly she had met the amateur photographer before and distrusted the species. I could not convince her I could produce a nice picture.

I never saw those "lovely little homes" either. They certainly were not to be found in my meaning of the words in Monrovia or any of the Coast towns, and up country I did not go; there was no way of doing so, save on my own feet, and I felt then I could not walk in such a hot climate. There may be such homes, I do not know, for between this good, kindly woman and me was the great unbridgeable gulf fixed, and our modes of thought were not the same. In judging things Liberian I try to remember that. Every day it was brought home to me.

The civilised black man, for instance, is often a great stickler for propriety, and I have known one who felt himself obliged to board up his front verandah because the white man who lived opposite was wont to stroll on *his* balcony in the early morning clad only in his pyjamas, and yet often passing along the street and looking up I saw men and women in the scantiest of attire lounging on their balconies doing nothing, unless they were thinking, which is doubtful.

Dress or want of dress, I find, strikes one curiously. I have times without number seen a black man working in a loin cloth or bathing as Nature made him, and not been conscious of anything wrong. He seemed fitly and suitably clad; he lacked nothing. But looking on those men in the balconies in only a pair of trousers, or women in a skirt pure and simple, among surroundings that to a certain extent spoke of civilisation, there was a wrong note struck. They were not so much barbaric as indecent. It was as if a corner of the veil of respectability had been lifted, the thin veneer of civilisation torn off, and you saw if you dared to look the possibilities that lie behind. I believed all the horrible stories of Vaudooism of America and the West Indies when I saw the naked chest and shoulders of a black man leaning over a balcony in Monrovia, and yet I have been only moved to friendliness when the fetish man of an Ashanti village, with greasy curls flying, with all his weird ornaments jingling, tom-toms beating, and excited people shouting, came dancing towards me and pranced round me with pointing fingers that I hope and believe meant a blessing. Can anyone tell me why this was? Was it because the fetish man was giving of his very best, while the half-civilised man was sinking back into barbarism and looking at the white woman gave her thoughts she would deeply have resented? Was it just an example of the thought-reading we are subconsciously doing every day and all day long without exactly realising it ourselves?

The people of Monrovia, there are over 4000 of them, seem always lounging and idling, and the place looks as if it were no one's business to knock in a nail or replace a board. It is falling into decay. It is not deserted, for the people are there, and presumably they live. They exist waiting for their houses to tumble about their ears. There is a market-place down in Waterside, the poorest, most miserable market-place on all the African coast. The road here, just close to the landing-place, is not made, but just trodden hard by the passing of many feet. Here and there the native rocks crop up, and no effort has been made to smooth them down. Above all, the stench is sickening, for the Coast negro, without the kindly, sometimes the stern guidance of the white man, is often intolerably dirty, and if my eyes did not recognise it, my nose would. In all the town, city they call it, there is not one garden or attempt at a garden. The houses are set wide enough apart; any fences that have been put up are as a rule broken-down, invariably in need of repair, and in between those houses is much wild growth. The scarlet hibiscus covers a broken fence; an oleander grows bushy and covered with pink roselike flowers; stately cocoa-nut palms, shapely mangoes are to be seen, and all over the streets and roadway in the month of January, I was there, as if it would veil man's neglect as far as possible, grew a creeping convolvulus with masses of pink cup-shaped flowers—in the morning hopeful and fresh and full of dew, in the evening wilted and shut up tightly as if they had given up the effort in hopeless despair. Never have I seen such a dreary, neglected town. It would be pitiful anywhere in the world. It is ten times more so here, where one feels that it marks the failure of a race, that it almost justifies the infamous traffic of our forefathers. It was all shoddy from the very beginning. It is now shoddy come to its inevitable end.

For all the great mark on the map, as I have said, the settlements at Monrovia do not extend more than thirty miles up the river; elsewhere the civilised negroes barely hold the sea-board. They are eternally at war with the tribesmen behind, and here in Monrovia I met half a dozen of the prisoners, dressed in rags, chained two and two with iron collars round their necks, and their guard, a blatant, self-satisfied person, was just about as ragged a scarecrow as they were. Not that the victory is by any means always to the Liberians, for a trader, an Englishman, who had been seeking fresh openings in the hinterland where no Liberian would dare to go, told me that though the tribes are not as a rule cannibals, they do make a practice of eating their best-hated enemies, and he had come across the hands and feet of not a few of the Liberian Mendi soldiery in pickle for future use.

To keep these tribesmen in check, the Liberian, who is essentially a man of peace—a slave—has been obliged to raise an army from the Mendis who inhabit the British protectorate to the west, and so he has laid upon himself a great burden. For, unfortunately, there is not always money in the treasury to satisfy this army of mercenaries when they get tired of taking out their pay in trade gin or tobacco. Poor Liberians, threatened with a double danger. If they have no soldiers the tribesmen within their borders eat them up, and if they have soldiers, war they must have, to provide an outlet for energies that otherwise might be misdirected.

I left my kind host with many regrets and Monrovia without any, and I went on board the *Chama* which was to call at Grand Bassa and Cape Palmas, and if I did not intend to view them entirely from the ship's deck, at least I felt after my visit to Monrovia it would hardly be necessary for me to stay in either of these towns.

A HOUSE IN LOWER BUCHANAN.

They bear a strong family resemblance to the capital, only they are "more so." The tribes see to it, I believe, that there is no communication with the capital except by sea, and the little communities with their pretensions to civilisation are far less ininteresting than the people of an Ashanti village who have seldom or never seen a white man.

I landed at Lower Buchanan, Grand Bassa, early one morning. The beach simply reeked of human occupancy. They do not trouble about sanitation in Liberia, and the town itself looked as if the houses had been set down promiscuously in the primeval bush. Perhaps there were more signs of wealth than in Monrovia, for I did see three cows and at least half a dozen hairy, razor-backed pigs on the track that was by courtesy the principal street, and it must require something to support all the churches.

I suppose it is the emotional character of the negro that makes him take so largely to religion, or rather, I think I may say, the observances of religion. The question of the missionaries is a vexed one, and on board the *Chama* was a missionary who made me think. She was a pretty young girl who had left home and father and mother and sisters and brothers and lover—ah, the lover was evidently hard where all had been hard—to minister to the spiritual needs of the people who dwelt behind Cape Palmas. She was sweetly ignorant of the world, of everything that did not apply to the little home in Canada that she had left with such reluctance, and was evidently immensely surprised to find the captain and officers of the ship kindly, honest gentlemen who treated her as tenderly and deferentially as they might have treated one of their own young sisters.

"I thought all sailors were bad men," she said wonderingly. "I have always been led to believe they were bad."

Now, what could such a nice, ignorant little girl as that teach the negro? And yet she had curiously hard ideas on some subjects. She talked about the missionary and his wife to whom she was going for five long years and to whom she was bringing out clothes for their baby.

"If it is alive," she added naively.

"Oh, I hope it will live," said I, the heathen who doubted the use of missionaries and all their works.

"Well, I don't know"—and the cynicism sat curiously on the sweet, young face—"poor little kiddie, perhaps it is better dead. What sort of a life could it have out there, and what sort of an upbringing? Its mother has other work to do."

And I tried to show her that one white child was worth a thousand problematical souls of negroes, and I tried in vain.

But if ever I saw the wrong side of Christianity I saw it here in Liberia. Monrovia had many churches, all more or less unfinished, all more or less in decay, and here in Lower Buchanan three corrugated-iron churches within a stone's throw of one another constituted one of the chief features of the town. It was early on a Tuesday morning, the best time for work in a tropical climate, if work is going to be done at all. On the beach the Kroo boys were bringing from surf boats the piassava, the fibre that grows in the swamps and constitutes a large part of the Liberian export, but in Lower Buchanan itself the greater part of the inhabitants that I saw were in church. I entered that church.

PRINCIPAL STREET, LOWER BUCHANAN.

Such a tatterdemalion crew! God forbid that I should scoff at any man's faith, but here cleanliness is practically divorced from godliness, and I can honestly say that never in my life have I seen dirtier bundles of rags than that congregation. A woman in a costume a scarecrow would have despised, her head adorned with a baby's hat, the dirty white ribbons fluttering down behind, was praying aloud with much unction, shouting that she was a miserable sinner, and calling upon the Lord to forgive her. The negro loves the sound of his own voice, and again I must claim that I do not scorn any man's sincere faith, but that negro lady was thoroughly enjoying herself, absolutely sure of her own importance. The ragged scarecrows who listened punctuated the prayer with groans of delight, and the only decent one amongst them was a small girl, whose nakedness was hidden by a simple blue-and-white cloth, and she was probably a household slave. For these descendants of a slave people make slaves in their turn, perhaps not men slaves, but women are saleable commodities among a savage nation, and for a trifling consideration, a bottle of trade gin or a few sticks of trade tobacco, they will hand over a girl-child who, taken into the household without pay, holds the position of a servant and is therefore to all intents and purposes a slave. This is really not as bad as it sounds; her position is probably quite as good as it would be in her own tribe, and as she grows older she either marries or forms some sort of alliance with a Liberian. Loose connections and divorce are both so common that she is no worse off than the ordinary Liberian woman, and the admixture of good, strong virile blood may possibly help the future race. At least that is what I thought as I watched the congregation at prayer. They sang hymn choruses so beautifully as to bring tears to my eyes, and then they came outside and abused me because I wanted to photograph them. Had I been they, I should have objected to going out to the world as specimens of their people, but they need not have reviled me in the blatant, coarse manner of the negro who has just seen enough of civilisation to think he rules the universe. I did not press the matter, because I felt it would be ungracious to make a picture of them against their will. But clearly the lovely little homes were not in Lower Buchanan. Nor were they in Cape Palmas.

Far be it from me to say that plantations of some useful description do not exist. They may; I can only say I have seen no evidences of them in three of their towns or near those towns. I will put it on record that I did see some cabbage stalks behind some broken railings opposite the President's house in Monrovia, but that was absolutely the only thing in the shape of a garden, vegetable, fruit, or flower, that I did see in the environs of the towns. You can buy no fruit in Monrovia, no chickens, no eggs. Bananas and limes have to be imported. Meat is only to be had at rare intervals, and living is so frightfully dear that when the British Consul had, during my stay, to provide for a distressed British subject who had been unfortunate enough to get adrift in the land, he had to pay six shillings and sixpence a day for his board and lodging—a bare room, not over-clean, with a rough bed in it, and board that did not include meat, but consisted chiefly of manioc or cassava which is what the majority of the Liberians live on themselves.

The country as a matter of fact lives on the Custom's dues which reach about £70,000 a year and are levied not only on the goods that they themselves use but on those the unfortunate natives of the hinterland require. No Liberian is a craftsman even of the humblest sort. The Kroo men are fishermen and boatmen; men from Sierra Leone, the Gold Coast, and Lagos, with an occasional Vai tribesman thrown in, are painters, smiths, and carpenters. The Liberian, the descendant of the freed slave, despises these things; he aspires to be a gentleman of leisure, to serve in the Government Service, or in the Church, to walk about in a black suit with a high collar and a silver-mounted cane. Then apparently he is happy even if he come out of the most dilapidated house in Monrovia. There are, I believe, exceptions. I wonder, considering their antecedents and the conditions under which they have had to exist, whether one could expect more. Possibly it should be counted to them for great righteousness if any good men be found among them at all. But taken as a whole the Liberians after close on ninety years of self-government must strike the stranger as an effete race, blatant and arrogant of speech, an arrogance that is only equalled by their appalling ignorance, a race that compares shockingly with the Mandingo or Jolloff of the Gambia, the stately Ashanti, a warrior with reserve power, or the busy agricultural Yoruba. These men are gentlemen in their own simple, untutored way, courteous and dignified. The Liberian is only a travesty of the European, arrogant without proper dignity, boastful with absolutely nothing in the world to boast about unless it be the amazing wealth of the country he mismanages so shamefully. For Liberia is a rich country; it has a soil of surpassing fertility, and it seems to me that almost anything in the way of tropical products might be produced there. That nothing is produced is due to the ignorance and idleness of these descendants of slaves who rule or misrule the land. Since the days of the iniquitous trade, that first brought her into touch with civilisation, West Africa has been exploited for the sake of the nations of the western world. No one till this present generation seems to have recognised that she had any rights. Now we realise that the black man must be considered at least as much as the white man, who has made himself his master. Now most settlements along the Coast are busy, prosperous, and, above all, sanitary. Only in Liberia, the civilised black man's own country, does a different state of things prevail; only here has the movement been retrograde.

An end must come, but who can say what this end will be.

The missionary girl who had given up all she held most dear, who had joined the noble band of martyrs and heroes for Africa, said she had done so because she had seen a letter from a black man just mentioning a chapter and verse of the New Testament. She had looked it up and read the prayer of the Macedonians. Strange, strange are the workings of the Unseen, cruel sometimes the penalties poor human nature takes upon itself. Who shall say that a Guiding Hand had not made that girl choose wisely for the development of her own character, and who shall say that some ultimate good may not yet come for beautiful, wealthy, poverty-stricken Liberia. That the civilised nations, sinking their own jealousies, may step in and save her despite herself, I think, is the only hope. But it must be as Paul would have saved, not as the pitiful Christ. For the pendulum has swung too far back; the fathers have eaten sour grapes and the children's teeth are set on edge. She does not know it herself, she will resent bitterly the imputation, but to me Liberia seems to be stretching out her hands crying dumbly to the white man the cry that came across the water of old, the cry the missionary girl listened to, the cry of Macedonia, "Come over and help us."

But I was one who only heard the cry in passing, who felt that I at least could not help. I went on in the *Chama* to Axim, interested with what I had seen, but forgetting much in what I thought was to be my first hammock-trip alone. For I wanted to go to Half Assinie, and since no one may be sure of landing all their gear in safety on that surf-bound coast, I had to land at Axim and go back overland the fifty miles to the French border, and I thought I should have to do it alone.

CHAPTER V
THE GUINEA COAST

Every man's duty—"Three deaths in two days"—An old Portuguese settlement—A troubled District Commissioner—What to do with a wandering white woman—The Judge's quarters—The kindly medical officer and his wife—A West-African town—"My outside wife"—Dangers ahead—The man who was never afterwards heard of—The Forestry officer's carriers—"Good man, bad man, fool man"—First night in the wilds—Hair in the soup.

A great German philosopher has remarked that you very seldom get a human being who has all the qualities of his own sex without a trace of the characteristics of the other. Such a being would be hardly attractive. At least I consoled myself with that reflection when I found stirring within me a very masculine desire to be out of leading strings and to be allowed to take care of myself. It is pleasant to be taken care of, but it is decidedly uncomfortable to feel that you are a burden upon men upon whom you have no claim whatever. They were looking after me because they were emphatically sure that the Coast is no place for a lone woman. At the bottom of my heart, grateful as I was to the individuals, I didn't like it. I thought my freedom was coming at Axim, but it didn't.

Every man felt it his duty to impress upon me the unhealthiness of the Coast, and every man did his duty manfully, forgetting that I have a very excellent pair of eyes and an inquiring mind. The hot, still morning we arrived at Axim the captain, having discussed matters with the Custom officer, came to me solemnly shaking his head.

"A terrible place, Mrs Gaunt, a terrible place. Three deaths in Axim in the last two days."

It was quite a correct Coast speech, and for the moment I was shocked, though not afraid, because naturally it never occurs to me that I will die, at least not just yet, and not because the people round me are dying. The captain was gloomily happy as having vindicated the evil reputation of the country, and I looked ashore and wondered what was wrong with so attractive a place.

The Portuguese, those mariners of long ago, chose the site and, as they always did, chose wisely. A promontory, on which is the white fort, juts out into the sea, and behind is all the luxuriant greenery of the Tropics, for the land rises just sufficiently to give beauty to the scene. I wondered why those three people had died, and I inquired. The whole incident is so characteristic of the loose talk that builds up an evil reputation for a country. Those deaths were held up to me as a warning. It would have been quite as much to the point if they had warned me against getting frost-bitten or falling into a cauldron of boiling sugar. One man died of a disease he had contracted twenty years before, and was exceedingly lucky to have lived so long, another had died of drink, and the third was a woman. She, poor thing, was the wife of a missionary from Sierra Leone, and had not been in a cooler climate for two years. There was a baby coming, and instead of going home she had come to Axim, had a bad go of blackwater, and when the baby came, her constitution could not stand the double strain, and she died. Only her death was directly attributable to the climate, and the exercise of a little common sense would have saved her.

So I landed and was not afraid.

But my arrival was a cause of tribulation to the District Commissioner. There was no hotel, so I appealed to him for quarters. It really was a little hard on him. He sighed and did his best, and the only time I really saw him look happy was about three weeks later when he saw me safely in a surf boat bound for the out-going steamer. But when I landed, the need for shelter was pressing, and he gave me a room in the Judge's quarters where it seems they bestow all homeless white strangers in Axim. Already the Forestry officer was there, and he had a sitting-room and a bedroom, so that I could only have a bedroom and a bathroom. Now, with a verandah and such a large room at my disposal, I could make myself more than comfortable; then, because I did not know African ways, I accepted the very kind invitation of the medical officer and his wife, the only white woman in Axim, to "chop" with them.

African ways are very convenient when you come to think of it. Here was a big empty room with a wardrobe and a little cane furniture in it. I went in with my brother's kit and set up my camp-bed, my bath, laid down my ground sheet and put up my table and chair, and I had all that was really necessary. Outside was the ragged garden, haunted they said, though I never saw the ghost, and because it was usually empty the big rats scrambled up the stairs, and the birds sat in the oleander bushes and called "Be quick, be quick" continually.

I couldn't take their advice because it is impossible to hurry things on the Coast and I must wait for the carriers.

The first night I had dinner—chop—with the medical officer and his wife and went to bed reflecting a little regretfully I had made no preparations for my early-morning tea. However, I concluded it might be good discipline to do without it. But it is a great thing to have a capable boy. Just as it began to get light Grant appeared outside my mosquito curtains as usual with a cup of tea and some fruit. The cup and teapot were my own; he had stolen all the materials from the Forestry officer next door, and I was much beholden to that young man when, on apologising, he smiled and said it was all right, he was glad I liked his tea.

Axim is a pretty little town with the usual handful of whites and the negroes semi-civilised with that curious civilisation which has probably persisted for centuries, which is not what we would call civilisation and yet is not savagery. It is hardly even barbarism. These Coast towns are not crowded with naked savages as many a stay-at-home Briton seems to imagine; they are peopled with artisans, clerks, traders, labourers, people like in many ways to those in the same social scale in other countries, and differing only when the marked characteristics of the negro come in. All along in these Coast towns the negroes are much the same. To their own place they are suitable; only when they try to conform too much to the European lines of thought do they strike one as *outré* or objectionable. I suppose that is what jars in the Christian negro. It is not the Christianity, it is the striving after something eminently unsuited to him. Left to himself though, he naturally goes back to the mode of life that was his forefathers', and sometimes he has the courage to own it. I remember a man who called in the medical officer about his wife. The ordinary negro has as many wives as he can afford, but the Christian is by way of only having one, and as this man was clothed in the ordinary garb of the European, unnecessary coat, shirt, and hat, I naturally set him down as a Christian.

"I Christian," he told me. "Mission-teacher once."

"Not now?"

"No, Swanzy's agent now. You savey my wife; she get well?"

I said I had no doubt she would, and I rejoiced in this sign of marital affection, when he dashed it all to the ground.

"She not my real wife; she my outside wife," said he as one who would explain their exact relations.

My views on negro homes received a shock, but after all if the women don't object, what matter? It is the custom of the country.

I looked round the town and took photographs, wasted many plates trying to develop in too hot a place, and declared my intention of going west just as soon as ever I could get carriers. I didn't quite know how I should manage, but I concluded I should learn by experience.

Even now, though I have travelled since then close on 700 miles in a hammock, I cannot make up my mind whether it would have been safe for me to go alone. Undoubtedly I should have made many mistakes, and in a country where the white man holds his position by his prestige it is perhaps just as well that a woman of his colour should not make mistakes.

"Not suitable," said one who objected strongly to the presence of any white women on the Coast.

"Hardly safe," said another.

"Not safe," said a third emphatically, and then they told a story. Axim has been settled and civilised many years, and yet only last year a man disappeared. He was one of a party dining with his friends. After dinner they started a game of cards, and up the verandah steps came this man's house-steward. His master was wanted. The company protested, but he left declaring he would return immediately. He did not return and from that day to this neither he nor his house-boy have been seen by mortal eyes. The story sounds fearsome enough. It sounded worse to me preparing to go along the Coast by myself, but now, thinking it over calmly, I see flaws. Investigated, I wonder if it would turn out like the story of the three people dead in two days; true, but admitting of quite a different construction being put upon it than that presented for my edification. One thing I do know and that is that I would feel very much safer in an Ashanti village that has only been conquered in the last ten years than I would alone in any of those little towns along the Guinea Coast, between Axim and Half Assinie, that have been in contact with the white man for the last three hundred years.

Anyhow, Axim decided for me I should not go alone, and the Forestry officer, like the chivalrous, gracious gentleman he was, came forward and pretended he had business at Half Assinie and that it would be a great pleasure to have a companion on the road. And so well did he play his part that it was not till we were bound back from the Border that I discovered he had simply come to look after me.

Then I was initiated into the difficulties of carriers. The Omahin, that is to say the Chief of Beyin, had sent me twenty men and women, and the Forestry officer had two separate lots of Kroo boys and Mendis, and early one morning in January we made preparations for a start. We didn't start early. It seems to me how ever carefully you lay your plans, you never do. First no carriers turned up; then some of the Forestry officer's men condescended to appear. Then the orderly, a man from the north with his face cut with a knife into a permanent sardonic grin, strolled up. He was sent out to seek carriers, and presently drove before him two or three women, one with a baby on her back, and these it appeared were the advance contingent of my gang. A Beyin woman-carrier or indeed any woman along the Coast generally wears a printed-cotton cloth of a dark colour round her by way of a skirt, and one of the little loose blouses that the missionaries introduced on to the Coast over a hundred years ago because they regarded it as indecent for a woman to have her bosom uncovered. Now her shoulders are often covered by the blouse, but that many a time is of such skimpy proportions that it does not reach very far, the skirt invariably slips, and there is a gap, in which case—well, shall we say the result is not all the originators desired. A woman can carry anything but a hammock, but these carriers of mine were not very good specimens of the class. They looked at the loads, they went away, they came back, they altered, they grumbled, and at last about two hours late we started, I going ahead, the Forestry officer fetching up the rear to round in all stragglers, and in between came our motley array of goods. There is a family resemblance among all travellers on the Gold Coast. They all try to reduce their loads to a minimum and they all find that there are certain necessaries of life which they must have, and certain other things which may be luxuries but which they cannot do without, and certain other little things which it would be a sin not to take as it makes all the difference between comfort and savagery. So the procession comes along, a roll of bedding, a chop box, a kitchen box with pots and pans, a bath, a chair, a table, the servant's box, a load of water, a certain amount of drink, whisky, gin, and if the traveller is very luxurious (I wasn't) some claret, a uniform case with clothes, a smaller one containing the heavier things such as boots and the various goods that pertain to the European's presence there. Before the Commissioner goes his orderly, carrying his silver-topped stick, the insignia of his rank. I had a camera and a lot of heavy plates but I don't think the Forestry officer had anything special except a tent which took three men to carry and which we could never set up because we found on the first night that the ridge poles had been left behind. It is not supposed to be well to sleep in native houses, but it did us no harm.

The carrier divides the masters he serves into three divisions. "He be good man," "he be bad man," and "he be fool man." My carriers decided I was a fool man and they were not far wrong. Less than an hour after leaving Axim, distance as yet is always counted by time in Africa, we came to the Ancobra River and my first difficulty arose. My hammock had not yet been brought across and I, walking on a little way, came to a swampy bit which it was difficult to negotiate without wetting my feet above the ankles. My headman stooped and offered a brawny, bare back for my acceptance. I hesitated. My clothes were not built for riding pick-a-back. I looked back; there was no hammock, neither, thank heaven, was there any sign of the Forestry officer. I tried to show them how to cross their hands and carry me as in a chair, but no, they would have none of my methods, and then I gave in hastily lest my travelling companion should appear, accepted the back, rode across most ungracefully, and was set down triumphantly on the other side. And then they, began to take advantage of me.

"Missus," explained one, "you walk small. If man tote hammock, plenty broken bottle cut feet."

And so I walked all through the outskirts of that little river-side village. It was the hottest part of a very hot day, the sand made the going heavy, and the sun poured down mercilessly out of a cloudless sky. I was soon exceedingly tired, but I was filled with pity for the unfortunates who had to carry me. They walked beside me happily enough or dawdled behind scorning the fool woman who employed them. I may say when I came back my men carried me over every foot of the path, but they set me down a dozen times that day, and when my companion came up and found me sitting under a cocoa-nut palm, as he did pretty frequently, he remonstrated with me and remonstrated with my men, but the thing rested with me. It took me all day long to learn that the men must do the work they had undertaken to do, and until I was convinced of it in my own mind they certainly were not. We had luncheon in the house of the headman of a fishing village; at afternoon tea-time we were sitting on the sand waiting for the tide to run out so that we might cross the Twin Rivers, and we waited nearly two hours, and at last as the darkness was falling we arrived at a village where we must stop the night. My first night in the wilds.

It was a small fishing village on the sands of the seashore, built of the stalks of the raffia palm which here the people call bamboo. The Chief had a compound cleared out for us, and I do not know now whether that compound was clean. In my mind it remains as clean, because till then I had always expected a native house to be most uninhabitable, and was surprised to find any simple comforts at all. The floors were of sand, the walls of the stalks of the raffia, and the thatch of the fronds. I prefer palm to mud for a wall; for one thing, it is nice and airy, the wind can blow right through it and you might almost be in the open air, but then again, you must make your toilet and have your bath in the dark, for if you have a light everything is as clearly visible to the outside world as if you had been placed in a cage for their special benefit. However, my bed was put up, my bath and toilet things set out, and I managed to dress and come outside for dinner which we had in the open. The grey sand was our carpet, the blue-black sky dotted with twinkling diamonds our canopy, and the flickering, chimneyless Hinkson lamp lighted our dinner-table. I was more than content. It was delightful, and then the serpent entered into our paradise.

"Kwesi," said the Forestry officer angrily, "there's a hair in the soup."

Kwesi had only brought the soup from the kitchen to the table, so it was hardly fair to blame him, but the average man, if his wife is not present, is apt to consider the nearest servant is always responsible for his little discomforts, and he does not change his character in Africa I find. Kwesi accepted the situation.

"It not ploper hair, sah," he protested as apologetically as if he had sought diligently for a hair without success and been obliged to do the best he could with negro wool.

I, not being a wife and therefore not responsible, was equal to suggesting that it probably came off the flour bag and he might as well have his dinner in peace, but he was not easily soothed.

That first night, absolutely in the open, everything took on a glamour which comes back to me whenever I think of it. A glorious night out in the open in the Tropics is one of the pure delights of life. A fire flickered in the centre of the compound; to the right in a palm-thatched hut we could see the cook at work, and we had *hors d'oeuvre*, which here they call small chop, and the soup which my companion complained of, and fish and chicken and sweets and fruit as good as if we had been in a London restaurant. Better, for the day's hammocking on the beach with the salt spray wetting our faces and the roar of the turbulent West-Coast surf in our ears had given us an appetite that required no tempting. The hair was but an incident; the sort of contrast that always marks West Africa. We dined luxuriously.

Around us were strewn our camp outfit, all the thousand and one things that are required to make two people comfortable. It had taken sixteen men to carry us twenty miles in our hammocks; it had taken five-and-twenty more to minister to our comfort. The headman of the village regarded us as honoured guests. He provided a house, or rather several houses in a compound, he told the carriers where they could get wood and water, he sold us chickens at exorbitant prices, but still chickens, and plantains and kenky and groundnuts for the men. And so we dined in comfort and talked over the incidents of the day.

CHAPTER VI
THE KING'S HIGHWAY

The burying of the village dead—For Ju-ju—The glory of the morning—The catastrophes by the way—The cook is condemned to death—Redeemed for two shillings—The thunderous surf—The charm of the shore—Traces of white blood—A great negro town—Our quarters—Water that would induce a virulent typhus in any but a negro community—The lonely German trader—Difficulties of entertaining a negro potentate—The lair of the hunted.

The King's Highway is along the shore here easy enough going when the tide is out and the golden sand is hard; very heavy indeed when the roaring waves break almost at the foot of the cocoa-nut palms that stand in phalanxes tall and stately, or bending somewhat towards the sea that is their life, all the way from Axim to Half Assinie, and beyond again to the French border. There is no other way than this way along the shore. Occasionally, if the "sea be too full," as the carriers say, they may go up to a rough path among the cocoa-nut palms, but it is a very rough path. Husks of the cocoa-nuts lie there, palm fronds drying and withering in the sun, a great creeping bean flings its wandering stalks across the path as a trap to the unwary, and when there is other greenery it stands up and stretches out thorny branches to clutch at the passer-by. Besides, the villagers—and there are many villages—bury their dead here, and they consider two feet a deep enough grave, so that the odour of decay rises on the hot air. All along the shore, which is the highway, just under the cocoa-nut palms, I saw tiny miniature sloping thatches over some pots—a sign that someone has been buried there. At first I was touched to think so many of the living mourned the dead; but my sentimental feelings are always receiving rude shocks, and I found that these thatches had not been raised in tender remembrance, but to placate the ghosts of the dead and to prevent them from haunting the living. They must be rather foolish ghosts, too, and easily taken in; for I observed that a bunch of cock's feathers evidently simulated a chicken, and the pots were nearly always rather elderly and often broken. There were more gruesome signs of Ju-ju too; a crow suspended with outspread wings, a kid with drooping head and hanging legs. I hope these things were not put up while they were alive and left to suffer in the tropical sunshine, but I fear, I fear. The negro is diabolically cruel.

When we were children we always ate the things we liked least first, bread and butter, and then cake; and there is much to be said for the plan. Afterwards I found it was much easier and nicer travelling in the bush, but on that first journey travelling along the shore had great charms for me. In the early morning a whitish mist hangs over the sea and veils the cocoa-nut palms, and there is a little chill in the air which makes travelling pleasant. We always got up before dawn. At the first streak of light we were having our breakfast, porridge and eggs and marmalade and fruit, bananas, pines, or oranges, quite as comfortably as if we were in civilised lands, though the servants were waiting to pack our breakfast equipage, and we watched our beds and boxes and baths borne away on men's heads as we drank our coffee. There were catastrophes sometimes, of course.

There was the morning when the coffee had been made on top of the early-morning tea, and the evening when the peaches were agreeably flavoured with household soap; the day when some unknown hand had conveyed native peppers, which are the hottest things in creation outside the infernal regions, into the sparklet bottle; and the day when the drinking water gave out altogether, and was replaced by the village water, black and greasy, and sufficient to induce in any but a negro community a virulent typhus. But all disasters paled before the day when neither the dinner nor the cook were forthcoming at Beyin.

The Forestry officer, in the kindness and hospitality of his heart, had asked me to be his guest, so that we always had chop together, and I gained experience without any trouble to myself.

I was sorry there was no dinner, because it seemed a long time since we had had tea, but otherwise I was not troubled.

"Where be cook, Kwesi?" asked the Forestry officer of his immediate attendant.

Kwesi spluttered and stammered; he was so full of news. Round at a little distance stood the people of the town of Beyin—men in cloths; women, some with a handkerchief round their heads, but some with a coiffure that suggested the wearer had been permanently surprised, and her hair had stood up on end and stayed there ever since; little children, who shyly poked their heads round their mothers' legs to look at the strange white woman. The truth was hardly to be told in Kwesi's agitated pigeon English. It was awful. The cook had marched into the town on business bent and demanded chickens for the white master and the white missus, and the inhabitants, with a view to raising the market price, had declared there was not a chicken within miles of the place, and they had not seen such a thing for years. Cook was aggravated, for the chickens were walking about under his very eyes, not perhaps well-bred Dorkings or Buff Orpingtons, but the miserable little runt about the size of a self-respecting pigeon that is known as a chicken all over West Africa, and the sight was too much for him. He seized one of those chickens and proceeded to pluck and dress it, and before he was half-through the Omahin's men had come down and hauled him off to durance vile, for he had committed the iniquitous offence of stealing one of the Omahin's guard's chickens, and public opinion was almost agreed that only death could expiate so grievous a crime. Of course, there was the white woman to be considered, an unknown quantity, for many of them had never seen a white woman before; and there was the Forestry officer, by no means an unknown quantity, for it was pretty certain he would resent any harm to his cook. Finally, with much yelling and shouting and tremendous gesticulation, the case was laid before him and the demand made that his cook should be handed over to the powers he had offended. I am bound to say that young man held the scales of justice with a niceness that is only to be properly appreciated when we remember that it was his dinner that was not forthcoming and his cook whose life was threatened. He listened to both sides, and then decreed that the cook was to be redeemed by the payment of two shillings, that the crowd was to disperse, and dinner to come up forthwith.

"Two shillings," said the next white man we met, the preventive officer at Half Assinie, close to the Border, "two shillings! I should think so indeed. The price of a chicken is sixpence, and it's dear at that."

They are such arrant savages, these people of the King's Highway; often enough they are stark save for a loin cloth, and I have seen men without even the proverbial fig leaf. The very decencies of life seem unknown to them, and yet they calculate in sixpences and shillings, even as the man in the streets in England does.

They have touched the fringe of civilisation for so many hundred years; for this is the Coast of the great days of the slave trade, and along this seashore, by this roaring surf, beneath the shade of these cocoa-nut palms, have marched those weary companies of slaves, whose descendants make the problem of America nowadays. It must have been the same shore, the very same. Here is the golden sand and the thunderous surf that only the men of the Coast will dare, and between Axim and the French Ivory Coast not always they. The white scallop shells are tossed aside by the feet of the carriers; the jellyfish that twinkle like lumps of glass in the strong sunshine must be avoided, for they sting; plover and little wading birds like snipe dart into the receding wave, or race back from its oncoming; and the little crabs, like brown pincushions on stilts, run to hide themselves in the water. Here are crows, too, with neat black coats and immaculate white waistcoats and white collars, who fly cawing round the villages. We saw an occasional vulture, like a ragged and very dissipated turkey, tearing at the carcass of a goat or sheep. Such is the shore now. So was it four hundred years ago. The people must have changed a little, but very, very little in this western portion of the Gold Coast, which is given over to the mahogany cutters, the gold-seekers, and the men who seek mineral oil. And the people are born, and live, and die, and know very, very little more than their forefathers, who lived in fear of the trader who would one day tear them from their homes, and force civilisation upon them with the cat and with the branding iron. In the old days they got much of their sustenance from the sea, and so do they get it still; and when the surf was not too bad we saw the dark men launching their great surf boats, struggling to get them into the surf, struggling to keep them afloat till they got beyond it, when they were things of life. And when the surf was too bad, as it was on many days, they contented themselves with throwing in hand-nets, racing back as the sea washed over them, racing forward as it receded; and the women and children gathered shell-fish just where sand and surf met, carrying in their hands calabashes, or cocoa-nut shells, or those enamelled iron-ware basins which are as common now on the Coast as they are in London town. It seems to me that enamelled iron ware is one of the great differences between now and the days when the English and Dutch and Portuguese adventurers came first to this coast trading for gold and ivory and slaves.

There are other traces of them, too, though they only built forts and dared hardly go beyond the shelter of their walls. Not infrequently the skin of the man who bore me was lightened to copper colour; every now and then I saw straight features and thin lips, though the skin was black, and I remembered, I must perforce remember, that these traders of old time made the dark women minister to their passions, and that the dark women bore them children with pride, even as they do to-day.

Beyin is one of the biggest purely negro towns along the Coast. It is close on the shore, a mass of negro compounds huddled close together; the walls of the compounds and of houses are alike made of raffia palm, and the roofs are thatched with the fronds, looking not unlike peasant cottages in Somerset or Brittany.

And the people who live in them are simple savages. They chatter and shriek, talking at the top of their voices about—God knows what; for it seems as if nothing in the nature of news could have happened since the long-ago slave-raiding days. In the street they pressed me close; only when I noticed any particular one, especially a woman or a child, that one fled shrieking to hide behind its neighbour. We sent our orderly forward to tell the Omahin we proposed to honour them with our presence for two days, and to ask for a house to live in. The house was forthcoming, a great two-storied house, built of swish, and whitewashed. It was right in the centre of the town, so closely surrounded by the smaller houses that, standing on the balcony, I could drop things easily on to the roofs below; but it had this advantage, that unless the people climbed on their roofs—they did as a matter of fact—we could not be overlooked. We had three rooms: an enormous centre room that someone had begun to paint blue, got tired, and finished off with splashes of whitewash, the council chamber of the town; and two side-rooms for bedrooms. And words fail me to describe those bedrooms. There were iron beds with mattresses, mattresses that looked as if they had been rescued from the refuse heap specially to accommodate us, and tables covered with dirt and the most wonderful collection of odds and ends it has ever been my fortune to come across. They were mostly the cheapest glass and china ornaments, broken-down lamps that in their palmy days must have been useless, and one of those big gaily painted china sitting hens that humble households sometimes serve up their breakfast eggs under. The first thing was to issue strict orders that not even the ground sheet was to touch that bed; the next was to clear away the ornaments, wipe down the table, cover it with clean paper and a towel, sweep the floor, lay down the ground sheet, put up the bed, and decide whether I would wash in sea water or in the black and greasy liquid which comes from a mile away across the swamp, and which was the only alternative. I may say I tried them both, and found them both unsatisfactory; and I finished with the sea water because I knew that, however uncomfortable, it was at least clean.

Here we used the last of our drinking water and had to beg a little from the only white trader in the town, who gave generously of his small store, as white men do help each other beyond civilisation. He was German, and somewhat difficult to understand at times when he grew excited; but he stood on the same side of the gulf as we other two, while the black people, those who served us, and those who stared at us, were apart on the other side. A weary, dreary life is the trader's. He had a house just on the edge of the surf. His "factory" was below it. His only companions were a beautiful green-crested clock-bird and a little old-man monkey with a white beard. The ghastly loneliness of it! Nothing to do but to sell cotton stuffs and enamel ware and gin to the native, and count the days till it was time to tramp to Axim and take the steamer that should bear him back to the Fatherland and all the joys of wife and children.

"I saw the homeward-bound steamer to-day," he said pathetically, though he did not know he was pathetic. "I always look for it."

"The steamer! I did not know it came close enough in."

"It doesn't. Of course it was only the smoke on the horizon."

Surely, surely, the tragedy of the exile's life lay in those words.

We had sent our orderly forward to say we were going to visit the Omahin, and soon after our arrival we called upon him. His palace is a collection of swish huts with palm-thatched roofs, built round a sanded compound; and we were ushered into a cramped, whitewashed room—his court. The population packed themselves into the body of the court to stare at the white people and native royalty; and the Omahin and his councillors were crowded up in the corner, whence, I presume, justice is dispensed. The exalted personage was clad in a dark robe of many-coloured silks, with a band of the same material round his black head. Round his neck was a great, heavy gold chain, on his arms bracelets of the same metal, and on his fingers heavy gold rings. Some of his councillors were also dressed in native robes, and they carried great horns of gold and the sticks that mark his rank with gold devices on top of them. The incongruity was provided by the "scholars" among his following—the linguists, the registrar, and other minor officials. These functionaries were clad in the most elderly of cast-off European garments, frock coats green with age, shirts that simply shrieked for the washtub, and trousers that a London unemployed would have disdained. However, they interpreted for us, and we explained to the Chief how pleased the white lady was with his country and how much she wished to visit the lake village, which was three hours away on the trade route to the back-country. He expressed his willingness to give us a guide through the swamp that lay behind the town, and then with a great deal of solemnity we took our leave and retired to our own somewhat delayed afternoon tea.

We were mistaken if we thought we were going to be allowed to have it in peace. We had not sat down a moment, the Forestry officer, the German trader, and I, when the ragged travesty of a Gold Coast policeman, who was the Omahin's messenger, came dawdling upstairs to announce that the Omahin was coming to return our call; and he and his councillors and linguists followed close on his heels. The linguist explained that it was the custom to return a ceremonial call at once, and custom rules the roost in West Africa. That might be, but our conversational powers had been exhausted a quarter of an hour before, and not the most energetic ransacking of our brains could find anything to say to this negro potentate, who sat stolidly in a chair surrounded by an ever increasing group of attendants. I asked him if he would have tea. No. Cake, suggested the Forestry officer frantically. No. Toast and butter we both offered in a breath. No; he had no use for toast and butter, or for biscuits or oranges, which exhausted our tea-table. And then the Forestry officer had a brilliant idea: "You offer him a whisky-and-soda." I did, and the dusky monarch weighed the matter a moment. Then he agreed, and a glass of whisky-and-soda was given him. We did not offer any refreshment to his followers. It would have left us bankrupt, and then not supplied them all. For a moment the Omahin looked at his whisky-and-sparklet, then he held out the glass, and aman stepped forward, and, bending low, took a sip; again he held out the glass, choosing his man apparently quite promiscuously from among the crowd, and again the man bent low and sipped. It was done over and over again. I did not realise that a glass could have held so much liquid as one after another, the chosen of the company, among whom was my most troublesome hammock-boy, sipped. At last there was but a teaspoonful left, and the Omahin put it to his own lips and drank with gusto, handed it to one of his attendants, took it back, and, tipping it up, drained the very last dregs; then, solemnly holding out a very hard and horny hand, shook hands with us and departed.

The next day we visited Lake Nuba. Beyin stands upon a narrow neck of land between the sea and a swamp that in the rainy season is only passable in canoes, but when I was there in the middle of the dry season a winding path took us through the dense swamp grasses to the place that is neither land nor water, and it is difficult to say whether a hammock or a canoe is the least dangerous mode of progression. Be it understood that this is a trade route. Rotting canoes lay among the grasses; and there passed to and fro quite an array of people laden with all manner of goods, plantains, and cassava, stinkfish (which certainly does not belie its name), piles of cotton goods for the interior, and great enamelled-ware basins piled with loam to make swish houses in Beyin. Most often these heavily laden folks are women who stalk along with a child up on their backs, or suckling it under their arms. They stared with wonder at the white woman in the hammock and moved into the swamp to let her pass, but I should think they no more envied me than I envy the Queen of England driving in the Park. Presently the way was ankle-deep in water, knee-deep in mud. Raffia palm, creepers, and all manner of swamp grasses grew so close that the hammock could barely be forced through, and only two men could carry it. We went up perhaps twenty feet in squelching, slippery mud. We came down again, and the greenery opened out into an expanse of water, where starry-white water-lilies opened cups to the sky above, and the great leaves looked like green rafts on the surface of the water. There were holes hidden by that water, but it is the trade route north all the same; and has been the trade route for hundreds of years since the Omahins of Beyin raided that way, and brought down their strings of slaves, carrying the tiny children lest they should be drowned, to the Dutch and Portuguese and English traders on the Coast. Presently we came to a more marked waterway, and here were canoes waiting for us. I draw a veil over the disembarking out of a hammock into an extremely crank and wet canoe. I was up to my knees in water, but the Forestry officer expressed himself as delighted. I held up a dripping skirt, and he made his men paddle over, and inspected. It was, of course, as we might have expected; the natives had seen that the most important person in their eyes, the man, got the only fairly dry canoe, and my kindly guardian was shocked, and insisted on an immediate change being made. And if it is necessary to draw a veil over the disembarking from a hammock to a canoe it is certainly necessary to draw one over the changing from one crank canoe to another. I can assure you it cannot be done gracefully. Even a mermaid who had no fear of being drowned could hardly accomplish that with elegance. But it was done at last, and we set off up the long and picturesque waterway fringed with lilies and palms and swamp grasses that led to Lake Nuba. And sometimes the waterway was deep, sometimes shallow. The canoe was aground, and every man had to jump overboard to help push it over the obstruction, but more than one man went over his head in slime and water. At each accident the lucky ones who had escaped roared and yelled with laughter as if it were the best of jokes. Perhaps it was. It was so hot that it could have been no hardship to have a bath, and they had nothing on to spoil. But at last we got out on the lake. It looked a huge sheet of water from the little canoe, and it took a good hour's paddling till we came to the lake village.

This is the lair of the hunted, though it does lie on the trade route. Behind it lies the swamp which is neither land nor water in the dry season, and it looks just a tangle of raffia palm and swamp grass, and all manner of tropical greenery. The huts, like the huts of Beyin are, are built of raffia palm, but they go one better than Beyin and the fishing villages, even the flooring is of the stems; and the whole village is raised on stakes, so that it hangs over the water, and the houses can only be reached by a framework of poles.

"If you *will* go exploring," said the Forestry officer, as I gathered up my skirts and essayed the frail ladder.

I here put it on record that I think savage life can by no manner of means be recommended, save and except for its airiness. There is plenty of air. It is easy enough to see through those lightly built walls of raffia palm, and the doings of the occupants must be fairly open to the public. Also, except in one room, where a hearth had been laid down about six feet by three in extent, the flooring is so frail that in trying to walk on it I slipped through, and was nipped tightly by the ankles. I couldn't rescue myself. I was held as in a vice till the grinning King's messenger and a Kroo-boy carrier got me out, wherefore I conclude the inhabitants of those villages must spend the most of their time on their backs. In the dry season there is a little bit of hard earth underneath the huts. In the wet season there is nothing but water and the raffia palm flooring or a crank canoe for a resting-place. No wonder even the tiny children seem as much at home in a canoe as I am in an easy chair. And yet the village is growing, so there must be a charm about it as a dwelling-place. We had "chop" on the verandah of the Chiefs house. The Chief had apparently quite recently buried one of his household, for at the end of the platform close against the dwelling-chambers was erected one of the miniature sloping roofs with offerings of cock's feathers, shells, and pots to placate the ghost. It was quite a new erection, too, for the palm-leaf thatch was still green; but where the dead body was I do not know, probably sunk in the swamp underneath, and why so close I do not know either, since the people evidently feared his ghost. However, even if we were lunching over a grave, it did not trouble us half so much as the fate of the toast which was being brought across from another hut in a particularly crank canoe, and was naturally an object of much curiosity.

The people were very courteous. It seems to me that the farther you get from civilisation the more courteous the population. Village children eager to see the lions in a circus could not have been more keen than the people of this lake village to see the white woman, but they did not even come and look till our linguist went forth and announced that the white people had had their chop, and were ready to receive the headman. He came, bringing his little daughter—a rough-looking, bearded old man, who squatted down in front of me and rammed the tail of his cloth into his mouth; and immediately there followed in his train, I should think, the entire village, men, women, and children, and ranged themselves in rows on the bamboo flooring, and looked their fill. Rows of eyes staring at one are embarrassing; I don't care whether they be those of a cultured people or of savages clad in scanty garments. If you stand up before an audience in a civilised land you know what you are there for, and you either succeed or fail, so the thing marches and comes to an end. But sitting before a subdued crowd clad in Manchester cotton or simply a smile, with all eyes centred on you, I at least feel that my rôle is somewhat more difficult. What on earth am I to do? If I move they chatter; if I single one out to be touched, he moves away, and substitutes a neighbour, who is equally anxious to substitute someone else, and the production of a camera causes a stampede. Looking back, I cannot consider that my behaviour at the lake village reflected any particular credit upon me. I felt I ought really to have produced more impression upon a people who had, many of them, never in their lives set eyes on a white woman before. They tell me, those who know, that for these people, whose lives move on in the same groove from the cradle to the grave, the coming of the Forestry officer and the white woman was a great event, and that all things will bear date from the day when the white missus and the white master had chop on the Chief's verandah.

Before we left Beyin, I promised to take the Omahin's photograph. Early in the morning, when we had sent on our carriers, we wended our way to his house, where an eager crowd awaited us. They kept us waiting, of course; I do not suppose it would be consistent with an African chief's dignity to show himself in any hurry. When I grew tired of waiting and was turning away, the linguist came out to know if I would promise a picture when it was taken. I agreed. Certainly. More waiting, and then out came the linguist with a dirty scrap of paper and a lead pencil in his hand, and demanded of the Forestry officer his name and address.

"Why?" asked the astonished young man.

"So we can write to you when pictures no come." It was lucky I was pretty sure of my own powers, but it was a little rough to make the Forestry officer responsible for any accident that might happen. It was a great relief to my mind when there came back to me from Messrs Sinclair a perfect picture of the Omahin and his following and his little son. I sent them the picture enlarged, but I never heard from that respectable linguist what they thought of it.

TO THE MEMORY OF THE DEAD.

CHAPTER VII
ON THE FRENCH BORDER

Very heavy going—-Half Assinie—The preventive service station—The energetic officer—Dislike of Africa—The Tano River—The enterprising crocodiles—The mahogany logs—Wicked waste—Gentlemen adventurers—A primitive dinner-party—Forced labour—The lost carrier—"Make die and chopped"—A negro Good Samaritan—A matrimonial squabble—The wife who would earn her own living—Dissatisfied carriers.

We were bound to Half Assinie and the French border and the way was all along the shore, which is a narrow strip of land between the roaring surf and a mangrove-fringed lagoon, and on this strip are the palm-built fishing villages and the cocoa-nut groves that are so typical of the Coast. The last day out from Half Assinie the way was very heavy going indeed. We had our midday meal in the street of a village with the eyes of the villagers upon us, and by the afternoon the "sea was too full," the sun was scorching, and the loose sand was cruel heavy going for the carriers and the hammock-boys. The sun went down, the cool of the evening came, but the bearers were staggering like drunken men before a shout went up. We had reached Half Assinie, the last important town in the Gold Coast Colony.

Half Assinie is just like any other Western Province Gold Coast town, built close down to the roaring, almost impassable surf, because the people draw much of their livelihood from the sea, and built of raffia-palm bamboo, because there is nothing else to build it of. Only there is this difference, that here is a preventive station, with a white man in command. There is a great cleared square, which is all sand and cocoa-nut palms, men in neat dark-blue uniforms pass to and fro, and bugle calls are heard the livelong day. We arrived long before the rest of our following, and we marched straight up to the preventive officer's house only to find that he was down with fever. But he was hospitable. All white men are in West Africa. The house was ours. It consisted of a square of sun-dried, white-washed mud, divided into three rooms with square openings for windows, mud floor and no ceiling, but high above the walls the palm-thatched roof is raised and carried far out beyond them to form a verandah where we could sit and eat and entertain visitors. It was big enough, never less than twelve and often quite eighteen feet wide, and could be made quite a comfortable living-room were a woman there, but Englishmen and the English Government do not encourage wives. The rooms assigned to the guests were of necessity empty, for men cannot carry furniture about in West Africa, and our host being sick and our gear not yet arrived, the Forestry officer and I, comforted with whisky-and-soda, took two chairs and sat out in the compound under the stars and watched for the coming of our carriers. The going had been so hard they straggled in one by one, bath and bed and chairs and tables and boxes, and it was nine o'clock before we were washed and dressed and in our right minds, and waiting "chop" at a table on the big verandah that the faithful Kwesi, who had been properly instructed, had decorated with yellow cannas from the garden.

There is something about Half Assinie that gives the impression of being at the end of the world. Of course I have been in places much farther from civilisation, but nowhere has the tragedy of the Englishman's life in West Africa so struck me as it did here, and again I must say I think it is the conditions of the life and not the climate that is responsible for that tragedy. The young man who ran that preventive station was cheerful enough; he got up from his bed of fever when he could hardly stagger across the room to entertain his visitors. When he could barely crawl, he was organising a game of cricket between some white men who had unexpectedly landed and the "scholars" among the black inhabitants; and he was energetic and good-tempered and proud of his men, but he hated the country and had no hesitation in saying so. He had no use for West Africa; he counted the days till he should go home. He would not have dreamt of bringing his wife out even if she had wished to come. He was, in fact, a perfect specimen of the nice, pleasant Englishman who is going the way that allows France and Germany to beat us in colonising all along the line. It was his strong convictions, many of them unspoken, that impressed me, his realisation of his own discontent and discomfort and hopelessness that have tinged my recollections of the place.

It should be a place of great importance, for it is but a short distance from the Tano River, and down the Tano River, far from the interior, come the great mahogany logs that rival the logs of Honduras and Belize and all Central America in value. They are cut far away in the forests of the interior; they are floated down the Tano River, paying toll to the natives who guide them over the falls and rapids; they come between tall, silk-cotton trees and fan palms and raffia palms, where the chimpanzee hides himself and the dog-faced monkeys whimper and cry, the crocodile suns himself on the mud-banks, and great, bell-shaped, yellow flowers lighten the greenery. They come past the French preventive station, that the natives call France, a station thriftily decorated with a tiny flag that might have come out of a cracker, past the English station built of raffia palm like the lake village, for this ground is flooded in the rains, through a saving canal, for the Tano River enters the sea in French territory, into a lagoon behind Half Assinie. The lagoon is surrounded by swamp, and the crocodiles, they say, abound, and are so fierce and fearless they have been known to take the paddler's arm as he stoops to his stroke. I did not know of their evil reputation as I sat on a box in the frail canoe, that seemed to place me in the midst of a waste of waters, rising up to the greenery in the far distance, and the blue-white sky above shut down on us like a lid. I was even inclined to be vexed with the men's reluctance to jump out and push when we ran ashore on a sand-bank. They should be able to grow rice in these swamps at the mouth of the Tano River and behind Beyin, and so raise up a new industry that shall save Half Assinie when the mahogany trade is a thing of the past.

"FRANCE."

From the lagoon to Half Assinie, a couple of miles away, the logs are brought on a tramway line, and where they land the men are squaring them, cutting off the butts where the journey down the river has split and marred them, and making them ready to be moved down to the beach by the toilsome application of many hands. It reminded me of the way they must have built the pyramids as I watched the half-naked men toil and sweat and push and shriek, and apparently accomplish so little. Yet all in good time the beach is strewn with the logs, great square-cut baulks of red timber with their owners' marks upon their butts and covered generally with a thatch of cocoa-nut palm fronds to keep them from the all-powerful sun. The steamer will call for them some day, but it is no easy thing to get them through the surf, and steamer after steamer calls, whistles, decides that the surf is too heavy to embark such timber, and passes on. And where they have been cut and trimmed, the mammies come with baskets to gather pieces of the priceless wood to build their fires. It seems to me that the trimming is done wastefully. The average savage and the ignorant white is always wasteful where there is plenty, and it is nothing to them that the mahogany tree does not come to maturity for something like two hundred and fifty years, and that the cutters have denuded the country far, far beyond the sea coast.

There are other phases of life in Half Assinie. Usually there is but one white man there, the preventive officer, but when I visited it actually ten white people sat down one night to dinner. For there had landed some white people bound on some errand which, as has been the custom from time immemorial in Africa, was veiled in mystery. They were seeking gold; they hoped to find diamonds; their ultimate aim was to trade with the natives, and cut out every other trading-house along the Coast. Frankly, I do not know what they had landed for—their leader talked of his wealth and how he grew bananas and pines and coffee, and created a tropical paradise in Devonshire, and meanwhile in Africa conferred the inimitable benefits of innumerable gramophones and plenty of work upon the guileless savage—but I only gathered he was there for the purpose of filling his pockets, how, I have not the faintest idea. His dinner suggested Africa in the primitive days of the first adventurers and rough plenty. Soup in a large bowl, from which we helped ourselves, a dozen tins of sardines flung on a plate, a huge tongue from a Gargantuan ox, and dishes piled with slices of pine-apple. The table decorations consisted of beer bottles, distributed at intervals down the table between the kerosene lamps; the boys who waited yelled and shrieked and shouted, like the untamed savages they were, and some of the white men were unshaven and in their shirt sleeves, and the shirts, to put it mildly, needed washing.

"Gentlemen adventurers," said I to my companion under my breath, thinking of the days of old and the men who had landed on these shores.

"Would you say gentlemen?" said he.

And I decided that one epithet would be sufficient.

How the bugles called. Every hour almost a man clad in the dark-blue preventive service uniform stood out in the square with his bugle and called to the surf and the sky and the sand and the cocoa-nut palms and the natives beyond, saying to them that here was the representative of His Britannic Majesty, here was the white man powerful above all others who kept the Borders, who was come as the forerunner of law and cleanliness and order. For these things do not come naturally to the native. He clears the land when he needs it and then he leaves it to itself and the quickly encroaching bush. The mosquito troubles him not. Dirt and filth and evil smells are not worth counting weighed in the balance against a comfortable afternoon's sleep, and so it came that when I commented on the neatness of Half Assinie, the preventive officer laughed.

BRITISH CONSULATE, TANO RIVER.

"Forced labour," said he. "The place was in a frightful state a month ago and I couldn't get anybody to do anything, so I just turned out my men, put a cordon round, and forced everyone to do an hour's labour, men, mammies, and half-grown children, till we got the place clear. It wasn't hard on anyone, and you see." He was right. Sometimes in Africa, nay, as a rule, the powers of a dictator are needed by the white man. If he is a wise and clever dictator so much the better, but one thing is certain, he must not be a man who splits hairs. Justice, yes, rough crude justice he must give—must have the sort of mind that sees black and white and does not trouble about the varying shades in between.

We came back from the Border by the road that we had gone, the road that is the King's Highway, and an incident happened that shows how very, very easily a wrong impression of a people may be gathered.

When we were in Beyin on our way out, the two headmen who were eternally at war with each other suddenly appeared in accord leading between them a man by the hands.

"This man be very sick."

This man certainly was very sick, and it seemed to the Forestry officer that the simplest thing would be to leave him behind at Beyin and pick him up on our return journey. He thought his decision would be received with gratitude. Not at all. The sick carrier protested that all he wanted was to be relieved of his load and allowed to go on. The men of Beyin were bad people; if he stayed they would kill him and chop him. The Forestry officer was inclined to laugh. Murder of an unoffending stranger and cannibalism on a coast that had been

- 74 -

in touch with civilisation for the last four hundred years; the idea was not to be thought of. But the frightened sick man stuck to his point and his brother flung down his load and declared if he were left behind he should stay with him. There was nothing for it then but to agree to their wishes. He was relieved of his load and he started, and he and his brother arrived at Half Assinie long after all the other carriers had got in. The gentlemen adventurers numbered among them a doctor, and he was called in and prescribed for the sick man. After the little rest there he was better, and started back for Axim, his brother, who was carrying the Forestry officer's bath, in close attendance. By and by we passed the bath abandoned on the beach, and its owner perforce put another man on to carry it.

That night there were no signs of the missing men, but next morning the brother, the man who ought to have carried the bath, turned up. His face was sodden with crying. A negro is intensely emotional, but this man had some cause for his grief. He had missed his brother, abandoned the bath, and gone right back to Half Assinie to look for him. The way was by the seashore, there is no way to wander from it; on one side is the roaring surf that no man alone may dare, and on the other, just beyond the line of cocoa-nut palms, a mangrove-fringed lagoon, and beyond that a bush, containing perhaps a few native farms to be reached by narrow tracks, but a bush that no stranger would lightly dare. But no trace of his brother could this man find. What had become of the sick carrier? That was the question we asked ourselves, and to that no answer could we find except the sinister verdict pronounced by his fellows, "Make die and chopped." And that I believed for many months, till just before I left the Coast the Forestry officer and I met again and he told me the end of the story. He had made every inquiry, telegraphed up and down the Coast, and given the man up for lost, and then after four or five weeks a miserable skeleton came crawling into Axim. The lost carrier. He had felt faint by the wayside, crawled into the shade of a bush and become insensible, and there had been found by some man, a native of the country and a total stranger to him. And this Good Samaritan instead of falling upon him and making him die as he fully expected, took him to his own house, fed and succoured him, and when he was well enough set him on his way. So he and I and all his fellows had wronged these men of the shore. Greater kindness he could not have found in a Christian land, and in all probability he might easily have found much less.

But Beyin too furnished another lesson for me, not quite so pleasant. All my carriers had come from here, and on our way back they struck. In plain words they wanted to see the colour of my money. Said the Forestry officer, "Don't pay them, else they'll all run away and you will have no one to carry your things into Axim." That was a contingency not to be thought of, so the ultimatum went forth—no pay until they had completed their contract. That night I regret to state there was a row in the house, a matrimonial quarrel carried on in the approved matrimonial style all the world over, with the mother-in-law for chorus and general backer-up. There was a tremendous racket and the principal people concerned seemed to be one of my women-carriers and the Omahin's registrar in whose house we were lodged. Then because Fanti is one of the Twi languages, and an Ashanti can understand it quite well, Kwesi interpreted for me. This woman, it appeared, was one of the registrar's wives, and he disapproved of her going on the road as a common carrier. It was not consistent with his dignity as an official of the court, he said at the top of his voice; he had given her a good home and she had no need to demean herself. She shrilly declared he had done no such thing, and if he had, had shamefully neglected her for that last hussy he had married, and her mother backed her and several other female friends joined in, and whether they settled the dispute or not to their own satisfaction I do not know, but the gentleman cuffed the lady and the lady had the extreme satisfaction of scattering several handfuls of his wool to the winds.

Next morning none of my carriers turned up; there lay the loads under a tree in front of the house with the orderly looking at them with his sardonic grin, but never a carrier. It was cool with the coolness of early morning. We had our breakfast in the great room, we discussed the disturbance of the night before, the things were all washed up, still no carriers; at last, just as it was getting hot and our tempers were giving out, came a message. The carriers would not go unless they were paid.

"And it's a foregone conclusion they won't go if they are paid," sighed the Forestry officer as he set off to interview the Omahin and tell him our decision. If the carriers did not come in at once, it ran, we would leave all the loads, making him, the Omahin, responsible for their safety, and we would push on with the Mendi and Kroo-boy carriers in the Forestry officer's employ. Those left behind not having carried out their contract of course would then get no pay at all, and this would happen unless they returned to work within a quarter of an hour. The effect was marvellous. The Omahin, of course, did not grasp how exceedingly uncomfortable it would have been for us to leave our gear behind us, and as we had sixteen Kroo boys and Mendi boys the feat was quite feasible, and promptly those Beyin people returned to work and were as eager to get their loads as they had before been to leave them. So I learned another lesson in the management of carriers, and we made our way without further incident back to Axim.

CHAPTER VIII
ALONE IN WEST AFRICA

Cinderella—A troubled Commissioner—Few people along the Coast—No hotels—Nursing Sister to the rescue—Sekondi—A little log-rolling—A harassed hedge—Carriers—Difficulties of the way—A funeral palaver—No dinner and no ligjit—First night alone—Unruly carriers—No breakfast—Crossing the Prah—A drink from a marmalade pot—"We no be fit, Ma"—The evolution of Grant—Along the Coast in the dark—Elmina at last—A sympathetic medical officer—"I have kicked your policeman."

West Africa is Cinderella among the colonies. No one goes there for pleasure, and of those who gain their livelihood from the country three-fourths regard themselves as martyrs and heroes, counting the days till the steamer shall take them home again for that long leave that makes a position there so desirable. The other quarter perhaps, some I know for certain, find much good in the country, many possibilities, but as yet their voice is not heard by the general public above that chorus that drowns its protest. That any man should come to the Gold Coast for pleasure would be surprising; that a woman should come when she had no husband there, and that she should want to go overland all along the sea-board, passed belief. "Why? why?" asked everyone. "A tourist on the Coast," a surprised ship's captain called me, and I disclaimed it promptly. My publisher had commissioned a book and I was there to write it. And then they could not make up their minds whether I or my publisher were the greater fool, for but very few among that little company saw anything to write about in the country.

In Axim the troubled Commissioner set his foot down. I had been to Half Assinie and he felt that ought to satisfy the most exacting woman; but since I was anxious to do more he stretched a point and took me as far as Prince's, an abandoned Branden-burgher fort that is tumbling into ruins, with a native farm in the courtyard, but no farther could I go. Carriers he could not get me, and for the first time I saw a smile on his face, a real relieved smile, when he saw me into the boat that took me to the steamer bound for Sekondi.

No one goes along the Coast except an occasional Public Works Department man or a School Inspector; nobody wants to, and it is not easy of accomplishment.

Even in the towns it is difficult for the stranger. I do not know what would happen if that stranger had not friends and letters of introduction, for though there are one or two hotels, as yet no one who is not absolutely driven to it by stern necessity stays in a West-African hotel. In Sekondi it is almost impossible, for at this town is the Coast terminus of the railway that runs to the mines at Tarkwa and Kumasi, and the miner both coming and returning seems to require so much liquid refreshment that he is anything but a desirable fellow-housemate, wherefore was I deeply grateful when Miss Oram, the nursing Sister at the Sekondi Hospital, asked me to stay in her quarters.

Sekondi straggles up and down many hills, and by and by if some definite plan of beautifying be followed may be made rather a pretty place. Even now at night, from some of the bungalows on the hillsides when the darkness gently veils the ugly scars that man's handiwork leaves behind, with its great sweep of beach, its sloping hillsides dotted with lights, the stars above and the lights in the craft on the water that lie just outside the surf, it has a wonderful charm and beauty that there is no denying. And yet there is no doubt Sekondi should not be there. Who is responsible for it I do not know, but there must have been some atrocious piece of log-rolling before Elmina and Cape Coast were deprived of the benefit of the railway to the north. At Sekondi is no harbour. It is but an open roadstead where in days gone past both the Dutch and English held small forts for the benefit of their trade. At Sekondi was no town. At the end of the last century the two little fishing villages marked the Dutch and English forts. Now the English fort is gone, Fort Orange is used as a prison, and a town has sprung into existence that has taken the trade from Cape Coast and Elmina. It is a town that looks like all the English towns, as if no one cared for it and as if everyone lives there because perforce he must. In the European town the roads are made, and down their sides are huge gutters to carry off the storm waters; the Englishman, let it be counted to him for grace, is great on making great cemented gutters that look like young rivers when it rains, and one enterprising Commissioner planted an avenue or two of trees which promise well, only here and there someone has seen fit to cut a tree or two down, and the gap has never been replaced. Some of the bungalows are fairly comfortable, but though purple bougainvillia, flame-coloured flamboyant trees, and dainty pink corrallitis will grow like weeds, decent gardens are few and far between. Instead of giving an impression of tropical verdure as it easily might, Sekondi looks somewhat hot and barren. This, it is only fair to say, I did not notice so much till I had visited German territory and seen what really could be done with the most unpromising material in a tropical climate. But German territory is the beloved child, planned and cared for and thought much of; English territory is the foster-child, received into the household because of the profit it will bring, and most of the towns of the Gold Coast shore bear these marks plain for everyone to read. They suffer, and suffer severely from the iniquitous system that is for ever changing those in authority over them in almost every department.

Sekondi Hospital for instance is rather a nice-looking building but it is horribly bare-looking and lacks sadly a garden and greenery. There is, of course, a large reserve all round it where are the houses of the medical officers and nursing Sisters, and in this reserve many things are growing, but the general impression is of something just beginning. This I hardly understood, since the place has been in existence for the last ten years, till I found out that in the last eight months there had been four different doctors head of that hospital, and each of those doctors had had different views as to how the grounds should be laid out. So round the medical officer's bungalow the hedge had been three times planted and three times dug up. Just as I left, the fourth unfortunate hedge was being put in. That, as I write, is nearly six weeks ago, so in all probability they are now considering some new plan. If only someone with knowledge would take in hand the beautifying of these West-African towns and insist on the plans being adhered to! In one of the principal streets of Sekondi is a tamarind tree standing alone, a pleasant green spot in the general glare and heat, a reminder of how well the old Dutch did, a reproach that we who are a great people do not do better. It seems to me it would want so little to make these towns beautiful places, the moral effect would be so great if they were.

But I had come to go along the Coast, and the question was carriers; I appealed to the transport. My friend, Mr Migeod, the head of the transport, was on leave, and his second in command shook his head doubtfully. The troops in the north were out on manoeuvres and they had taken almost very carrier he could lay his hands on; but he would see what he could do. How few could I do with? Seventeen, I decided, with two servants, was the very fewest I could move with, and he said he would do his best. I wanted to start on the following Monday, and I chose the hour of ten; also because this was my first essay entirely alone I decided I would not go farther than Chama, nine miles along the Coast to the east.

So, on a Monday morning early in March, behold me with all my goods and chattels, neatly done up into loads not weighing over 60 lbs., laid out in a row in the Sister's compound, and waiting for the carriers. I had begged a policeman for dignity, or protection, I hardly know which, and he came first and ensconced himself under the house, and I sat on the verandah and waited. Presently the carriers came and began gingerly turning over the loads and looking at me doubtfully. They were Mendis and Timinis, not the regular Government carriers, but a scratch lot picked up to fill up gaps in the ranks. I didn't like the looks of them much, but there was nothing else to be done so I prepared to accept them. But it always takes two to make a bargain, and apparently those carriers liked me less than I liked them, for presently they one and all departed, and I began a somewhat heated discussion across the telephone with the head of the transport. Looking back, I don't see what he could have done more than he did. It is impossible to evolve carriers out of nothing, but then I didn't see it quite in that light. I wanted carriers; I was looking to him to produce them, and I hadn't got them. He gave me to understand he thought I was unreasonable, and we weren't quite as nice to each other as we might have been. The men, he said, were frightened, and I thought that was unreasonable, for there was nothing really terrifying about me.

At three o'clock another gang arrived with a note from the transport officer. They were subsisted for sixteen days, and I might start there and then for Accra.

I should have preferred to have subsisted my men myself; that is, given them each threepence daily, as I had on the way to the French border, seeing that they were not regular Government men; but as the thing was done there was nothing for it but to make the best of it, and I went down, hunted up my policeman, and saw the loads on to the men's heads. I saw them start out in a long string, and then the thing that always happens in Africa happened. Both my servants were missing.

Zacco, a boy with a scarred face from the north, did not much matter, but Grant knew my ways and I could trust him. Clearly, out in the wilds by myself with strange carriers and without even a servant, I should be very badly off, and I hesitated. Not for long though. If I were going to let little things connected with personal comfort stand in my way I knew I should never get to Accra, so I decided to start; my servants might catch me up, and if they did not, I would rely on the ministrations of the hammock-boys. If the worst came to the worst, I supposed I could put my dignity in my pocket and cook myself something, or live on tinned meat and biscuits; and so, leaving directions with my hostess that those boys were to be severely reprimanded when they turned up, I got into my hammock and started.

The road to Accra from Sekondi is along the seashore, and so, to be very Irish, there is no road. Of a truth, very few people there are who choose to go by land, as it is so much easier to go by steamer, and the way, generally speaking, is along the sand. Just outside Sekondi the beach is broken by huge rocks that run out into the sea, apparently barring the way effectually, and those rocks had to be negotiated. My hammock-boys stopped, and I got out and watched my men with the loads scrambling over the rocks, and one thing I was sure of, on my own feet I could not go that way. I mentioned that to my demurring men, and insisted that over those rocks they had to get me somehow, if it took the eight hammock-boys to do it. And over those rocks I was got without setting foot out of my hammock, and I fairly purred with pride, most unjustly setting it down to my own prowess and feeling it marked a distinct stage on my journey eastwards. We were, all of us, pleased as we went on again in all the glare of a tropical afternoon, and I mentally sniffed at the men who had hinted I was not able to manage carriers. There was not a more uplifted woman in all Africa than I was for about the space of half an hour. It is trite to say pride goes before a fall. We have all heard it from our cradles and I ought to have remembered it, but I didn't. Presently we came to a village, or rather two villages, with a stream dividing them, and there was a tremendous tom-toming going on, and the monotonous sound of natives chanting. The place was surrounded by thick greenery, only there was a broad way between the houses, a brown road with great waterways and holes in it, and the occasional shade-tree, under which the village rests in the heat of the day, and holds its little markets and its little councils and even does a stray job of cooking. The tom-toming went on, and men appeared blowing horns. They were evidently very excited, and I remember still, with a shudder, the staring, bloodshot eyes of two who passed my hammock braying on horns. Most of my men could speak a little English, so I asked not without some little anxiety, "What is the matter?"

"It be funeral palaver, Ma."

Oh, well, a funeral palaver was no great matter, surely. I had never heard of these Coast natives doing anything more than drink palm wine to celebrate the occasion. Some of those we passed had evidently drunk copiously already, and I was thankful we were passing. We came to the little river, we crossed the ford, and then we stopped.

"We go drink water, Ma," said my men.

I ought to have said "No," but it was a very hot afternoon, and the request was not unreasonable. They had had to work hard carrying me over those rocks so I got out and let them go. And then, as I might have known, I waited. I grew cross, but it is no good losing your temper when there is no one to be made uneasy by it, and then I grew frightened; but, if it is foolish to lose one's temper, it is the height of folly to be afraid when there is no help possible. I was standing on the bank of the little river that we had just forded, my hammock was at my feet, all around was greenery, tropical greenery of palm and creeper, not very dense compared to other bush I have seen, but dense enough to prevent one's stepping off the road; before me was the village, with its mud walls and its thatched roofs, and behind me were the groves of trees on the other side of the water that hid the village, from which came the sound of savage revelry. Never have I felt more alone, and yet Sekondi was a bare five miles away. I comforted myself with the reflection that nothing would be likely to happen, but the thought of those half-naked men with the bloodshot, staring eyes was most unpleasantly prominent in my mind. Some little naked boys came and bathed and stared at me; I didn't know whether to welcome them as companions or not. They understood no English, and when asked where were my men only stared the harder. I tried to take a photograph, but the policeman, who carried my stand, was also absent at the funeral, and I fear my hand shook, for I have never seen that picture. Then, at last, when I was absolutely despairing, a hammock-boy turned up. He was a most ragged ruffian, with a printed cloth by way of trousers, a very openwork singlet, all torn away at one arm, a billycock hat in the last stages of dilapidation, and a large red woollen comforter with a border of black, blue, and yellow. That comforter fascinated me, and I looked at it as I talked to him, and wondered where it had been made. It had been knitted, and many of the stitches had been dropped, and I pictured to myself the sewing-party sitting round the fire doing useful work, while someone read aloud one of Father Benson's books. My hammock-boy looked at me as if he wondered how I was taking it, and wiped his mouth with the tail of the comforter, where they had used up the odd bits of wool. He flung it across his shoulder and a long, dropped red stitch caught over his ear.

"Where be the men?" I was very angry indeed, which was very rough on the only one of the crowd who had turned up. He was very humble, and I suggested he should go and look for them, and tell them that if "they no come quick, they get no pay." He departed on his errand, and I waited with a sinking heart. Even if there was no danger, and I was by no means sure of that, with that tom-toming and that chant in my ears, I could not afford to go back and announce that I had failed. All my outlay had been for nothing. Another long wait, and more little boys to look at me. The evening was coming; here in the hollow, down among the trees, the gloom was already gathering, and I began to think that neither Chama nor Sekondi would see me that night. I wondered what it would be like to spend the night under the trees, and whether there were any beasts that might molest me.

"Toom, toom, toom," went the village drum, as if to remind me there might be worse things than spending the night under the trees, and then my friend with the comforter appeared, leading two of the other hammock-boys; one wore a crocheted, red tam-o'-shanter that fell over his face—probably made at the same sewing-party. It was the same wool.

I talked to those three men. Considering they were the best behaved of the lot, it comes back to me now that I was rather hard on them. I pointed out the dire pains and penalties that befell hammock-boys who did not pay proper attention to their duties, and I trusted that the fact that I was utterly incapable of inflicting those penalties was not as patent to them as it was to me, and then I decreed that my friend with the comforter should go back and try and retrieve a fourth man while the other two stayed with me. After another long wait he got that fourth man and we started off, I dignifiedly wrathful—at least I hope I was dignified; there was no doubt about the wrath—and they bearing evident marks of having consumed a certain quantity of the funeral palm wine.

It was dark when we reached Chama, at least as dark as it ever is on a bright, starlight night in the Tropics, and we came out of the gloom of the trees to find a dark bungalow raised high on stilts on a cement platform, looming up against the star-spangled sky, and then another surprise, a comforting surprise, awaited me: on that cement platform were two white spots, and those white spots rose up to greet me, shamefaced, humble, contrite, my servants. They had evidently slunk past me without being seen, and I was immensely relieved. But naturally I did not say so. I mentioned that I was very angry with them, and that it would take a long course of faithful service to make up for so serious a lapse, and they received my reproof very humbly, and apparently never realised that I was just about as lonely a woman as there was in the world at that moment, and would gladly have bartered all my wild aspirations after fame and fortune for the comfortable certainty that I was going to spend a safe night. It certainly does not jump with my firm faith in thought transference that none of those men apparently ever discovered I was afraid. I should have thought it was written all over me, but also, afraid as I was, it never occurred to me to turn back; so, if the one thought impressed them, perhaps the other did too.

Then I waited on that dark verandah. There was some scanty Government furniture in the rest-house, and my repentant servant fetched me out a chair, and I sat and waited. I looked out; there was the clearing round the house, the gloom of the dense greenery that grew up between the house and the seashore, while east ran the road to the town of Chama, about a ten minutes' walk distant, and on the west a narrow track hardly discernible in the gloom came out of the greenery. Up that I had come and up that I expected my men. And it seemed I might expect them. No one was going to deny me that privilege. Still, I began to feel distinctly better. At least I had arrived at Chama, and four hammock-boys and two servants were very humbly at my service. I wasn't going to spend the night in the open at the mercy of the trees and the unknown beasts, and I laughed at the idea of being afraid of the trees, though to my mind African trees have a distinct personality of their own. Well, there was nothing to be done but wait, and I waited in the dark, for as no carriers had come in there was no possibility of a light, or of dinner either for that matter. Grant was extremely sympathetic and most properly shocked at the behaviour of the carriers. No punishment could be too great for men who could treat his missus in such an outrageous manner. In the excitement and bustle of getting off I had eaten very little that day, so I was very hungry now; it added to my woes and decreased my fear. Nothing surely could be going to happen to a woman who was so very commonplacely hungry. At last, about ten o'clock, I saw my loads come straggling out of the gloom of the trees on to the little path up to the platform, and then, before I quite realised what was happening, the verandah was full of carriers, drunk and hilarious, and not at all inclined to recognise the enormity of their crime. Something had to be done, I knew. It would be the very worst of policies to allow my verandah to be turned into pandemonium. The headman had lighted a lantern, that I made Grant take, and by its flickering light I singled out my policeman, cheerfully happy, but still, thank goodness, holding on to the sticks of my camera. Him I tackled angrily. How dared he allow drunken carriers on my verandah, or anywhere near me? Everyone, on putting down his load, was to go downstairs immediately. How we cleared that verandah I'm sure I don't know. The four virtuous haminock-boys and Grant and Zacco, I suppose, all took a hand, backed by their stern missus, and presently I and my servants had it to ourselves with a humble and repentant policeman sitting on the top of the steps, and Grant set about getting my dinner. It was too late, I decided, to cook anything beyond a little coffee, so I had tinned tongues and tinned apricots this my first night alone in Africa. Then came the question of going to bed. There were several rooms in the rest-house, but the verandah seemed to me a pleasanter place where to sleep on a hot night. Of course, I was alone, and would it be safer inside? The doors and windows were frail enough, besides it would be impossible to sleep with them shut, so I, to my boy's intense astonishment, decided for the verandah, and there I set up my bed, just an ordinary camp-bed, with mosquito curtains over it, and I went to bed and wondered if I could sleep.

First I found myself listening, listening intently, and I heard a thousand noises, the night birds calling, the skirl of the untiring insects, a faint tom-toming and sounds of revelry from the village, which gave things an unpleasant air of savagery, the crash of the ceaseless surf on the beach. I decided I was too frightened to sleep and I heartily wished myself back in England, writing mystery stories for a livelihood, and then I began to think that I was most desperately tired, that the mosquito curtains were a great protection, and before I realised I was sleepy was sound asleep and remembered no more till I awakened wondering where I was, and saw the first streaks of light in the east. Before the first faint streaks of light and sunrise is but a short time in the Tropics, and now I knew that everything depended upon me, so I flew out of bed and dressed with great promptitude, and there was Grant with early-morning tea and then breakfast. But no carriers; and I had given orders we were to start at half-past five. It was long past that; six o'clock, no carriers, half-past. I sent Zacco for the headman and he like the raven from the ark was no more seen. I sent Grant and he returned, not with an olive branch but with the policeman.

"Where are the carriers?" I demanded.

"They chop," said he nonchalantly, as if it were no affair of his.

"Chop! At this hour in the morning?" It was close on seven.

He signified that they did.

"Bring the headman." And I was a very angry white missus indeed. Since I had got through the night all right I felt I was bound to do somthing today and I was not nearly so afraid as I had been.

The headman wept palm-wine tears. "They chop," he said and he sobbed and gulped and wiped his face with the back of his hand like a discomfited Somersetshire laburer. His condition immensely improved my courage. I was the white woman all over dealing with the inferior race, and I had not a doubt as to what should be done.

"Policeman, you follow me."

He did not like it much, my little Fanti policeman, because he feared these Mendis and Timinis who could have eaten him alive, but he followed me however reluctantly. I wanted him as representing law and order. The thinking I intended to do myself.

We walked down to the village and there in the middle of the road were my carriers in two parties, each seated round a large enamelled-iron basin full of fish and rice. They did chop. They looked up at me with a grin, but I had quite made up my mind.

"Policeman," I said, "no man chops so late. Throw away the chop."

He hesitated. He could not make up his mind which he was most afraid of, me or the men. Finally he decided that I was the most terrifying person and he gingerly picked up one of those basins and carefully put it down under a shrub.

"Policeman," I said, and I was emphatic, "that's not the way to throw away chop. Scatter it round," and with one glance at me to see if I meant what I said, he scattered it on the ground. What surprised me was that the men let him. Certainly those round the second dish seized it and fled up towards the rest-house, and we came after them. When we arrived the men were still eating, but there was still some rice in the dish, and I made the policeman seize it and fling it away, and then every one of those men came back meekly to work, picked up their loads or waited round the hammock for me.

I saw the loads off with the headman, and told him to get across the Prah River if he could and on to Kommenda, where I proposed to have my luncheon, and then I stayed behind to take some photographs of the old fort. It took me some time to take my pictures. The heat was intense, and beyond the fort, which is quaintly old-world, there is not much to see. The town is the usual Coast village built of clay, which they call swish, with thatched roofs; the streets between the houses are hot and dry and bare, and little naked children disport themselves there with the goats, sheep, pigs, and chickens. There are the holes from which the earth has been taken to make

the swish—man-traps in the night, mosquitobreeding places at all times—
and there are men and women standing gossiping in the street, wondering at
the unusual sight of a white woman, just for all the world as they might do in
a remote Cornish village if a particularly smart motor passed by. They are
fishing villages, these villages along the Coast, living by the fishing, and
growing just a little maize and plantains and yams for their own immediate
needs; and it is a curious thing to say, but they give one the same sleepy, out-
of-the-world feeling that a small village in Cornwall does. There is not in
them the go and the promise there is in an Ashanti village, the dormant
wealth waiting to be awakened one feels there is along the Volta. No, these
places were exploited hundreds of years ago by the men who built the fort
that frowns over them still, and they are content to live on from day to day
with just enough to keep them going, with the certain knowledge that no man
can die of starvation, and when a young man wants distraction I suppose he
goes to the bigger towns. So I found nothing of particular interest in Chama,
and I went on till I reached the Prah River, just where it breaks out across
the sands and rushes to meet the ocean.

I wondered in that journey to Accra many times whether my face was set
hard, whether my lips were not one firm, stern line that could never unbend
and look kindly again. My small camp mirror that I consulted was exceedingly
unflattering, but if I had not before been certain that no half-measures were
of any use I should have been certain of it when I reached the river. There
lay my loads, and sitting down solemnly watching them like so many crows,
rather dissipated crows, were my men. They rose up as my hammock came
into view.

"Missus, men want drink water. It be hot."

It was hot, very hot, and the river it seemed was salt; moreover, the only
house in sight, and that was a good way off, was the hut apparently belonging
to the ferryman. I looked at them, and my spirits rose; it was borne in on me
that I had them well in hand, for there was no reason why they should not
have gone off in a body to get that much-needed water.

But I gave the order, "One man go fetch water."

Why they obeyed me I don't know now, and why they didn't take the bucket
I don't know now. I ought to have sent one man with a bucket; but
experience always has to be bought, and I only realised that I was master of
the situation, and must not spoil it by undue haste. So I solemnly stood there
under my sun umbrella and watched those men have a drink one by one out
of an empty marmalade pot. Whenever, in the future, I see one of those
golden tins, it will call up to my memory a blazing hot day, a waste of sand
and coarse grass, a wide river flowing through it, and a row of loads with a
ragged company of black men sitting solemnly beside them waiting while one

of their number brought them a drink. That drink was a tremendous piece of business, but we were through with it at last, and though I was rather weary and very hot I was inclined to be triumphant. I felt I had the men fairly well in hand.

Still, they weren't all that I could have desired. The road was very, very bad indeed, sometimes it was down on the heavy sand, sometimes the rocks were too rough—the hammock had to be engineered up and down the bank by devious and uncomfortable ways, sometimes we stopped to buy fruit in a village, and sometimes the men stopped and declared: "Missus, oder hammock-boy, he no come."

Then I was hard. I knew it was no good being anything else.

"If hammock-boy no come you go on. I no stop."

And they went, very slowly and reluctantly, but they went. It seemed cruel, but I soon grasped the fact that if I once allowed them to wait for the relief men who lingered there always would be lingerers, and we should crawl to Accra at the rate of five miles a day.

They sang songs as they went, and this my first day out the song took a most personal turn.

"If man no get chop," they intoned in monotonous recitative, "he go die. Missus frow away our chop———-"

The deduction was obvious and I answered it at once. "All right, you go die. I no care. If men no come to work they may die."

But they went very badly indeed, and it was after two o'clock in the afternoon before we arrived at Kommenda on the seashore, where there is a village and a couple of old forts falling into decay. Here, inside the courtyard of one of them, which is Ju-ju, I had my table and chair put out and my luncheon served. The feeling of triumph was still upon me. Already I was nearer Elmina than Sekondi and I felt in all probability, bad as they were, the men would go on. But, before I had finished my luncheon, my serenity received another shock. Of course no one dared disturb so terrible a person at her chop, but, after I had finished, while I was endeavouring to instruct Zacco in the way in which a kettle might be induced to boil without letting all the smoke go down the spout—I wanted some coffee—Grant came up with a perturbed countenance and said the headman wanted to speak to me. I sent for him.

"Missus," he began propitiatingly, "man be tired too much. You stop here to-night; we take you Cape Coast to-morrow."

COURTYARD, KOMMENDA FORT.

For the moment I was very properly wrathful. Then I reflected—the white men did not understand, the majority of them, my desire to see Elmina, the most important castle on the Coast, how then should these black men understand. There was a tiny rest-house built on the bastion of the fort here, and looking at it I decided it was just the last place I should like to spend the night in. I did not expect to meet a white man at Elmina, but at least it must be far nearer civilisation than this.

I looked at my headman more in sorrow than in anger. He was a much-troubled person, and evidently looked upon me as a specimen of the genus "Massa." I said:

"That is a very beautiful idea, headman, and does you credit. The only drawback I see to it is that I do not want to go to Cape Coast to-morrow, and I do want to go to Elmina to-night."

He scratched his head in a bewildered fashion, transferring a very elderly tourist cap from one hand to the other in order that he might give both sides a proper chance.

"Man no be fit," he got out at last.

"Oh, they no be fit. Send for the Chief," and I turned away and went on with Zacco's instructions in the art of making coffee. Still, in my own mind, I was very troubled. That rest-house on the bastion was a horrid-looking hole, and I had heard it whispered that the men of Kommenda were very truculent. If I had been far from a white man at Chama, I was certainly farther still now at Kommenda. Still, my common sense told me I must not allow I was dismayed.

Presently I was told the Chief had arrived, and I went outside and interviewed him. He wasn't a very big chief, and his stick of office only had a silver top to it with the name of the village written on it in large letters. He could speak no English, but with my headman and his linguist he soon grasped the fact that I wanted more carriers, and agreed to supply them. Then I went back inside the fort and he joined the group outside who had come to look at the white woman, and who, I am glad to say, all kept respectfully outside. I seated myself again and sent for the headman.

"Headman, you bring in man who no be fit."

The headman went outside and presently returned with the downcast, ragged scarecrow who had been carrying my bed.

"You no be fit?"

"No, Ma."

I pointed out a place against the wall.

"You go sit there. You go back to Sekondi. I get 'nother man. Headman, fetch in other man who no be fit."

The culprit sat himself down most reluctantly, afraid, whether of me or the Ju-ju that was supposed to reign over the place, I know not, and the headman brought in another man.

"You no be fit?"

"No, Ma"; but it was a very reluctant no.

"Sit down over there. Another man, headman," but somehow I did not think there would be many more. And for once my intuitions were right. The headman came back reporting the rest were fit. I felt triumphant. Then the unfortunate scare-crows against the wall rose up humbly and protested eagerly: "we be fit."

But I was brutally stern. It cost me dear in the end, but it might have cost me dearer if I had taken them on. However, I had no intention of doing any such thing. They had declared themselves of their own free will "no fit." I was determined they should remain "no fit" whatever it cost me to fill their places. I must rule this caravan, and I must decide where we should halt. I engaged two Kommenda men to carry the loads, and when I had taken photographs of the fort—how thankful I was that they turned out well, for Kommenda is one of the most unget-at-able places I know, and before a decent photographer gets there again I don't suppose there will be one stone left on another—I started after my men to Elmina.

The carriers who were "no fit" came with us. Why, I hardly know, but they were very, very repentant.

It was four o'clock before we left Kommenda, and since we had twelve miles to go I hardly expected to arrive before dark, but I did think we might arrive about seven. I reckoned without my host, or rather without my carriers. There was more than a modicum of truth in the statement that they were no fit. The dissipation of the day before, and the lack of chop to-day—carriers always make a big meal early in the morning—were beginning to tell; besides they were very bad specimens of their class, and they lingered and halted and crawled till I began to think we should be very lucky indeed if we got into Elmina before midnight. The darkness fell, and in the little villages the lights began to appear—these Coast villagers use a cheap, a very cheap sort of kerosene lamp—and more than once my headman appealed to me. "We stop here, Ma."

I was very tired myself, now, very tired, indeed, and gladly would I have stopped, but those negro houses seen by the light of a flickering, evil-smelling lamp were impossible; besides I realised it would be very bad to give in to my men. Finally we left the last little village behind, and before us lay a long, crescent-shaped bay, with a twinkling point of light at the farther horn—Elmina, I guessed. It was quite dark now, sea and sky mingled, a line of white marked the breakers where the water met the sands, and on my left was the low shore hardly rising twenty feet above the sea-level, and covered with short, wiry sea-grasses, small shrubs, and the creeping bean. The men who were carrying me staggered along, stumbling over every inequality of the ground, and I remembered my youthful reading in "Uncle Tom's Cabin," and felt I very much resembled Legree. There was, too, a modicum of sympathy growing up in my mind for Legree and all slave-drivers. Perhaps there was something to be said for them; they certainly must have had a good deal to put up with. Presently my men dropped the hammock, and I scrambled out and looked at them angrily. The carriers were behind, the policeman—my protection and my dignity—was nowhere to be seen, my two servants were just behind, where they ought to have been, and my four hammock-boys looked at me in sullen misery.

"We no be fit."

The case was beyond all words at my command, and I set my face to the east, and began to walk in the direction of the feeble little light I could see twinkling in the far distance, and which I concluded rightly, as it turned out, must be Elmina.

My servants overtook me, and Grant, who had been a most humble person when first I engaged him, who had been crushed with a sense of his own unworthiness the night before, now felt it incumbent upon himself to protest.

"You no walk, Ma. It no be fit."

How sick I was of that "no be fit."

"Grant," I said with dignity, at least I hope it was with dignity, abandoning pigeon English, "there is no other way. Tell those boys if I walk to Elmina they get no pay," and I stalked on, wishing at the bottom of my heart I knew something of the manners and customs of the African snake. In my own country I should have objected strongly to walking in such grass, when I could not see my way, and it just shows the natural selfishness of humanity that this thought had never occurred to me while my hammock-boys were carrying me. I don't suppose I had gone half a mile when Grant and the boys overtook me.

"Ma," said Grant with importance, the way he achieved importance that day was amazing, "you get in. They carry you now."

"They no be fit."

"They carry you," declared he emphatically.

"We try, Ma," came a humble murmur from the boys, and I got in once more and we staggered along.

How I hated it all, and what a brute I felt. I thought to offer a little encouragement, so I said after a little time, when I thought the light was getting appreciably larger: "Grant, which of these men carry me best?" and thought I would offer a suitable reward.

"They all carry you very badly, Ma," came back Grant's stern reply; "that one," and he pointed to the unfortunate who bore the lefthand front end of the hammock, "carry you worst."

Now, here was a dilemma. The light wasn't very far away now, and I could see against the sky the loom of a great building.

"Very well," I said, "each of the other three shall have threepence extra," and the lefthand front man dropped his end of the hammock with something very like a sob, and left the other three to struggle on as best they might. We were close to Elmina now. There was a row of palms on our right between us and the surf, and I could see houses with tiny lights in them, and so could the men.

"I will walk," I said.

But the three remaining were very eager. "No, Ma; no, Ma, we carry you."

Then there appeared a man in European clothes, and him I stopped and interviewed.

"Is that the Castle of Elmina?"

"Yes," said he, evidently mightily surprised at being interviewed by a white woman.

"Who is in charge?" and I expected to hear some negro post office or Custom official.

"Dr Dove," said the stranger in the slurring tones of the negro.

"A white man?"

"Yes, a white man."

For all my weariness, I could have shouted for joy. Such an unexpected piece of good luck! I had not expected to meet a white man this side of Cape Coast. I had thought the great Castle here was abandoned to the tender mercies of the negro official.

"You can get in," went on my new friend; "the drawbridge is not down yet."

A drawbridge! How mediaeval it sounded, quite in keeping with the day I had spent, the day that had begun in Chama fifty years ago.

We staggered along the causeway, the causeway made so many hundreds of years ago by the old Portuguese adventurers; the sentry rose up in astonishment, and we staggered across it into the old courtyard; I got out of my hammock at the foot of a flight of broad stone steps, built when men built generously, and a policeman, not mine, raced up before me. All was in darkness in the great hall, and then I heard an unmistakable white man's voice in tones of surprise and unbelief.

"A missus, a———"

I stepped forward in the pitchy darkness, wondering what pitfalls there might be by the way.

"I am a white woman," I said uncertainly, for I was very weary, and I had an uneasy feeling that this white man, like so many others I had met, might think I had no business to be there, and I didn't feel quite equal to asserting my rights just at that moment, and then I met an outstretched hand. It needed no more. I knew at once. It was a kindly, friendly, helpful hand. Young or old, pretty or plain, ragged, smart, or disreputable, whatever I was, I felt the owner of that hand would be good to me. Dr Duff, for the negro had pronounced his name after his kind, led me upstairs through the darkness, with many apologies for the want of light, into a big room, dimly lighted by a kerosene lamp, and then we looked at each other.

"God bless my soul! Where on earth did you come from?" said he.

"No one told me there was a white man in Elmina," said I; "and the relief of finding one was immense."

But not till I was washed and bathed, dressed, fed, and in my right mind did we compare notes, and then we sat up till midnight discussing things.

It seemed to me I had sounded the depths, I had mastered the difficulties of African travel. My new friend listened sympathetically as he drank his whisky-and-soda, and then he flattered my little vanities as they had never been flattered since I had set out on my journeyings.

"Not one woman in ten thousand would have got through."

I liked it, but I think he was wrong. Any woman who had once started would have got through simply and solely because there was absolutely nothing else to be done. It is a great thing in life to find there is only one way.

Then Dr Duff descended to commonplace matters.

"I hope you don't mind," said he; "I've kicked your policeman."

"That," said I, "is a thing he has been asking someone to do ever since we left Sekondi a thousand years ago."

CHAPTER IX
AN OLD DUTCH TOWN

But one man of the ruling race—Overlooked Elmina—Deadly fever—The reason why—Magnificent position—Ideal for a capital—Absence of tsetse—Loyal to their Dutch masters—Difficulty in understanding incorruptibility of English officials—Reported gold in Elmina—The stranded school-inspector—"Potable water"—Preferred the chance of guinea-worm to trouble—Stern German head-teacher—Cape Coast—Wonderful native telegraphy—Haunted Castle—Truculent people.

Elmina means, of course, the mine, and the reason for the name is lost in the mist of ages. Certain it is there is no mine nearer than those at Tarkwa, at least two days' journey away, but in the old Portuguese and Dutch days Elmina was a rich port. It is a port still, though an abandoned one, and you may land from a boat comfortably on to great stone steps, as you may land in no other place along the Guinea Coast. On the 17th of May in this year of our Lord, 1911, there raged along the Coast a hurricane such as there has not been for many a long day, and the aftermath of that hurricane was found in a terrific surf, which for several days made landing at any port difficult, in some cases impossible. The mail steamer found she could land no mails at Cape Coast, and then was forgotten, neglected Elmina remembered, and the mails were landed there, eight miles to the west, and carried overland to their destination.

Yet is there but one man of the ruling race in Elmina, and the fine old Castle, where the Portuguese and Dutch governors of Guinea reigned, is almost abandoned to the desecrating hand of the negro officials—Custom and post office men! Why, when the Gold Coast was looking for a capital, they overlooked Elmina is explained usually by the declaration that yellow fever was very bad there; and I conclude it was for the same reason that they passed it by when they wanted a seaport for the inland railway. Somehow it seems an inadequate reason. It would have been cheaper surely to search for the cause of the ill-health than to abandon so promising a site. The reason lies deeper than that. It is to be found in that strong feeling in the Englishman—that feeling which is going to ruin him as a colonising nation now that rivals are in the field, unless he looks to his ways—that one place in "such a poisonous country" is as good or as bad as another, and therefore if people die in one place, "let's try another beastly hole." Die they certainly did in Elmina. It was taken over from the Dutch in 1874, and in 1895 the records make ghastly reading. "Yellow fever, died," you read, not once but over and over again. Young and strong and hopeful, and always the record is the same, and now, looking at it with seeing eyes and an understanding mind, the explanation is so simple, the cure so easy.

Round this great Castle is a double line of moats, each broad and deep and about half a mile in extent, and these moats were full to the brim of water, stagnant water, an ideal breeding place for that entirely domesticated animal, the yellow-fever mosquito—*stegmia*, I believe, is the correct term. Get but one yellow-fever patient, let him get bitten by a mosquito or two, and the thing was done. But sixteen years ago they were not content with such simple ways as that. It seems there was a general sort of feeling then along the Coast, it has not quite gone yet, that chill was a thing greatly to be dreaded, and so instead of taking advantage of the magnificent position so wisely chosen by the Portuguese mariners, where the fresh air from the ocean might blow night and day, they mewed themselves up in quarters on the landward side of the Castle, so built that it is almost impossible to get a thorough draught of air through them. The result in such a climate is languor and weariness, an ideal breeding ground for malaria or yellow fever. And so they died, God rest their souls; some of them were gallant gentlemen, but they died like flies, and Elmina, for no fault of its own, was abandoned.

ELMINA.

And yet the old Portuguese were right. It is an ideal site for a capital. The Castle is on a promontory which juts out into the sea, and is almost surrounded by water, for the Sweetwater River, which was very salt when I was there, runs into the sea in such a fashion as to leave but a narrow neck of land between the Castle and the mainland. The land rises behind the town, it is clear of scrub and undergrowth, so that horses and cattle may live, as there is no harbour for that curse of West Africa, the tsetse fly; there is sufficient open space for the building of a large town, and it is nearer to Kumasi, whence comes all the trade from the north, than Sekondi, which was chosen, instead of it, as a railway terminus. A grievous pity! It is England's proud boast that she lets the man on the spot have a free hand, knowing that he must be the better judge of local conditions and needs; it is West Africa's misfortune that she had so evil a reputation that the best and wisest men did not go there; and hence these grave mistakes.

I had always believed that every coloured man was yearning to come under the British flag, therefore was I much astonished to hear that in 1874, when Britain took over this part of the Coast, the natives resented the change of masters very bitterly. They would not submit, and the big village to the west of the fort, old Elmina native town, was in open rebellion. At last the guns from the fort were turned upon it, the inhabitants evacuated it hastily, it was bombarded, and the order went forth that no one should come back to it.

Even now, thirty-seven years later, the old law which prohibits the native from digging on the site of the old town is still in force, and since the natives were in the habit of burying their wealth beneath their huts, great store of gold dust is supposed to be hidden there. Again and again the solitary official in charge of Elmina has been approached by someone asking permission to dig there, generally with the intimation that if only the permission be granted, a large percentage of the hidden treasure shall find its way into the pockets of that official.

"It is hard," said Dr Duff, "for the native mind to grasp the fact that the English official is incorruptible, and the law must be kept—but I confess," he added, "I should like to know if there really is gold in old Elmina."

The town has been a fine town once. The houses are substantially built of stone, they are approached by fine flights of stone steps, there are the ruins of an old casino, and picturesque in its desolation is an old Dutch garden. If I were to describe the magnificent old Castle, I should fill half the book; it is so well worth writing about. I walked up the hill behind the Castle where they have built up the roadway with discarded cannon, and there I took photographs and wished I had a little more time to spare for the place, and vowed that when I reached England the British Museum should help me to find out all there is to be known about this magnificent place and the men who have gone before.

A STREET IN ELMINA.

For the man of the present it must be a little difficult to live in, if it is only for the intense loneliness. It must be lonely to live in the bush with the eternal forest surrounding you, but at least there a man is an outpost of Empire, the trade is coming to him, he may find interest and amusement in the breaking of a road or the planning of a garden, while the making of a town would fill all his time, but in Elmina there are no such consolations. The place is dead, slain by the English; the young men go away following the trade, and the old mammies with wrinkled faces and withered breasts lounge about the streets and talk of departed glories.

I had not expected to find one white man here, and I found two, the other being a school-inspector who was on his way along the Coast inspecting the native schools. He was in a fix, for he had sent on his carriers and stores and could get no hammock-boys. They had promised to send them from Cape Coast and they had not come. The medical officer made both us strangers hospitably welcome, but stores are precious things on the Coast and one does not like to trespass, so he was a troubled school-inspector.

"I think I'll walk on to Kommenda," said he.

"I wouldn't," said I, the only one who knew that undesirable spot.

We made a queer little party of three in that old-world Castle, in the old Dutch rooms that are haunted by the ghosts of the dead-and-gone men and women of a past generation. At least, I said they were haunted, the school-inspector was neutral, and the medical officer declared no ghosts had ever troubled him. I don't know whether it was ghosts that troubled me, but the fact remains that I, who could sleep calmly by myself in the bush with all my carriers drunk, could not sleep easily now that my troubles were over, and I set it down to the haunting unhappy thoughts of the people who had gone before me, who were dead, but who had lived and suffered in those rooms; and yet in the day-time we were happy enough, and the two men instructed me as one who had a right to know in things African. The school-inspector was very funny on the education of the native. His great difficulty apparently was to make the rising generation grasp the fact that grandiloquent words of which they did not understand the meaning were not proofs of deep knowledge. The negro is like the Hindoo Baboo dear to the heart of Mr Punch. He dearly loves a long word. Hygiene is a subject the Government insist upon being taught, only it seems to me they would do more wisely to teach it in the vernacular so that it might be understood by the common people. As it is, said my school-inspector, the pupils are very pat; and when solemnly asked by the teacher what are the constituents of drinking water, rap out a list of Latin adjectives the only one of which he can understand is "potable."

"Tut, tut," said the inspector, "run along, Kudjo, and bring me a glass of drinking water"; and then it was only too evident that that youthful scion of the Fanti race who had been so glib with his adjectives did not understand what "potable" meant.

STREET IN ELMINA.

Afterwards in the eastern portion of the Colony I was told of other difficulties and snares that lie in the way of the unlucky schoolmaster. In Africa it is specially necessary to be careful of your water, as in addition to many other unpleasant results common in other lands there is here a certain sort of worm whose eggs may apparently be swallowed in the water. They have an unpleasant habit of hatching internally and then working their way out to the outer air, discommoding greatly their unwilling host. Therefore twice a week in every English school the qualities of good water and the way to insure it are insisted upon by the teacher. But does that teacher practise what he preaches? He doesn't like guinea-worm, but neither does he like trouble, wherefore he chooses the line of least resistance and chances his water. If the worst come to the worst and he has guinea-worm, a paternal Government will pay his salary while he is ill.

At least up till lately it always has. But a change is coming over the spirit of the dream. The other day there arose in Keta, a town in the Eastern Province, a German head-teacher who got very tired of subordinates who were perpetually being incapacitated by guinea-worm, a perfectly preventable disease, and, as the Germans are nothing if not practical, there went forth in his school the cruel order that any teacher having guinea-worm should have no salary during his illness. There is going to be one more case of guinea-worm in that school, then there is going to be a sad and sorry man fallen from his high estate and dependent on his relatives, and then the teachers will possibly learn wisdom and practise what they preach. But in Elmina my school-inspector seemed to think the Golden Age was yet a long way off.

I left him and the medical officer with many hopes for a future meeting, and one afternoon took up my loads and having sent a telegram to the Provincial Commissioner—how easy it seemed now—set out for Cape Coast eight miles along the shore.

There is very little difference in the scenery all along the shore here. The surf thunders to the right, and to the left the land goes back low and sandy, covered with coarse grass and low-growing shrubs, while here and there are fishing villages with groves of cocoa-nuts around them, only the houses instead of being built of the raffia palm are built of swish, that is mud, and as you go east dirtier and dirtier grow the villages.

It took us barely two hours and a half to reach Cape Coast, one of the oldest if not the oldest English settlement on the Coast. It was the original Capo Corso of the Portuguese, but the English have held it since early in the seventeenth century, and the natives, of course, bear English names—in Elmina they have Dutch names—and remember no other masters.

Cape Coast is a great straggling untidy town with rather an eastern look about it which comes, I think, from the fact that many of the houses have flat roofs.

But it is a drab-looking town without any of the gorgeous colouring of the east. The Castle is built down on the seashore behind great walls and bastions, and here are the Customs, the Commissioner's Court, the Post Office, all the mechanism required for the Government of a people, but the old cannon are still there, piles of shot and shell and great mortars, and in the courtyards are the graves of the men and women who have gone before, the honoured dead. Here lies the lady whom the early nineteenth century reckoned a poet, L. E. L., Laetitia Landor, the wife of Captain Maclean who perished by some unexplainable misadventure while she was little more than a bride, and here lies Captain Maclean himself, the wise Governor whom the African merchants put in when England, in one of her periodic fits of thriftless economy, would have abandoned the Gold Coast, and here are other unknown names Dutch and English, and oh, curious commentary on the hygiene of the time, in the same courtyard is the well whence the little company of whites, generally surrounded by a people often hostile, must needs in time of siege or stress always draw their water.

They say Cape Coast like Elmina is haunted, and men have told me tales of unaccountable noises, of footsteps that crossed the floor, of voices in conversation, of sighs and groans and shrieks for help that were unexplained and unexplainable. One man who had been D.C. there told me he could keep no servant in the Castle at night they were so terrified, but as I only paid flying visits to take photographs I cannot say of my own knowledge whether there is anything uncanny about it. There ought to be, for there are deep dungeons underground, dark and uncanny, where in old days they possibly kept their slaves and certainly their prisoners-of-war. There was no light in them then, there is very little now, only occasionally someone has knocked away a stone from the thick walls, and you may see a round of dancing sunlight in the gloom and hear the sound of the ceaseless surf. An officer in the Gold Coast regiment told me he wanted to have a free hand to dig in the earth here, for he was sure the pirates who owned it in the old days must have buried much treasure here and forgotten all about it, but he was a hopeful young man and looked forward to the days when the Ashantis should come down and besiege Cape Coast again as they had done in the old days, and he pointed out the particular gun on the bastion that in case of such an event he should train on the Kumasi road and blow those savages into the next world. I have seen those fighting men of Ashanti since then and I do not think they are ever coming to Cape Coast, at least as enemies, which perhaps is just as well, for the gun which that gay young lieutenant slapped so affectionately and called "Old Girl" is pretty elderly and I fancy might do more damage to those loading than to those at the other end of her muzzle.

But I did not lodge at the fort. The medical officer, it was always the medical officer to the rescue, very kindly took charge and I was very comfortably lodged in the hospital. And here I had proof of the wonderful manner in which news is carried by the birds of the air in West Africa. I had thought that the Provincial Commissioner was going to put me up, and I instructed my boys to that effect.

"Ask way to Government House," which I thought lay to the west of the town. As we passed the first houses a man sprang up.

"Dis way, Ma, I show you," and off he went, we following, and I thought my men had asked the question. Clearly Government House was not to the west, for we went on through the town and up a hill and up to a large bungalow which I was very sure was not Government House, unless we had arrived at the back.

I got out protesting, but my boys were very sure and so was our guide.

"Dis be bungalow, Ma. Missus come."

Then I knew they were wrong, for I knew the Commissioner had no wife. But they weren't after all, for down the steps breathing kindly welcome came the medical officer's wife, a pretty bride of a couple of months, and she smilingly explained that the Commissioner had asked her to take me in because it would be so much more comfortable for me where there was another woman. "I suppose he sent you on," said she.

But not only had he not sent me on, but he knew nothing of my coming, and was waiting in Government House for my arrival. The town, then, knew of my expected coming and his intentions with regard to me almost before he had formulated them himself. At any rate, it was none of his doing or his servants' doings that I went straight to the hospital, and the telegram stating my intention had only been sent that morning. So much for native telegraphy.

Round Cape Coast, in my mind, hangs a mist of romance which will always sharply divide it from the town as I saw it. When I think of it I have to remind myself that I have seen Cape Coast and that, apart from kindly recollections of the hospitality with which I was received, I do not like it. The people are truculent and abominably ill-mannered, and I do not think I would ever venture to walk in the streets again without the protection of a policeman.

There were two white women there, so they had hardly the excuse of curiosity, as we must have been familiar sights, yet they mobbed me in the streets, and when I tried to take photographs of the quaint, old-world streets, hustled and crowded me to such an extent that it was quite out of the question. And they did this even when I was accompanied by my two servants and my hammock-boys.

"These Fanti people catch no sense," said Grant angrily, when after a wild struggle I had succeeded in photographing a couple of men playing draughts, and utterly failed to get a very nice picture of a man making a net. I quite agreed with Grant; these Fanti people do catch no sense, and I got no photographs, for which I was sorry, for there are corners in that old town picturesque and quaint and not unlike corners in the towns along the Sicilian coast. What they said of me I do not know, but I am afraid it was insulting, and if ever my friends the Ashantis like to go through Cape Coast again I shall give them a certain amount of sympathy. At least it would give me infinite satisfaction to hear of some of them getting that beating I left without being able to inflict.

I do not think a white woman would be safe alone in Cape Coast, and this I am the more sorry for because it has belonged so long to the English. Perhaps Dr Blyden is right when he says, and I think he spoke very impartially when speaking of his own people, that the French have succeeded best in dealing with the negro, I beg his pardon, the African. They have succeeded in civilising him, so says Dr Blyden, with dignity. The English certainly have not.

PLAYING DRAUGHTS, CAPE COAST.

CHAPTER X
IN THE PATHS OF THE MEN OF OLD

The glory of the morning—The men who have passed along this road—The strong views of the African pig—An old-world Castle—Thieving carriers—The superiority of the white man—Annamabu—A perfect specimen of a fort—A forlorn rest-house—A notable Coast Chief—Tired-out mammies—The medical officer at Salt Ponds—The capable German women—The reason of the ill-health of the English women—Kroo boys as carriers—Tantum—A loyal rest-house—Filthy Appam—A possible origin for the yellow fever at Accra—Winne-bah—A check—The luckless ferryman—Good-bye to the road.

The carriers from Kommenda were only to come as far as Cape Coast, so here I had to find fresh men or rather women to replace them. I know nothing more aggravating than engaging carriers. Apparently it was a little break in the monotony of life as lived in an African town to come and engage as a carrier with the white missus, come when she was about to start, an hour late was the correct thing, look at the loads, turn them over, try to lift them, say "We no be fit," and then sit down and see what would happen next. The usual programme, of course, was gone through at Cape Coast, the mammies I had engaged smiling and laughing as if it were the best joke in the world, and I only kept my temper by reflecting that since I could not beat them, which I dearly longed to do, it was no good losing it. They had had three days to contemplate those loads and they only found "we no be fit" as I wanted to start. Of course the men who had come on from Sekondi with me were now most virtuous; they bore me no ill-will for my harsh treatment, indeed they respected me for it, and they regarded themselves as my prop and my stay, as indeed they were.

With infinite difficulty I got off at last, taking three new carriers, mammies, where two had sufficed before.

Travelling in the early morning is glorious. The dew is on all the grass; it catches and reflects the sunbeams like diamonds, and there is a freshness in the air which is lost as the day advances. I loved going along that coast too.

I was thrown upon myself for companionship, for my followers could only speak a little pigeon English, and of course we had nothing in common, but the men and women who had gone before walked beside me and whispered to me tales of the strenuous days of old. Perhaps the Phoenicians had been here, possibly those old sea rovers, the Normans, and certainly the Portuguese; they had marched along this shore, even as I was marching along, only their own homes were worlds away and the bush behind was peopled for them with unknown monsters, such as I would not dream of. They had feared as they walked, and now I, a woman, could come alone and unarmed.

Leaving Cape Coast that still, warm, tropical morning, we passed the people coming into town to the markets with their wares upon their heads, all carried in long crates, chickens and fowls and unhappy pigs strapped tightly down, for the African pig, like the pig in other lands, has a mind of his own; he will not walk to his own destruction, he has to be carried. These traders were women usually, and they looked at me with interest and no little astonishment, for I believe that never before had a white woman by herself gone alone along this path.

CHICKENS FOR THE MARKET.

My carriers had been instructed to go to Accra and to Accra they went by the nearest way, sometimes cutting off little promontories, and thus it happened that, looking up on one of these detours, I saw on a hill, between me and the sea, a ruined fort. Of course I stopped the hammock and got out. I had come to see these forts, and here I was passing one. I wanted to go back. My headman demurred. Had I not distinctly said I wanted to go to Accra, and were we not on the direct road to Accra? To get to that old fort, which he did not think worth looking at, we should have to go back an hour's journey, and the men "no be fit." I am regretful now that I only saw that fort from a distance. It was very very hot, and I don't think I felt very fit myself; at any rate, the thought of two hours extra in the hammock dismayed me and I decided to take a long-distance photograph from where I stood. It was an old Dutch fort—Fort Mori—and was built on high ground overlooking a little bay. I think now it would have been easier for me to do that two hours than to climb as I did, with the assistance of Grant and my headman, to the highest point on the roadside, through long grass, scrub, and undergrowth,

- 104 -

there to poise myself uneasily to get a photograph of the ruins. An ideal place, whispered the men of old, for a fort in the bygone days, for it overlooked all the surrounding country, there was no possibility of surprise, and at its feet was a little sheltered bay. Now, on the yellow sands, in the glare of the sunshine, I could see the great canoes that dared the surf drawn up, the thatched roofs of the native town that drew its sustenance from the sea and in old times owed a certain loyalty to the fort and derived a certain prestige from the presence of the white men.

Regretfully I have only that distant memory of Fort Mori, and I went on. Those men who were "no fit" to take me back behaved abominably. Whenever they neared a village they endeavoured to steal from the inhabitants—a piece of suger-cane, a ball of kenky, or a few bananas—and again and again a quarrel called me to intervene. It is very curious how soon one gets an idea of one's own importance. In England, if I came across a crowd of shouting, furious, angry men, I should certainly pass by on the other side, but here in Africa when I was by myself I felt it my bounden duty to interfere and inquire what was the matter. It was most likely some trouble connected with my carriers. I disliked very much making enemies as I passed, and I endeavoured to catch them and make them pay for what they had stolen. And now I understood at last how it is white people living among a subject race are so often overwhelmed in a sudden rising. It is hard to believe that these people whom you count your inferiors will really rise against you. Here was I, alone, unarmed, only a woman, and yet immediately I heard a commotion I attended at once and dispensed justice to the very best of my ability. I fully expected village elders to bow to my decision, and I am bound to say they generally did.

Most of the villages along the Coast bore a strong family resemblance to the one in which I had spent an unhappy hour while my men attended the funeral palaver, and all the shore is much alike. Between Axim and Sekondi is some rough, rugged, and pretty country, but east and west of those points the shore is flat, and the farther east you go the flatter it becomes, till at the mouth of the Volta and beyond it is all sand and swamp. The first day out from Cape Coast it was somewhat monotonous, possibly if I went over it again I should feel that more; but there was growing up in me a feeling of satisfaction with myself—I do trust it was not smug—because I was getting on. I was doing the thing so many men had said I could not possibly do, and I was doing it fairly easily. Of course, I was helped, helped tremendously by the freehanded hospitality of the people in the towns through which I passed, for which kindness I can never be sufficiently grateful, but here with my carriers I was on my own, and I began to regard them as the captures of my bow and spear, and therefore I at least did not find the country uninteresting. Who ever found the land he had conquered dull?

In due course I arrived at Annamabu, an old English fort that the authorities on the Gold Coast hardly think worth preserving, and have given over to the tender mercies of the negro Custom and post office officials. Like Elmina, I could write a book about Annamabu alone, and I was the more interested in it because it is the most perfect specimen of the entirely English fort on the Coast, and is built at the head of a little bay, where is the best landing on the Coast for miles round.

There is a curious difference between the sites chosen by the different nations. The other nations apparently always chose some bold, commanding position, while the English evidently liked, as in this instance, the head of a little bay and a good landing.

Annamabu is quite a big native town, ruled over, I believe, by a cultured African, a man who is well read and makes a point of collecting all books about the Coast, and has, so they say, some rare old editions. I tried to see him and went to his house, a mud-built, two-storied building, where I sat in a covered courtyard and watched various members of his family go up and down a rickety staircase that led to the upper stories, but the Chief was away on his farm, and even though I waited long he never made his appearance. I should like to have seen the inside of his house, seen his books; all I did see was the courtyard, all dull-mud colour, untidy and unkempt, with a couple of kitchen chairs in it, a goat or two, some broken-down boxes and casks, and the drums of state that marked his high office piled up outside the door.

In the fort itself is the rest-house on the bastion, as untidy and dirty as the Chiefs courtyard. There are three rooms opening one into the other, and in the sitting-room, a great high room with big windows—those men of old knew how to build—there is a table, some chairs, a cupboard, and a filter, on which is written that it is for the use of Europeans only, and behind in the bedroom is the forlornest wreck of a bed, and some remnants of crockery that may have been washed about the time when Mrs Noah held the first spring cleaning in the ark, but apparently have never been touched since. It is only fair to say that every traveller, they are like snow in summer, carries his own bedding, and in fact all he needs, so that all that is really wanted for these rest-houses along the shore is a good broom and a good stout arm to wield it, and if a place is left without human occupancy the dirt is only clean dust, for the clean air along these coasts is divine.

But at Annamabu the usual difficulties came in my way; my old men were well broken-in now, but my new mammies were—well—even though I am a woman, and so by custom not permitted to use bad language, I must say they were the very devil. They carried on with the men and then they complained of the men's conduct, and when they arrived at Annamabu— late, of course, and one of them had the chop box—they sent in word to say they "no be fit" to go any farther, and there and then they wanted to go back to Cape Coast.

I said by all means they might go back to Cape Coast, but the loads would have to be left here and sent for from Salt Ponds, and therefore, as they had not completed their contract, they should be paid nothing.

They came and lay down before me in attitudes of intense weariness calculated to move the heart of a sphinx, but I came to the conclusion I must be a hard-hearted brute, for I was adamant, and those weeping women decided they would go on to Salt Ponds.

At Salt Ponds there is a little company of white people, and, so says report, the very worst surf on the Coast, with perhaps the exception of Half Assinie. The D.C. was away, so the Provincial Commissioner had telegraphed to the medical officer asking him to get me quarters. I arrived about three o'clock on a Sunday afternoon, when the place was apparently wrapped in slumber; the doctor's bungalow was pointed out to me, built on stilts on a cement foundation, and on that foundation I established myself and my loads, and made my way upstairs. A ragged and blasphemous parrot, with a very nice flow of language, was in charge, and he did not encourage me to stop, nor did he even hint at favours to come, so I went down again and waited. Apparently I might wait; towards evening I made my way—I was homeless— towards another bungalow, where a white man received me with astonishment, gave me the nicest cup of tea I have ever drunk, and sent for the medical officer, who had lunched off groundnut soup and had gone into the country to sleep it off. We all know groundnut soup is heavy.

The medical officer remains in my mind as a man with a grievance; he was kind after his fashion, but he did hate the country. If I had listened to him, I should have believed it was unfit for human habitation, and I couldn't help wondering why he had honoured it with his presence. In his opinion it was exceedingly unbecoming in a woman to be making her way along the Coast alone. To drive in these facts he found me house-room with the only white woman in the place, the charmingly hospitable wife of the German trader who had been on the Coast for a couple of years, who was perfectly well, healthy, and happy, who always did her own cooking, and who gave me some of the most delicious meals I have ever tasted. Thus I was introduced to the German element in West Africa, and began to realise for the first time that efficiency in little things which is going to carry the Germans so far. This fair-haired, plump young woman, with the smiling young face, was one of a type, and I could not help feeling sorry there were not more English women like her. I do not think I have ever met an English woman, with the exception of the nursing Sisters, who has spent a year on the Coast. The accepted theory is they cannot stand it, and in the majority of cases they certainly can't. They get sick. With my own countrywomen it is different; the Australian stays, so does the German, so does the French woman. At first I could not understand it at all, but at last the explanation slowly dawned upon me.

"*Haus-fraus,*" said many a woman, and man, too, scornfully, when I praised those capable German women who make a home wherever you find them, and it is this *haus-frau* element in them that saves them. A German woman's pride and glory is her house, therefore, wherever she is she has to her hand an object of intense interest that fills her mind and keeps her well. An Australian does not take so keen an interest in her house, perhaps, but she has had no soft and easy upbringing; from the time she was a little girl she has got her own hot water, helped with the cooking, washing, and all the multifarious duties of a houshold where a servant is a rarity, therefore, when she comes to a land where servants are plentiful, if they are rough and untaught, she comes to a land of comfort and luxury. Besides, it is the custom of the country that a woman should stand beside her husband; she has not married for a livelihood, men are plentiful enough and she has chosen her mate, wherefore it is her pleasure and her joy to help him in every way. She is as she ought to be, his comrade and his friend, a true helpmate. God forbid that I should say there are not English women like that, because I know there are, but the conditions in England are also very different. The girl who has been brought up in an English household, even if it be a poor one, is not only brought up in luxury, but is the victim of many conventions. Any ruffled rose leaf makes her unhappy. The servants that to the Australian are a luxury to be revelled in are very bad indeed to her. Whenever I saw one of these complaining English women, I used to think of the Princess of my youth. We all remember her. She was wandering about lost, as royalty naturally has a habit of doing, and she came to a little house and asked the inmates to give her shelter because she was a princess. They took her in, but being just a trifle doubtful of her story—when I was a little girl I always felt that was rather a slur upon those dwellers in the little house—they put on the bed a pea and then they put over it fourteen hair mattresses and fourteen feather beds—it doesn't seem to have strained the household to provide so much bedding—and then they invited the princess to go to bed, which she did. In my own mind I drew the not unnatural conclusion that princesses were accustomed to sleeping in high beds. Next morning they asked her how she slept. She, most rudely, I always thought, said she had not been able to sleep at all, because there was such a hard lump in the bed. And so they knew that her story was true, and she was a real princess. Now, the English women in West Africa always seem to me real princesses of this order. Certain difficulties there always are for the white race in a tropical climate, there always will be, but there is really no need to find out the peas under twenty-eight mattresses.

manless country like England, many a woman marries not because the
ho asks her is the man she would have chosen had she free right of

choice, but because to live she must marry somebody, and he is the first who has come along. He may be the last. Her African house interests her not, her husband does not absorb her, she has no one to whom to show off her newly wedded state, no calls to pay, no afternoon teas, no *matinées*, in fact she has no interest, she is bored to death; she is very much afraid of "chill," so she shuts out the fresh, cool night air, and, as a natural result, she goes home at the end of seven months a wreck, and once more the poor African climate gets the credit.

No, if a woman goes to West Africa there is a great deal to be said for the German *haus-frau*. At least they always seem to make a home, and I have seen many English women there who cannot.

At Salt Ponds one of my carriers came to me saying he was sick and wanting medicine, and I regret to say, instead of sending him at once to the doctor, I casually offered him half a dozen cascara tabloids, all of which to my dismay he swallowed at one gulp. The next morning he was worse, which did not surprise me, but I called in the medical officer and found he was suffering from pneumonia—cascara it appears is not the correct remedy—and I was forced to leave him behind. The mammies I had engaged at Cape Coast also declined to go any farther, so I had to look around me for more carriers, and carriers are by no means easy to come by. Finally the Boating Company came to the rescue with four Kroo boys, and then my troubles began.

I set out and hoped for the best, but Kroo boys are bad carriers at all times. These were worse than usual. One of my hammock-boys hurt his foot, or said he had, and had for the time to be replaced by a Kroo boy, and we staggered along in such a fashion that once more I felt like a slave-driver of the most brutal order. Again and again we stopped for him to rest, and my hammock-boys remarked by way of comforting me:

"Kroo boy no can tote hammock."

"Why can Kroo boy no tote hammock?"

"We no know, Ma. We no be Kroo boy."

We scrambled along somehow, out of one village into another, and at every opportunity half the carriers ran away and had to be rounded up by the other half. In eight hours we had only done fifteen miles. I felt very cheap, very hungry, very thirsty, and most utterly thankful when we arrived late in the afternoon at a dirty native town called Tantum. The carriers straggled in one by one, and last of all came my chop box, so that, for this occasion only, luncheon, afternoon tea, and dinner were all rolled into one about six o'clock in the evening.

The rest-house was a two-storied house, built of swish and white-washed, and was inside a native compound, where both in the evening and in the morning the women were most industriously engaged in crushing the corn, rolling it on a hard stone with a heavy wooden roller.

And the rest-house, though very loyal, there were four coloured oleographs of Queen Alexandra round the walls of the sitting-room and two at the top of the stairs, all exactly alike, was abominably dirty. It had a little furniture—two mirrors, well calculated to keep one in a subdued and humble frame of mind, a decrepid bed that I was a little afraid to be in the same room with lest its occupants would require no invitation to get up and walk towards me, a table, and some broken-down chairs. Also on the wall was a notice that two shillings must be paid by anyone occupying this rest-house. Someone had crossed this out and substituted two shillings and sixpence, and that in its turn had been erased, so, as the sum went on increasing at each erasure, at last eighteen shillings and sixpence had been fixed as the price of a night's lodging in this charming abode. I decided in my own mind that two shillings would be ample, and that if the people were civil I should give them an extra threepence by way of a dash.

I photographed Tantum with the interested assistance of a gentleman clad in a blue cloth and a tourist cap. He seemed to consider he belonged to me, so at last I asked him who he was.

"P'lice," said he with a grin, and then I recognised my policeman in unofficial dress.

I didn't like that village. The people may have been all right, but I didn't like their looks and I made my "p'lice" sleep outside my door. My bedroom had the saving grace of two large windows, and I put my bed underneath one of them in the gorgeous moonlight; but a negro town is very noisy on a moonlight night and the tom-toms kept waking me. I always had to be the first astir else my following would have cheerfully slumbered most of the day, but on this occasion so bright was the moonlight, so noisy the town, that I proceeded to get up at two o'clock, and it was only when I looked at my travelling clock, with a view to reproaching Grant with being so long with my tea, that I discovered my error and went back to bed and a troubled rest again.

Two shillings was accepted with a smile by the good lady of the house, who was a stout, middle-aged woman with only one eye, a dark cloth about her middle, and a bright handkerchief over her head. She gave me the impression that she had never seen so much money in her life before. Possibly she had only recently gone into the rest-house business, say a year or two back, and I was her first traveller with any money to spend. We parted with mutual compliments, and I bestowed on her little grand-daughter the munificent dash of threepence.

There is a story told of a man who went out to India, and as he liked sunshine used to rise up each morning and say to his wife with emphasis, "Another fine day, my dear."

Now, she, good woman, had been torn from her happy home in England, and loved the cool grey skies, so at last much aggravated she lost her temper, and asked: "What on earth else do you expect in this beastly country?"

So, along the Guinea Coast in the month of March, the hottest season, there is really nothing else to expect but still, hot weather: divine mornings, glorious evenings, but in between fierce hot sunshine. And of course it was not always possible to travel in the coolest part of the day. To sit still by the roadside in the glare of the sunshine, or even under a tree, with a large crowd looking on, was more than I could have managed. So I started as early as I could possibly induce my men to start—one determined woman can do a good deal—and then went straight on if possible without a stop to my next point. I would always, when I am by myself, rather be an hour or two late for luncheon than bother to stop to have it on the way, and if a breakfast at half-past five or six and a morning in the open air induces hunger by eleven, it is easily stayed by carrying a little fruit or biscuits or chocolate to eat by the way.

It was fiercest noonday when I came to a town called Appam, where once upon a time was an old Dutch lodge worth keeping, if only to show what a tiny place men held garrisoned in the old days. It is hardly necessary to say that the Gold Coast Government do not think so, and have handed this old-time relic over to negro Custom and post office officials; and, judging by the condition of the rest of the town, much has not been required of them, for Appam is the very filthiest town I have ever seen. The old lodge is on the top of a hill overlooking the sea, splendidly situated, but you arrive at it by a steep and narrow path winding between a mass of thatched houses, and it stands out white among the dark roofs. As a passer-by, I should say the only thing for Appam is to put a fire-stick in the place; nothing else but fire could cleanse it. Many of the young people and children were covered with an outbreak of sores that looked as if nasty-looking earth had been scattered over them and had bred and festered, and they told me the children here were reported to be suffering and dying from some disease that baffled the doctors, what doctors I do not know, for there is no white man in Appam. It seems to me it is hardly necessary to give a name to the disease. I should think it was bred of filth pure and simple, and my remedy of the fire-stick would go far towards curing it. But there is a graver side to it than merely the dying of these negro children. Appam is not very far from Accra; communication by surf boat must go on weekly, if not daily, and Appam must be an ideal breeding ground for the yellow-fever mosquito. I know nothing about matters medical, but I must say, when I heard Accra was quarantined for yellow fever, I was not surprised. I had come all along the Coast, and filthier villages it would be difficult to find anywhere, and of these filthy villages Appam, a large town, takes the palm. I left it without regret, and though I should like to see that little Dutch lodge again, I doubt if I ever shall.

My carriers were virtue itself now. The Kroo boys were giving so much trouble that they posed as angels. I must admit they were a cheery, good-tempered lot, and it was impossible to bear malice towards them. They had forgotten that I had ever been wrathful, and behaved as if they were old and much-trusted servants. Munk-wady, a Ju-ju hill on the shore between Appam and Winnebah, is steep and the highest point for many miles along the Coast, and over its flank, where there was but a pretence at a road, we had to go.

"You no fear, Ma; you no fear," said the men cheerily, "we tote you safe"; and so they did, and took me right across the swamp that lay at the other side and right into the yard of the Basel Mission Factory at Winnebah, where a much-astonished manager made me most kindly welcome. It amused me the astonishment I created along the road. No one could imagine how I could get through, and yet it was the simplest matter. It merely resolved itself into putting one foot before the other and seeing that my following did likewise. Of course, there lay the difficulty. "Patience and perseverance," runs the old saw, "made a Pope of his reverence"; and so a little patience and perseverance got me to Accra, though I am sometimes inclined to wonder if it wasn't blind folly that took me beyond it.

VIEW FROM BASEL MISSION FACTORY, WINNEBAH.

But at Winnebah I received a check. Those Kroo boys gave out, and it was plain to be seen they could travel no longer with loads on their heads. I had no use for their company without loads. There were white men in Winnebah, but none of them could help me, for the cocoa harvest in the country behind was in full swing, and carriers there were not. The only suggestion was that there was a ship in the roadstead, and that I should embark on her for Accra. There seemed nothing else for it, and, regretful as I was, I felt I must take their advice. The aggravating part was that it was only a long day's journey from Winnebah to Accra, but as I had no men to carry my loads I could not do it. One thing I was determined to do, however, and that was to visit an old Dutch fort there was at a place called Berraku, about half-way to Accra. I could do it by taking my hammock-boys and my luncheon, and that I did.

That day's journey is simply remarkable for the frolicsomeness of my men and for the extreme filth of the fishing villages through which we passed. They rivalled Appam. As for the fort, it was built of brick, there was a rest-house upon the bastion for infrequent travellers, and it was tumbling into disrepair. There will be no fort at Berraku presently, for the people of the town will have taken away the bricks one by one to build up their own houses. But it must have been a big place once, and there is in the town a square stone tomb, a relic of the past. The inscription is undecipherable, but it was evidently erected in memory of some important person who left his bones in Africa, and lies there now forgotten.

There was a river to cross just outside the town of Winnebah, and crossing a river is a big undertaking in West Africa, even when you have only one load. I'm afraid I must plead guilty to not knowing my men by sight; for a long time a black man was a black man to me, and he had no individuality about him. Now they all crowded into the boat to cross the river, and it was evident to my mind that we were too many; then as no one seemed inclined to be left behind, I exercised my authority and pointed out the man who was to get out, and out he got, very reluctantly, but cheerily helped by his unfeeling fellows. It took us about a quarter of an hour to cross that river, for it was wide and we had to work up-stream, and once across they all proceeded to go on their way without a thought for the man left behind. And then I discovered what I had done. I had thrown the ægis of my authority over, putting the unfortunate ferryman out of his own boat, and to add injury to insult my men were quite prepared to leave him on one side of the stream and his boat on the other. When I discovered it was the ferryman I had put out I declared they must go back for him, and my decision was received with immense surprise.

"You want him, Ma?" as if such a desire should be utterly impossible; but when they found I really did, and, moreover, intended to pay him, two of them took the boat and he was brought to me with shouts of laughter, and comforted with an extra dash, which was more than he had expected after my high-handed conduct.

One could not help liking these peasant peoples; they were such children, so easily pleased, so anxious to show off before the white woman. Here all along the beach the people were engaged in fishing, and again and again I saw a little crowd of men launching a boat, or hauling it in and distributing their catch upon the beach. I always got out and inspected the catch, and they always made way to let me look when they saw I was interested. Of course, we could not speak to each other, but they spread out the denizens of the deep and pointed out anything they thought might be specially curious. I can see now one flat fish that was pulled out for my benefit. One man, who was acting as showman, caught him by the tail and held him out at arm's length. He was only a small fish about the size, I suppose, of a large dish, but that thorny tail went high over the man's head while the body of the fish was still flapping about on the sand, and the lookers-on all laughed and shouted as if they had succeeded in showing the stranger a most curious sight, as indeed they had.

LAUNCHING A SURF BOAT.

I was sorry to turn my back on the road, sorry to go back to Winnebah—Winnebah of the evil reputation, where they say if a white man is not pleasing to the people the fetish men poison him—sorry to pay off my men and send them back, sorry to take ship for Accra; but I could not get carriers, there was nothing else for it, and by steamer I had to go, and very lucky indeed was I to find a steamer ready to take me, so I said good-bye to the road for some considerable time and went to Accra.

CHAPTER XI
THE CAPITAL OF THE GOLD COAST COLONY

The pains and penalties of landing in Accra—Negro officials, blatant, pompous, inefficient—Christiansborg Castle—The ghost of the man with eyes like bright stones—The importance of fresh air—Beautiful situation of Accra—Its want of shade-trees—The fences of Accra—The temptation of the cooks—Picturesque native population—Striking coiffure—The expensive breakwater—To commemorate the opening of the waterworks—The forlorn Danish graveyard—A meddlesome missionary—Away to the east.

I don't like landing in Accra. There is a good deal of unpleasantness connected with it. For one thing, the ships must lie a long way off for the surf is bad, and the only way to land is to be put into a mammy-chair, dropped into a surf boat, and be rowed ashore by a set of most excellent boatmen, who require to be paid exorbitantly for their services. I don't know what other people pay, but I have never landed on Accra beach under a ten-shilling dash to the boat boys, and then I had to pay something like sixpence a load to have my things taken up to the Custom house. In addition to that you get the half-civilised negro in all his glory, blatant, self-satisfied, loquacious, deadly slow, and very inefficient. As well as landing my goods from the steamer, I wanted to inquire into the fate of other goods that I had, with what I considered much forethought, sent on from Sekondi by a previous steamer, and here I found myself in a sea of trouble, for, the negro mind having grasped the fact that a troublesome woman was looking for boxes that had probably been lost a couple of months ago, each official passed me on from one department to another with complacency. Accra is hot, and Accra is sandy, and Accra as yet does not understand the meaning of the text, "the shadow of a great rock in a thirsty land," so for a couple of hours I was hustled about from pillar to post, finding traces of luggage everywhere, and no luggage. Then, a little way from the port office, a large placard in blue and white, announcing "Post and Telegraph Office" caught my eye, so I thought I would by way of refreshment and interlude send a telegram telling of my safe arrival to my friends in Sekondi, and, in all the heat of a tropical morning, I toiled down one flight of steps and up another and at last found that the telegraph office, in spite of that big placard, was not at the port at all but at Victoriaborg, about a couple of miles away. I could not believe it, but so it was. Whether that placard is previous, or hints at past greatness, I cannot tell. I also found later on that you cannot send a telegram after four o'clock in the afternoon in the Gold Coast. Government takes a most paternal care of its negro subordinates and sees that the poor things are not worked too hard, but when I found they closed for luncheon as well, I was apt to inquire why it should be so hard-hearted as ever to require them to open at all. I think this matter should be inquired into by someone who has the welfare of the negro race at heart.

CHRISTIANSBORG CASTLE.

When my temper was worn to rags, and I was thoroughly hot and unhappy, wishing myself with all my heart out in the open again with only carriers who "no be fit" to deal with, at last a surprised white man found me, straightened things out in a moment, and assured me that I should have evening dresses to wear at Government House.

The Acting Governor and his wife put me up for a day or two, and then found me quarters, and I hereby put it on record that I really think it was noble of the Acting Governor, for he had no sympathy with my mission, and I think, though he was too polite to say so, was inclined to regard a travelling woman as a pernicious nuisance. I am sure it would have been more convenient for him if I had gone straight on, but I did not want to do the capital of the Colony like an American tourist, and so protested that I must have somewhere where I could rest and arrange my impressions.

Government House is old-world. It is Christiansborg Castle, which was bought from the Danes, I think, some time in the seventies, when a general rearrangement of the Coast took place. It is one of the nicest castles on the Coast, bar, of course, Elmina, which none can touch, and has passed through various vicissitudes. I met at Kumasi the medical officer who had charge of it some years back, when it was a lunatic asylum.

"Such a pity," said he, "to make such a fine place a lunatic asylum. But it was a terrible care to me. I was so afraid some of the lunatics would smash those fine old stained-glass windows."

I stared. Stained-glass windows on the Coast! But there is not a trace of them now, nor have I ever met anyone else who knew of them. I suppose they are some of those things no one thought worth caring about.

AUTHOR'S BUNGALOW, CHRISTIANSBORG.

There are ghosts at Christiansborg too. It used to be Government House, and then, because some Governor did not like it, a lunatic asylum, and Government House again. A man once told me how, visiting it while it was a lunatic asylum, he spoke to the warder in charge and said, "You must have an easy time here."

"No, sah; no, sah," said the man earnestly, "it no be good."

"Why?" asked my curious friend.

And then the negro said that as soon as the place was locked up quiet for the night, and he knew there could not possibly be any white men within the walls, two white men, he described them, one had eyes like bright stones, walked up and down that long corridor. And the strange part of the story, said my friend, was that he described unmistakably two dead-and-gone English Governors, men who have died in recent years, one, I think, in the West Indies, and the other on the way home from West Africa!

Christiansborg Castle is close down on the seashore, so close that the surf tosses its spray against its windows, and thus it came about that I learned what seems to me the secret of health in West Africa.

All along the Coast I had wondered; sometimes I felt in the rudest health, as if nothing could touch me, sometimes so weary and languid it was an effort to rouse myself to make half a dozen steps, and here in Christiansborg Castle I was prepared to agree with all the evil that had ever been said about the climate.

"In the morning thou shalt say, 'Would to God it were even,' and at even thou shalt say, 'Would to God it were morning.'"

That just about expressed my feelings while I was staying at Christiansborg Castle. My room, owing to the exigencies of space was an inside one, and though the doors were large, wide, and always open, still it had no direct communication with the open air. All the windows along the sea side of the Castle were tight closed, for the Acting Governor's wife did not like her pretty things to be spoiled by the damp sea breeze, so she stirred her air by a punkah. But at night of course there was no punkah going and I spent nights of misery. The heat was so oppressive I could not sleep, and I used to get up and wander about the verandah, where the air was cool enough, but I could not sleep there as it was by way of being a public passage-way. After a day or two they very kindly gave me for my abode a tumble-down old bungalow, just outside the Castle walls. It was like a little fort, and probably had been built for defence in the days that were passed and gone. There was a thick stone wall round the front of a strongly built stone house, that was loopholed for defence, and here lodged some of the Government House servants and their families, but on top of this stone house had been built a wooden bungalow, now rapidly falling into decay. Here were two big rooms and wide verandahs with a little furniture, and here I lodged, engaging a cook, and running my own establishment, greatly to my own satisfaction. The bungalow was as close to the seashore as the Castle, and I opened all the windows wide, and let the cool, health-giving fresh air blow over me day and night.

After the first night the languor and weariness at once disappeared and I felt most wonderfully well, a feeling that I kept always up so long as I could sleep in the uninterrupted fresh air. Put me to sleep in a closed-in room with no possibility of a direct draught and I was tired at once, wherefore I believe and believe firmly that to insure good health in West Africa you must have plenty of fresh air. I go further and would advise everybody to sleep as much in the open as possible, or, at the very least, in a good, strong draught. After that experience, I began to notice. I had a habit of getting up very early in the morning and going out for walks and rides in my cart, and as I went down the streets of towns like Sekondi, Tarkwa, and Accra, it was surprising the number of shutters I saw fast closed against the health-giving air. I concluded the people behind were foolishly afraid of chills and preferred to be slowly poisoned, and I looked too later on in the day at the pallid, white-faced men and women who came out of those houses. For myself, West Africa agreed with me. I have never in my life enjoyed such rude health as I found I had there.

I set the reason down to the care I took to live always in the open. The conclusion I draw is this—of course I may be wrong—the margin of health in West Africa is narrow and therefore you cannot do without a supply of the invigorating elixir supplied by Nature herself. Could I live in England as I did there it is quite likely my health would be still better. Now, when I hear a man is ill in West Africa, I ask several questions before I condemn the place. First, of course, there is the unlucky man who would be ill in any climate, then there is the dissipated man who brings his ailments upon himself, and, while in Africa men set his illness down to the right cause, when they are this side of the water they are only too ready to add another nail to their cross and pity the poor devil who has succumbed to the terrible climate they have to face. Next comes the man who, while not exactly dissipated, does himself too well, burns the candle at both ends, and puts upon his constitution a strain it certainly could not stand in a cooler climate, and then, when all these eliminated, there is to my mind the man and the woman, for the women are still greater offenders, who will sleep in too sheltered a spot, and spend their sleeping hours in the vitiated air of a mosquito-proof room.

AUTHOR IN HER CART AT CHRISTIANSBORG.

Of course other things tend to ill-health—loneliness, want of occupation for the mind, that perpetual strain that is engendered when a man is not contented with his surroundings and is for ever counting the slowly moving days till he shall go home; but that must come in any land where a man counts himself an exile, and I finally came to the conclusion that pretty nearly half the ill-health of West Africa would be cured if men would but arrange their sleeping-quarters wisely.

At any rate, in this old tumble-down bungalow I was more than happy. I engaged a cart and boys, and I used to start off at six o'clock in the morning, or as near to it as I could get those wretches of Kroo boys to come, and wander over the town.

Accra, which is the principal town of the Ga people, must have been for some centuries counted a town of great importance, for three nations had forts here. The English had James Fort, now used as a prison, the Dutch had Fort Crêvecoeur, now called Vssher Fort and used as a police barracks, and the Danes had Christiansborg Castle close to the big lagoon and three miles away from the town of Accra. And in addition to these forts all along the shore are ruins of great buildings. Till I went to Ashanti, between Christiansborg and Accra was the only bit of good road I had seen on the English coast of Guinea, and that was probably made by the Danes, for there is along part of it an avenue of fine old tamarind trees, which only this careful people would take the trouble to plant. They are slow-growing trees, I believe, and must be planted for shelter between other trees which may be cut down when the beautiful tamarinds grow old enough to take care of themselves. Some of the trees are gone and no one has taken the trouble to fill in the gaps, but still with their delicate greenery they are things of beauty in hot, sun-stricken Accra. For if ever a town needed trees and their shade it is this capital of the Gold Coast.

THE LAGOON, CHRISTIANSBORG

Accra might be a beautiful city. The coast is not very high, but raised considerably above sea-level, and it is broken into sweeping bays; the country behind gradually rises so that the bungalows at the back of the town get all the breeze that comes in from the ocean and all that sweeps down from the hills. In consequence, Accra, for a town that lies within a few degrees of the Equator, may be counted comparatively cool. The only heat is between nine o'clock in the morning and four o'clock in the afternoon; at night, when I was there, the hottest time of the year, March and the beginning of April, there was always a cool sea breeze. A place is always bearable when the nights are cool.

But on landing, Accra gives the impression of fierce heat. Shade-giving trees are almost entirely absent, the sun blazes down on hot, yellow sands, on hot, red streets lined with bare, white houses, and the very glare makes one pant. In the roadways, here and there, are channels worn by the heavy rainfall, the streets are not very regular, and many of the houses are ill-kept, shabby, and sadly in need of a coat of paint; when they belong to white men one sees written all over them that they are the dwellings of men who have no permanent abiding place here, but are "just making it do," and as for the native houses, every native under English rule has yet to learn the lesson that cleanliness and neatness make for beauty. When in the course of my morning's drive I looked at the gardens of Accra, for there are a good many ill-kept gardens, I fancied myself stepping with Alice into Wonderland. The picket fences are made of the curved staves that are imported for the making of barrels, and therefore they are all curved like an "S," and I do not think there is one whole fence in all the town; sometimes even the posts and rails are gone, but invariably some of the pickets are missing.

"All the good cooks in Accra," said a man to me with a sigh, "are in prison for stealing fences."

"Not all," said his chum; "ours went for stealing the post office, you remember. He'd burnt most of it before they discovered what was becoming of it." They say they are importing iron railings for Accra to circumvent the negro; for the negro, be it understood, does not mind going to prison. He is well-fed, well-sheltered, and the only deprivation he suffers is being deprived of his women; and when he comes out he feels it no disgrace, his friends greet him and make much of him, much as we should one who had suffered an illness through no fault of his own, therefore the cook who has pocketed the money his master has given him to buy wood, and stolen his neighbour's fence, begins again immediately he comes out of prison, and hopes he will not be so unlucky as to be found out this time.

RUINS ON THE SEASHORE, CHRISTIANSBORG.

This is the capital of a rich colony, so in business hours I found the streets thronged, and even early in the morning they were by no means empty, for the negro very wisely goes about his business while yet it is cool. Here, away from the forest, is no tsetse fly, so horses may be seen in buggies or drawing produce, but since man's labour can be bought for a shilling a day, it is cheaper, and so many people, like I was, are drawn by men. I, so as to feel less like a slave-driver, bought peace of mind in one way and much aggravation in another by having three, but many men I saw with only two, and many negroes, who are much harder on those beneath them than the white men, had only one. Produce too is very often taken from the factory to the harbour in carts drawn by eight or a dozen men, and goods are brought up from the sea by the same sweating, toiling, shouting Kroo boys.

They are broad-shouldered, sinewy men, clad generally in the most elderly of European garments cast off by some richer man, but always they are to be known from the surrounding Ga people by the broad vertical band of blue tattooing on their foreheads, the freedom mark that shows they have never been slaves. In Accra the white people are something under two hundred, the Governor and his staff, officials, teachers, merchants, clerks, missionaries, and artisans, and there are less than thirty white women, so that in comparison the white faces are very few in the streets. They are thronged with the dark people who call this place home. Clad in their own costumes they are very picturesque, the men in toga-like cloths fastened on one shoulder, the women with their cloths fastened under the arms, sometimes to show the breasts, sometimes to cover them, and on their head is usually a bright kerchief which hides an elaborate coiffure.

When I was strolling about Christiansborg one day I saw a coiffure which it was certainly quite beyond the power of the wearer to hide under a handkerchief. She was engaged in washing operations under a tree, and so I asked and obtained permission to photograph her. It will be seen by the result that, in spite of her peculiar notions on the subject of hair-dressing, she is not at all ungraceful. Indeed, in their own clothes, the Africans always show good taste. However gaudy the colours chosen, never it seems do natives make a mistake—they blend into the picture, they suit the garish sunshine, the bright-blue sky, the yellow beach, the cobalt sea, or the white foam of the surf breaking ceaselessly on the shore; only when the man and woman put on European clothes do they look grotesque. There is something in the tight-fitting clothes of civilisation that is utterly unsuited to these sons and daughters of the Tropics, and the man who is a splendid specimen of manhood when he is stark but for a loin cloth, who is dignified in his flowing robe, sinks into commonplaceness when he puts on a shirt and trousers, becomes a caricature when he parts his wool and comes out in a coat and high white collar.

Money is spent in Accra as it is spent nowhere else in the Colony. Of course I do not know much about these matters, therefore I suppose I should not judge, but I may say that after I had seen German results, I came to the conclusion that money was not always exactly wisely spent. Most certainly the people who had the beautifying of the town were not very artistic, and sometimes I cannot but feel they have lacked the saving grace of a sense of humour.

THE ONLY AVENUE IN THE CAPITAL OF THE GOLD COAST.

The landing here was shockingly bad; it is so still, I think, for the last time I left I was drenched to the skin, so the powers that be set to work at enormous cost to build a breakwater behind which the boats might land in comparative safety. Only comparative, for still the moment the boat touches the shore the boatmen seize the passenger and carry him as swiftly as possible, and quite regardless of his dignity, beyond the reach of the next breaking wave.

"Ah," said a high official, looking with pride at the breakwater, "how I have watched that go up. Every day I have said to myself, 'something accomplished, something done'"; and he said it with such heartfelt pride that I had not the heart to point out the sand pump, working at the rate of sixty tons a minute, that this same costly breakwater had necessitated, for the harbour without it would fill up behind the breakwater; not exactly, I fancy, what the authorities intended. The breakwater isn't finished yet, but the harbour is filling fast; by the time it is finished I should doubt whether there will be any water at all behind it.

I did Accra thoroughly. I lived in that little bungalow beside the fort, and I went up and down the streets in my cart and I saw all I think there was to be seen. But for one good friend, a medical officer I had known before, the lady who was head of the girls' school, a thoroughly capable, practical young woman, and the one or two friends they brought to see me, I knew nobody, and so I was enabled to form my opinions untrammelled, and I'm afraid I had the audacity to sit in judgment on that little tropical capital and say to myself that things might really be very much better done. The Club may be a cheerful place if you know anyone, but it is very doleful and depressing if the only other women look sidelong at you over the tops of their papers as if you were some curious specimen that it might perhaps be safer to avoid, and I found the outside of the bungalows, with their untidy, forlorn gardens, the houses of sojourners who are not dwellers in the land, anything but promising. Yet money is spent too—witness the breakwater—and in my wanderings I came across a tombstone-like erection close to James Fort, which I stopped and inspected. Indeed it is in a conspicuous place, with an inscription which he who runs may read. At least he might have read a little while ago, but the climate is taking it in hand. The stone is of polished granite, which must have cost a considerable amount of money, and by the aid of that inscription I discovered that it was a fountain erected to commemorate the opening of the waterworks in Accra. Oh Africa! Already it is difficult to read that inscription; the unfinished fountain is falling into decay, and the water has not yet been brought to the town! When future generations dig on the site of the old Gold Coast town, I am dreadfully afraid that tombstone will give quite a wrong impression. Now it is one of the most desolate things I know, more desolate even than the forlorn Danish graveyard which lies, overgrown and forgotten, but a stone's throw from my bungalow at Christiansborg. A heavy brick wall had been built round it once, but it was broken down in places so that the people of Christiansborg might pasture their goats and sheep upon it, and I climbed through the gap, risking the snakes, and read the inscriptions. They had died, apparently most of them, in the early years of the nineteenth century, men and women, victims probably to their want of knowledge, and all so pitifully young. I could wish that the Government that makes so much fuss about educating the young negro in the way he should go, could spare, say ten shillings a year to keep these graves just with a little respect. It would want so little, so very little. Those Danes of ninety years ago I dare say sleep sound enough lulled by the surf, but it would be a graceful act to keep their graves in order, and would not be a bad object-lesson for the Africans we are so bent on improving.

A REMARKABLE COIFFURE.

Behind the town are great buildings—technical schools put up with this object in view. They are very ugly buildings, very bare and barren and hot-looking. Evidently the powers who insist so strongly upon hand and eye training think it is sufficient to let the young scholars get their ideas of beauty and form by sewing coloured wools through perforated cards or working them out in coloured chalks on white paper; they have certainly not given them a practical lesson in beauty with these buildings. They may be exceedingly well-fitted for the use to which they are intended, but it seems to me a little far-fetched to house young negroes in such buildings when in such a climate a roof over a cement floor would answer all purposes.

If I had longed to beat my hammock-boys, my feelings towards them were mild when compared with those I had towards my cart-boys. They were terriblelooking ruffians, clad in the forlornest rags, and they dragged me about at a snail's pace. What they wanted of course was a master who would beat them, and as they did not get it, they took advantage of me. It is surprising how one's opinions are moulded by circumstances. Once I would have said that the man who hit an unoffending black man was a brute, and I suppose in my calmer moments I would say so still, but I distinctly remember seeing one of my cart-boys who had been on an errand to get himself a drink, or satisfy some of his manifold wants, strolling towards me in that leisurely fashion which invariably set me longing for the slave-driver's whip to hasten his steps. In his path was a white man who for some reason bore a grudge against the negro, and, without saying a word, caught him by the shoulder and kicked him on one side, twisted him round, and kicked him on the other side, and I, somewhat to my own horror, found myself applauding in my heart. Here was one of my cart-boys getting his deserts at last. The majority of white men were much of my way of thinking, but of course I came across the other sort. I met a missionary and his wife who were travelling down to inquire into the conditions of the workers in the cocoa plantations in Ferdinando Po. I confess I thought them meddlesome. What should we think if Portugal sent a couple of missionaries to inquire into the conditions of the tailoring trade in the East End of London, or the people in the knife trade in Sheffield? I have seen both these peoples and seen just as a passer-by far more open misery than ever I saw on the coast of West Africa. The misery may be there, but I have not seen it, as I may see it advertising itself between Hyde Park Corner and South Kensington any day of the week. Since I was a tiny child I have heard the poor heathen talked of glibly enough, but I have never in savage lands come across him.

JAMES FORT AND THE BREAKWATER THAT COST A MILLION OF MONEY.

After nearly a month at Accra I decided I must go on, and then I found it was impossible to get carriers to go along the beach eastward; the best I could do was to go up by the Basel Mission motor lorry to a place called Dodowah, and here the Acting Governor had kindly arranged with the Provincial Commissioner at Akuse to send across carriers to meet me and take me to the Volta.

So one still, hot morning in April I packed up bag and baggage in my nice little bungalow, had one final wrangle with my cart-boys, a parting breakfast with the Basel Mission Factory people whose women-kind are ideal for a place like West Africa and make a home wherever you find them, and started in the lorry north for Dodowah in the heart of the cocoa district.

CHAPTER XII
BLOOD FETISH OF KROBO HILL

To Dodowah by motor lorry—Orchard-bush country—Negro tortures—The Basel Mission factor—A personally conducted tour—Great hospitality—A dinner by moonlight—Plan a night journey—The roadway by moonlight—Barbarous hymns—Carriers who "no be fit" once more—Honesty of the African carrier—Extraordinary obedience—The leopard that cried at Akway Pool—A hard-hearted slave-driver—Krobo Hill—Blood fetishes—Terror of the carriers—Story of the hill—The dawning of a new day—Unexplained disappearances—Akuse at last—The arrival of a whirlwind—The fire on Krobo Hill.

Inland from Accra the country is what they call orchard bush, that is to say, it was rather flat country sloping in gradual gradation to the hills behind, covered now, in the end of the dry season, with yellow grass and dotted all over with trees, not close together as in the forest country but just far enough apart to give it a pleasant, park-like look. There were great tall ant heaps too, or rather the homes of the termite, the white ant which is not an ant at all I believe, and these reminded me of the ghastly form of torture sometimes perpetrated by the negroes. A Provincial Commissioner once told me that he had several times come across on these hills, which are often ten or twelve or twenty feet high, the skeleton of a man who had undoubtedly been fastened there while he was alive; and another went one better and told me how another form of torture was to place a man on the ant heap without any fastening whatever and then to surround it with men and women with knives, so that when he tried to escape he was promptly driven back. In this last case I am glad to think that the torturers are bound to have run their share of risk, and must have received many a good hard nip. But the negro mind seems to rather revel in secret societies, trial by ordeal, and tortures. Christianity, the religion of love and pity, has been preached on the Coast for many a long day now, and yet in this year of our Lord 1911 there is behind the Church of England in Accra, down on the sea beach, a rock which is generally known as Sacrifice Rock, and here those who know declare that every yam festival, which takes place just after the rains in September, they sacrifice a girl in order that the crops may not fail.

SACRIFICE ROCK, ACCRA.

Riding in a lorry I had plenty of time to consider these matters. My kind Basel Mission Factory *haus-frau* had provided me with luncheon to eat by the way, and I knew that all my goods and chattels would arrive safely at their destination without my having to worry about them. Grant was the only servant I had left. I had dismissed the cook, and Zacco had quarrelled with Grant and dismissed himself, and so while I sat on the front seat of the lorry alongside the negro driver, Grant and my goods and chattels were packed away in odd corners on top of the merchandise that was going to Dodowah. The road was bad, deeply cut by the passing of these lorries, but I arrived there about midday and was cordially received by a Basel Mission Factory man who told me my carriers had arrived, and suggested I should come to his house and have luncheon.

He was a kindly, fair-haired young German who had been in the Colony about a month and was learning English on Kroo-boy lines. The result was a little startling, but as it was our only means of communication I was obliged to make the best of it.

My carriers had been here waiting for me since Friday; this was Monday, and they wanted "sissy" money. I paid up and declared I should start the moment they had broken their fast. Meanwhile my German friend undertook to show me the sights.

Dodowah is a very pretty little place at the foot of the hills; it is embowered in palm trees and is the centre of the cocoa industry. In the yard of the factory the cocoa was lying drying in the blazing sun, and when I had been duly instructed in its various qualities, my host suggested I should "walk small."

"I take you my house."

It was very kind of him, but I was cautious. I do not like walking in the blazing noonday.

"How far is it?" I asked.

"Small, small," said he, with conviction.

Grant was a very different person now from the boy in a pink pyjama coat, meek and mild and bullied by Kwesi, whom I had engaged in the distant past. He was my body servant; evidently supposed by everyone else who came in contact with me to hold a position of high trust, and thinking no end of himself. So to him I gave strict instructions. All the loads were to start at once, the hammock-boys were to follow me to the factor's house, and he was to go on with the carriers. We had left the protection of the "p'lice" behind, and on the whole I thought I could do just as well without.

So I set out with my new friend and accompanied by my new headman who evidently thought it his duty to follow in my wake, though he could understand no English and I could understand not one word of his tongue. That walk remains in my mind as one long nightmare; I only did one worse, and then I thought I must be going to die. We left the plain country and plunged uphill, it was blazing noonday in April, and though there were palms and much growth on either side of the road, on the road itself was not a particle of shade. Still we went up and up and up.

"I show you, I show you," said my friend.

Frankly I wished he wouldn't. It was a splendid view from that hillside, with the town nestling embowered in palms at our feet, but a personally conducted walking-tour on the Coast at midday on an April day was the very last thing I desired.

I was dripping with perspiration, I was panting and breathless before we had been on that road five minutes; in the next five I would have bartered all my prospects in Africa for a glass of iced water, and then my companion turned. "You like go through bushway, short cut." It looked cooler, so I feebly assented and we turned into the bush which was so thin it did not shut out the sun, and the walking was very much rougher. I had given up all hopes of ever coming to the end when my companion stopped, flung up his head like a young war-horse, and said cheerfully, "Oh I tink I go lookum road."

I sank down on a log; my new headman, an awful-looking ruffian, stood beside me, and that aggressively active young German went plunging about the bush till he returned still cheerful and remarking, "I tink we lose way. We go back."

I draw a veil over the remainder of that walk. We did arrive at his house finally after two and a half hours' march over very rough country, and then he gave me wine to drink and fed me and was good to me, but I was utterly tired out and didn't care for the moment what became of me. He showed me a bedroom and I lay down and slept, rose up and had a bath, and felt as if I might perhaps face the world again. At half-past four we had some tea and I contemplated all my new hammock-boys sitting in a row under some palm trees on the other side of the road. They looked strapping, big, strong men, and I was thankful, for Akuse they said was twenty-seven miles away and I had to do it in one march. The question was, when I should start?

"If you start now," said the factor, "you get there one—half-past one in the morning—very good time."

Now I really could not agree with him. To launch yourself on totally unknown people at halfpast one in the morning and ask them to take you in is not, I think, calculated to place you in a favourable light, and I demurred. But what was I to do? I did not want to inflict myself any longer on this hospitable young man, and already I had paid my carriers for four days while they did nothing. It was a full moon. Last night had been gorgeous; this night promised to be as fine. I asked the question, why could I not travel all night?

"Oh yes, moon be fine too much"; and then he went on to tell me a long story about his Kroo boys being frightened to travel that road by themselves. "But it all be foolishness." It took me so long to discover the meaning of the words that I really paid no attention to the gist of what he was saying, besides I could not see that a Kroo boy being afraid was any reason why I should be. Finally we figured it out that I should start at nine o'clock, which would bring me to Akuse at a little after six in the morning. This did not seem so bad, and I agreed and cordially thanked the kindness which made him plan a nice little dinner in the moonlight on the verandah. It comes back to me as one of the most unique dinners I ever had; we had no other light but that of the moon, the gorgeous moonlight of the Tropics. It shone silver on the fronds of the palms, the mountains loomed dimly mysterious like mountains in a dream, and the road that ran past the house lay clear and still and warm in the white light.

My host asked leave to dine in a cap; he said the moon gave him a headache, and strongly advised me to do likewise, but though I have heard other people say the moon affects them in that manner, it never troubles me and I declined. And he translated his German grace into English for my benefit, and I could not even smile so kindly was the intention; and we ate fruit on the verandah, and nine o'clock came and I had the top taken off my hammock and started.

"Yi, yi, yi, ho, ho, ho," cried the hammock-boys, clapping their hands as they went at a fast trot, far faster than the ordinary man could walk without any burden on his head, and we were off to Akuse and the Volta. The night was as light as day, and it never occurred to me that there was any danger in the path. We went through the town, and here and there a gleam of fire showed, and here and there was a yellow light in one of the window places, and the people were in groups in the streets, dancing, singing, or merely looking on. Generally they sang, and no one knows how truly barbaric a hymn can sound sung by a line of lightly clad people keeping time with hands and feet to the music. It might have been a war song, it might have been a wail for those about to die; it was, I realised with a start, "Jesu, lover of my soul," in the vernacular. I suppose the missionaries know best, but it always seems to me that the latest music-hall favourite would do better for negro purposes than these hymns that have been endeared to most of us by old association. These new men were splendid hammock-men; they stopped for no man, and the groups melted before them.

A happy peasant people were these, apparently with just that touch of mysterious sadness about them that is with all peasant peoples. Their own sorrows they must have, of course, but they are not forced upon the passer-by as are the sordid sorrows of the great cities of the civilised world. At the outside ring of these dancers hung no mean and hungry wretches having neither part nor parcel with the singers.

Through the town and out into the open country we went, and the trees made shadows clear-cut on the road like splashes of ink, or, where the foliage was less dense, the leaves barely moving in the still night air made a tracery as of lace work on the road beneath, and there was the soft, sleepy murmur of the birds, and the ceaseless skirl of the insects. Occasionally came another sound, penetrating, weird, rather awe-inspiring, the cry of the leopard, but the hammock-boys took no heed—it was moonlight and there were eight of them.

"Yi, yi, yi, ho, ho, ho." They clapped their hands and sang choruses, and by the time we arrived at the big village of Angomeda, a couple of hours out, I was fairly purring with satisfaction. I have noticed that when things were going well with me I was always somewhat inclined to give all the credit to my perfect management; when they went wrong I laid the blame on Providence, my headman, or any other responsible person within reach. Now my self-satisfaction received a nasty shock.

The village of Angomeda was lying asleep in the moonlight. The brown thatch glistened with moisture, the gates of the compounds and the doors of the houses were fast shut; only from under the dark shadow of a great shade-tree in the centre of the village came something white which resolved itself into Grant apologetic and aggrieved.

"Carriers go sleep here, Ma. They say they no fit go by night."

My fine new carriers "no fit." How are the mighty fallen! And I had imagined them pretty nearly at Akuse by now! Clearly, they could not be allowed to stay here. I have done a good many unpleasant things, but I really did not feel I could arrive at Akuse at six o'clock in the morning without a change of clothing.

But I restrained myself for the moment.

"Why?"

"I not knowing, Ma."

I debated a moment. I realised the situation. I was a woman miles from any white man, and I could not speak one word of the language. Still, I had sent those carriers to Akuse and I could not afford to be defied, therefore I alighted.

"Where are those carriers?"

Nine pointing fingers indicated the house. Evidently the hammock-boys had been here before, and one of them pushed open a door in the wall. Black shadows and silver-white light was that compound. Heaped in the middle, not to be mistaken, were my loads, and from under the deeper shadows beneath the surrounding sheds came tumbling black figures which might or might not have been my erring carriers. I did not know them from the people about them, neither did I know one word of their language, and only one of my hammock-boys spoke any pigeon English. But that consideration did not stay me. I singled out my headman, and him I addressed at length and gave him to understand that I was pained and surprised at such conduct. Never in the course of a long career had I come across carriers who slept when they should have been on the road, and before I was half-way through the harangue those sleepy and reluctant men and women were picking up the loads. I confess I had been doubtful. Why should these carriers pay any attention to me? Now that I know what they risked by their obedience I have no words to express my astonishment. I did not know the carriers, but I did know the loads, and before I got into my hammock I stood at the gate and counted them all out. I need not have worried. The African carrier is the most honest man I have ever met. Never have I lost the smallest trifle entrusted to him. When my goods were well on the road I got into my hammock and started again.

Oh, such a night! On such a night as this Romeo wooed Juliet, on such a night came the Queen of the Fairies to see charm even in the frolicsome Bottom.

All the glories of the ages, all the delights of the world were in that night. The song of the carriers took on a softness and a richness born of the open spaces of the earth and the glorious night, and for accompaniment was the pad-pad of their feet in the dust of the roadway, and in one long, musical monotonous cadence the cheep of the insects, and again a sharper note, the cry of a bat or night bird.

It was orchard-bush country that lay outspread in the white light, with here and there a cocoa plantation. Here a tree cast a dark shadow across the road, and there was a watercourse through which the feet of the men splashed— only in German West Africa may you always count on a bridge—and, again, the trees would grow close and tunnel-like over the road with only an occasional gleam of moonlight breaking through. But always the hammock-boys kept steadily on, and the carriers kept up as never before in two hundred miles of travel had carriers kept up. We went through sleeping villages with whitewashed mud walls and thatched roofs gleaming wetly, and even the dogs and the goats were asleep.

It was midnight. It was long after midnight; the moon was still high and bright, like a great globe of silver, but there had come over the night that subtle change that comes when night and morning meet. It was night no longer; nothing tangible had changed, but it was morning. The twitter of the birds, the cry of the insects, had something of activity in it; the night had passed, another day had come, though the dawning was hours away. And still the men went steadily on.

A great square hill rose up on the horizon, and we came to a clump of trees where the moonlight was shut out altogether; we passed through water, and it was pitch-dark, with just a gleam of moonlight here and there to show how dense was that darkness. It was Akway Pool, and a leopard was crying in the thick bush close beside it. It was uncanny, it was weird; all the terror that I had missed till now in Africa came creeping over me, and the men were singing no longer. Very carefully they stepped, and the pool was so deep that lying strung up in the hammock I could still have touched the water with my hand. Could it be only a leopard that was crying so? Might it not be something even worse, something born of the deep, dark pool, and the night? Slowly we went up out of the water, and we stood a moment under the shade of the trees, but with the white light within reach, and Krobo Hill loomed up ahead against the dark horizon. The only hammock-boy who could make himself understood came up.

"Mammy, man be tired. We stop here small."

It was a reasonable request, but the leopard was crying still, and the gloom and fear of the pool was upon me.

"No, go on." They might have defied me, but they went on, and to my surprise, my very great surprise, the carriers were still with us. Presently we were out in the moonlight again; I had got the better of my fears and repented me. "Wait small now."

"No, Mammy," came the answer, "this be bad place," and they went on swiftly, singing and shouting as if to keep their courage up, or, as I gathered afterwards, to give the impression of a great company. Only afterwards did I know what I had done that night. Krobo Hill grew larger and larger at every step, and on Krobo Hill was one of the worst, if not the worst blood fetish in West Africa. Every Krobo youth before he could become a man and choose a wife had to kill a man, and he did it generally on Krobo Hill. There the fetish priests held great orgies, and for their ghastly ceremonies and initiations they caught any stranger who was reckless enough to pass the hill. How they killed him was a mystery; some said with tortures, some that only his head was cut off. But the fear in the country grew, and at the end of the last century the British Government interfered; they took Krobo Hill and scattered the fetish priests and their abominations, and they declared the country safe. But the negro revels in mystery and horror, and the fear of the hill still lingers in the minds of the people; every now and then a man disappears and the fear is justified. Only three years ago a negro clerk on his bicycle was traced to that hill and no further trace of him found. His hat was in the road, and the Krobos declared that the great white baboons that infest the hill had taken him, but it is hardly reasonable to suppose that the baboons would have any use for a bicycle, whereas he, strong and young, and his bicycle, together emblems of strength and swiftness, made a very fitting offering to accompany to his last resting-place the dead chief whose obsequies the Krobos were celebrating at the time. Always there are rumours of disappearances, less known men and women than a Government clerk and scholar, and always the people know there is need of men and women for the sacrifices, sacrifices to ensure a plenteous harvest, a good fishing, brave men, and fruitful women.

My men were afraid—even I, who could not understand the reason, grasped that fact; very naturally afraid, for it was quite within the bounds of possibility that a straggler might be cut off.

"Would they have touched me?" I asked afterwards.

"Not with your men round you. Some might escape, and the vengeance would have been terrible."

"But if I had been by myself?"

"Ah, then they might have said that the baboons had taken you; but you would not have been by yourself."

No, it was extremely unlikely I should be here by myself, but here were my men, sixteen strong and afraid. Akway Pool had been the last water within a safe distance from the hill, and I had not let them halt; now they dared not. A light appeared on the hill, just a point of flickering fire on the ridge, above us now, and I hailed it as a nice friendly gleam telling of human habitation and home, but the men sang and shouted louder than ever. I offered to stop, but the answer was always the same: "This be bad place, Mammy. We go."

At last, without asking my leave, they put down the hammock, and the carriers flung themselves down panting.

"We stop small, Mammy"; and I sat on my box and watched the great, sinewy men with strapping shoulders as they lay on the ground resting. They had been afraid I was sure, and I knew no reason for their fear.

But the night was past and it was morning, morning now though it was only half-past three and the sun would not be up till close on six o'clock. On again. The moon had swung low to the dawn, and the gathering clouds made it darker than it had yet been, while the stars that peeped between the clouds were like flakes of newly washed silver. People began to pass us, ghostlike figures in the gloom. Greetings were exchanged, news was shouted from one party to the other, and I, in spite of the discomfort of the hammock, was dead with sleep, and kept dropping into oblivion and waking with a start to the wonder and strangeness of my surroundings. Deeper and deeper grew the oblivion in the darkness that precedes the dawn, till I wakened suddenly to find myself underneath a European bungalow, and knew that for the first time in my experience of African travel I had arrived nearly two hours before I expected to.

My people were wild with delight and triumph. I had forced them to come through the Krobo country by night, but my authority did not suffice to keep them quiet now they had come through in safety. They chattered and shouted and yelled, and a policeman who was doing sentry outside the Provincial Commissioner's bungalow started to race upstairs. I tried to stop him, and might as well have tried to stop a whirlwind. Indeed, when I heard him hammering on the door I was strongly of opinion that the Commissioner would think that the whirlwind had arrived. But presently down those steps came a very big Scotchman in a dressing-gown, with his hair on end, just roused from his sleep, and he resolved himself into one of those courteous, kindly gentlemen England is blessed with as representatives in the dark corners of the earth.

Did he reproach me? Not at all. He perjured himself so far as to say he was glad to see me, and he took me upstairs and gave me whisky-and-soda because it was so late, and then tea and fruit because it was so early. And then in the dawning I looked out over Krobo Hill, and my host told me its story.

"I cleared them out years ago. I have no doubt they have their blood sacrifices somewhere, but not on Krobo Hill. But the people are still afraid."

"I saw a fire there last night."

He shook his head unbelieving.

"Impossible; there is a fine of fifty pounds for anyone found on Krobo Hill."

The dawn had come and the sun was rising rosy and golden. The night lay behind in the west.

I looked out of the window at the way I had come and wondered. I am always looking back in life and wondering. Perhaps it would be a dull life where there are no pitfalls to be passed, no rocks to climb over.

"I see smoke there now." In the clear morning air it was going up in a long spiral; but again my host shook his head.

"Only a cloud."

But there were glasses lying on the table, and I looked through them and there was smoke on Krobo Hill.

So I think my men were right to fear, and I am lost in wonder when I remember they obeyed me and came on when they feared.

And then when the sun had risen and another hot day fairly begun, I went over to the D.C.'s house; he had a wife, and they were kindly putting me up, and I had breakfast and a bath and went to bed and slept I really think more soundly than I have ever in my life slept before.

CHAPTER XIII
THE FEAR THAT SKULKED BENEATH THE MANGO TREE

Up the Volta—Svvanzy's trusting agent at Akuse—Amedika, the port of Akuse on the Volta—The trials of a trolley ride—My canoe—Paddling up-river—Rapids that raise the river thirty-four feet—Dangers of the river—Entrancingly lovely scenery—A wealthy land—The curious preventive service—Fears—Leaving the river—Labolabo—A notable black man—The British Cotton-growing Experimental Farm—The lonely white man—The fear that was catching—The lonely man's walk.

At Akuse I changed my plans. I had intended to come here, drop down the Volta in the little river steamers that run twice a week to Addah, and then pursue my way along the coast to Keta where there was an old Danish castle, and possibly get across the German border and see Lome, their capital. But there is this charm or drawback—which ever way you like to look at it—about Africa: no one knows anything about the country beyond his immediate district. The Provincial Commissioner had gone to Addah, and I discussed my further progress with the D.C. and his wife as we sat on the verandah that night and looked over the country bathed in the most gorgeous moonlight. The D.C.'s wife, a pretty little woman who had only been out a couple of months, was of opinion that the vile country was killing her and her husband, that it was simply a waste of life to live here, and she could not get over her surprise that I should find anything of interest in it. The D.C. thought it wouldn't be half bad if only the Government brought you back to the same place, so that you might see some result for your labours, and he strongly advised me to go a day or two up the river in a canoe just to see the country.

"It is quite worth seeing," said he, and his wife smiled. She had seen all she intended to see of the country at Akuse, and did not want to go farther in.

The next day I went into the town, the official quarters are some distance away, and called on a couple of the principal merchants.

The factor at Miller Bros, put a new idea into my head.

"Oh yes, go up the Volta," said he; "you can get up as far as Labolabo, then cut across-country and come out at Ho in German territory. You can get to Palime from there, and that is rail-head, so you can easily make your way down to Lome."

It sounded rather an attractive programme.

"You go and see Rowe about it," he suggested.

So I went and called upon Swanzy's agent, a nice young fellow, who first laughed, then looked me up and down doubtfully, and finally said it could be done. Mr Grey, one of their principals, had come across that way the other day, but it was very rough going indeed. No one else that he knew of had ever ventured it.

AMEDIKA, VOLTA RIVER.

If I liked to try he would get me a canoe to go up the river in, and give me letters to their black agents, for I must not expect to meet any white men. And again he looked doubtful.

If I liked; of course I liked. I am always ready to plunge in and take any risks in the future, provided the initial steps are not too difficult, and once he found I wanted to go, Mr Rowe made the initial steps very easy indeed.

First he very nobly lent me twenty-five pounds in threepenny bits, for I had got beyond the region of banks before I realised it, and had only two pounds in hand; he engaged a canoe and six men for me; he gave me letters to all Swanzy's agents in the back-country; and finally, when I had said goodbye to the D.C. and his wife, he gave me luncheon and had me rolled down on a trolley by the little hand railway, if I may coin a word, that runs through the swamp and connects Akuse with its port Amedika on the Volta.

This was a new mode of progression rather pleasant than otherwise, for as it was down-hill to the river it couldn't have been hard on the men who were pushing. I had come from the Commissioner's to the town on a cart, proudly sitting on top of my gear, and drawn by half a dozen Kroo boys; now my

- 141 -

luggage went before me on another trolley, and my way was punctuated by the number of parcels that fell off. My clothes were in a tin uniform case supposed, mistakenly, I afterwards found, to be air-tight and watertight, and I did not want this to fall off and break open, because in it I had stowed all my money—twenty-five pounds all in threepenny bits is somewhat of a care, I find. It escaped, but my bedding went, making a nice cushion for the typewriter which followed it.

The port Amedika, as may be seen from the picture, is very primitive, and though twice a week the little mail steamer comes up coaly and black as her own captain, on the occasion of my departure there were only canoes in the harbour.

My canoe was one of the most ordinary structures, with a shelter in the middle under which I had my chair put up. My gear was stowed fore and aft, and six canoe-men took charge.

AMEDIKA, VOLTA RIVER.

Starting always seems to be a difficulty in Africa, and when I was weary of the hot sun and the glare from the water, and was wondering why we did not start, the canoe-men, true to their kind, found they had no chop, and they had to wait till one of their number went back and got it. But it was got at last and I was fairly afloat on the Volta.

To be paddled up a river is perhaps a very slow mode of progression, but in no other way could I have seen the country so well; in no other way could I have grasped its vast wealth, its wonderful resources. It is something of an adventure to go up the Volta too, for as soon as we started its smooth, wide reaches were broken by belts of rock that made it seem well-nigh impassable. Again and again from the low seat in the canoe it looked as if a rocky barrier barred all further progress, but here and there the water rushed down the narrow chasm as in a mill-race. Wonderful it was to find that a canoe could be poled up those rocky stairways against the rushing water. The rapids before you reach Kpong are innumerable; it seems as if the going were one long struggle. But the river is wonderfully beautiful; it twists and turns, and first on the right hand and then on the left I could see a tall peak, verdure-clad to its very summit, Yogaga, the Long Woman. First the sun shone on it brilliantly, as if it would emphasise its great beauty, and then a tornado swept down, and the mist seemed to rise up and swallow it. The Senchi Rapids raise the river thirty-four feet in a furlong or two, and the water, white and foaming, boils over the brown rocks like the water churned up in the wake of a great ocean steamer. I could not believe we were going up there when we faced them, but the expert canoe-men, stripped to a loin cloth, with shout and song defying the river, poled and pulled and pushed the canoe up to another quiet reach, and when they had reached calm water flung themselves down and smoked and chattered and looked back over the way we had come. We seemed to go up in a series of spasms; either the men were working for dear life or they were idling so as to bring down upon them the wrath of Grant who, after that trip along the Coast, felt himself qualified to speak, and again and again I had to interfere and explain that if anybody was going to scold the men it must be me. But indeed they worked so hard they needed a spell.

AUTHOR'S CANOE, VOLTA RIVER.

Many a time when the canoe was broadside on and the white water was boiling up all round her, I thought, "Well, this really looks very dangerous," but nobody had told me it was, so I supposed it was only my ignorance, but I heard afterwards that I was right, it is dangerous. Many a bag of cotton has gone to the bottom here, and many a barrel of oil has been dashed to pieces against the rocks, and if many a white man's gear has not gone to the bottom too, it is only because white men on this river are few and far between. I had one great advantage, I did not realise the danger till we were right in it, and then it was pressing, it absorbed every thought till we were in smooth water again, with the men lying panting at the bottom of the canoe, so that I really had not time to be afraid till it was all over. Frankly, I don't think I could enter upon such a journey again so calmy, but I am glad I have gone once, for it was such a wonderful and enchanting river. Some day they dream the great waterway will be used to reach Tamale, a ten days' journey farther north, but money must be spent before that happy end is arrived at, though I fancy that if the river were in German hands something would be attempted at once, for the country is undoubtedly very rich.

"Scratch the earth it laughs a harvest." Cocoa and palm oil and rubber all come to the river or grow within a short distance of its banks, and all tropical fruits and native food-stuffs flourish like weeds. Beauty is perhaps hardly an asset in West Africa, but the Volta is a most beautiful river. The Gambia is interesting, the Congo grand, but the Volta is entrancingly lovely. I have heard men rave of the beauty of the Thames, and it certainly is a pleasant river, with its smooth, green lawns, its shady trees, and its picturesque houses; but to compare it to the Volta is to compare a pretty little birch-bark canoe to a magnificent sailing ship with all her snowy canvas set, heeling over to the breeze. Sometimes its great, wide, quiet reaches are like still, deep lakes, in whose clear surface is mirrored the calm, blue sky, the fleecy clouds, the verdure-clad banks, and the hills that are clothed in the densest green to their very peaks. Sometimes it is a raging torrent, fighting its way over the rocks, and beneath the vivid blue sky is the gorgeous vegetation of the Tropics, tangled, luxuriant, feathery palms, tall and shapely silk-cotton trees bound together with twining creeper and trailing vine in one impenetrable mass. A brown patch proclaims a village, and here are broad-leaved bananas, handsome mangoes, fragrant orange trees, lighter-coloured cocoa patches, and cassada that from the distance might be a patch of lucerne. Always there are hills, rising high, cutting the sky sharply, ever changing, ever reflected faithfully in the river at their feet. There is traffic, of course, men fishing from canoes, and canoes laden with barrels of oil or kernels, or cocoa going down the river, the boats returning with the gin and the cotton cloths for the factories run by the negro agents of the great trading-houses; and every three or four hours or so—distance is as yet counted by time in West Africa—are the stations of the preventive service.

SENCHI RAPIDS, VOLTA RIVER.

This preventive service is rather curious, because both banks of the river, in the latter part of its course, are owned by the English, and the service is between the two portions of the Colony. But east of the Volta, whither I was bound, the country is but little known, and apparently the powers that be do not feel themselves equal to cope with a very effective preventive service, so they have there the same duties, a 4 per cent, one that the Germans have in Togo land, while west of the Volta they have a 10 per cent. duty.

I hope there is not much smuggling on the Volta, for with all apologies to the white preventive officers, I doubt the likelihood of the men doing much to stop it. The stations match the river. They have been picturesquely planned—the plans carefully carried out; the houses are well kept up, and round them are some of the few gardens, in English hands, on the Gold Coast that really look like gardens. Though I did not in the course of three days' travel come across him, I felt they marked the presence of some careful, capable white man. The credit is certainly not due to the negro preventive men. In the presence of their white officer they are smart-looking men; seen in his absence they relax their efforts and look as untidy and dirty as a railway porter after a hard day's struggle with a Bank Holiday crowd. After all one can hardly blame the negro for not exerting himself. Nature has given him all he absolutely requires; he has but to stretch out his hand and take it, using almost as little forethought and exertion as the great black cormorants or the little blue-and-white king-fishers that get their livelihood from the river.

And I was afraid of those men. I may have wronged them for they were quite civil, but I was afraid. Again and again they made me remember, as the ordinary peasants never did, that I was a woman alone and very very helpless.

Nothing would have induced me to stay two nights at one of those stations. These men were half-civilised. They had lost all awe of a white face, and, I felt, were inclined to be presuming. What could I have done if they had forgotten their thin veneer of civilisation, and gone back to pure savagery. Nothing—I know it—nothing. At Adjena I had to have my camp-bed put up on the verandah, because I found the house too stuffy, and the moonlit river was glorious to look upon, but I was anything but happy in my own mind; I wondered if I wanted help if my canoe-men, who were very decent, respectable savages, would come to my help. I wonder still. But the morning brought me a glorious view. The sun rose behind Chai Hill, and flung its shadow all across the river, and I attempted feebly to reproduce it in a photograph, and gladly and thankfully I went on my way up the river, and I vowed in my own mind that never if I could help it would I come up here again by myself. If any adventurous woman feels desirous of following in my footsteps, I have but one piece of advice to give her—"Don't." I don't think I would do it again for all the money in the Bank of England. I may do him an injustice, but I do not trust the half-civilised black man. I got through, I think, because for a moment he was astonished. Next time he will not be taken by surprise, and it will not be safe.

CHAI HILL, VOLTA RIVER.

At Labolabo I left the river. Dearly I should have loved to have gone on, to have made my way up to the Northern Territories, but for one thing, my canoe-men were only engaged as far as Labolabo; for another, I had not brought enough photographic plates. I really think it was that last consideration that stopped me. What was the good of going without taking photographs? Curiously enough, the fact that I was afraid did not weigh much with me. I suppose we are all built alike, and at moments our mental side weights up our emotional side. Now, my mental side very much wanted to go up past the Afram plain. I should have had to stay in the preventive service houses, which grew farther and farther apart, and I was afraid of the preventive service men, afraid of them in the sordid way one fears the low-class ruffian of the great cities, but there was that in me that whispered that there was a doubt, and therefore it might be exceedingly foolish to check my search after knowledge for a fear that might only be a causeless fear. But about the photographic plates there was no doubt; I had not brought nearly enough with me, and therefore I landed very meekly at Labolabo.

There was rather a desolate-looking factory, but it did not look inviting enough to induce me to go inside it, so I sat down under a tree on the high bank of the river and interviewed the black factor to whom Swanzy's agent had given me a letter. He was mightily surprised, but I was accustomed to being received with surprise now, and began to consider the making of a cup of tea. Then the factor brought another man along and introduced him to me as Swanzy's agent at Pekki Blengo, Mr Olympia. And once more I feel like apologising to all the African peoples for anything I may have said against them. Mr Olympia came from French Dahomey. He was extremely good-looking, and had polished, courteous manners such as one dreams of in the Spanish hidalgos of old. If you searched the wide world over I do not think you could wish to find a more charming man than Swanzy's black agent at Pekki Blengo. I know very little of him. I only met him casually as I met other black men, men outside the pale for me, a white woman, but I felt when I looked at him there might be possibilities in the African race; when I think of their enormous strength and their wonderful vigour, immense possibilities.

I explained to Mr Olympia that I wanted to get to the rest-house at Anum, that I had arranged for my canoe-men to carry my kit there, and that Mr Rowe had told me that he, Mr Olympia, could get me carriers on to Ho. He said certainly, but he thought I ought at least to go up to the British Cotton-growing Experimental Farm, about ten minutes' walk away from the river. He felt that the white man in charge would be much hurt if I did not at least call and see him.

A white man at Labolabo! How surprised I was. Of course I would go, and Mr Olympia apologising for the absence of hammock or cart, we set off to walk.

Those African ten minutes! It took me a good forty minutes through the blazing heat of an African afternoon, and then I was met upon the steps of the bungalow by a perfectly amazed white man in his shirt sleeves, who hurriedly explained that when he had seen the luggage coming along in charge of the faithful Grant, who made the nearest approach to a slave-driver I have ever seen, he had asked him, "Who be your master?"

"It be no massa," said Grant, "it be missus."

"And then," said my new friend, "I set him at the end of the avenue and told him he was to keep you off till I found a coat. But I couldn't find it. I don't know where the blamed thing's got to."

He went on to inquire where I had come from and how I had come. I told him, "Up the river."

"But," he protested, "it requires a picked crew of ten preventive service men to come up the Volta."

I assured him, I was ready to take my oath about it, you could do it fairly easily with six ordinary, hired men, but he went on shaking his head and declared he couldn't imagine what Rowe was thinking of. He thought I had really embarked on the maddest journey ever woman dreamt of, and while getting me a cool drink, for which I blessed him, went on murmuring, "Rowe must have been mad." I think his surprise brought home to me for the first time the fact that I was doing anything unusual. Before that it had seemed very natural to be going up the river, to be simply wanting to get on and see the great waterway and the country behind.

I did not go on to Anum as I had intended. It was Easter Saturday, and my new friend suggested I should spend Easter with him. I demurred, and he said it would be a charity. He had no words to express his loneliness, and as for the canoe-men, who could not stay to carry my things to Anum, let them go. He would see about my gear being taken up there. And so I stayed, glad to see how a man managed by himself in the wilderness.

The British Cotton-growing Experimental Farm at Labolabo is to all intents and purposes a failure. It was set there in the midst of gorgeously rich country to teach the native to grow cotton, and the native seeing that cocoa, with infinitively less exertion, pays him very much better, naturally firmly declines to do anything of the sort. So here in this beautiful spot lives utterly alone a solitary white man who, with four inefficient labourers, tries desperately to keep the primeval bush from swallowing up the farm and entirely effacing all the hard work that has been done there. This farm should be a valuable possession besides being a very beautiful one. The red-roofed bungalow is set in a bay of the high, green hills, which stretch out verdure-clad arms, threatening every moment to envelop it. The land slopes gently, and as I sat on the broad verandah, through the dense foliage of the trees I could catch glimpses of the silver Volta a mile and a half away, while beyond again the blue hills rose range after range till they were lost in the bluer distance. Four years ago this man who was entertaining me so hospitably had planted a mile-long avenue to lead up to his bungalow, and now the tall grape-fruit and shaddock in front of his verandah meet and have regularly to be cut away to keep the path clear. I am too ignorant to know what could be grown with profit, only I can see that the land is rich and fruitful, and should be, with the river so close, a most valuable possession. As it is, it is one of the most lonely places in the world. I sympathised deeply with the man living there alone. The loneliness grips. If I went to my room I could hear him tramping monotonously up and down the verandah. "Tramp, tramp, tramp," and when I went out he smiled queerly.

BRITISH COTTON GROWING EXPERIMENTAL FARM, LABOLABO.

"I can't help doing it," said he; "it's the lonely man's walk. And when I can't see those two lines," he pointed to two boards in the verandah, "I know I'm drunk and I go to bed."

It was like the story of the man who kept a frog in his pocket and every time he had a drink he took it out and looked at it.

"What the dickens do you do that for?" asked a companion.

"Well, when I see two frogs," said he, "I know I've had enough."

Now I don't believe my friend at Labolabo did exceed, judging by his looks, but if ever man might be excused it was he. He had for servants a very old cook and a slave-boy with a much-scarred face; the marks upon his face proclaimed his former status, but no man could understand the unintelligible jargon he spoke, so no man knew where he came from. It was probably north of German territory. At any rate, he flitted about the bungalow a most inadequate steward.

And he laid the table in the stone house—or rather the shelter with two stone walls, a stone floor, and a broken-down thatch roof, where we had our meals. It was perhaps twenty yards from the bungalow, and on the garden side grew like a wall great bushes of light-green feathery justitia with its yellow, bell-like flowers, while on the other side a little grass-grown plain stretched away to the forest-clad hills behind.

Oh, but it was lonely! and fear is a very catching thing.

"There is nothing to be afraid of in Africa," said my host, "till the moment there is something, and then you're done."

Whether he was right or not I do not know, but I realised as I had never done before why men get sick in the bush, worse, why they take to drink and why they go mad. I looked out from the verandah, and when I saw a black figure slip silently in among the trees I wondered what it portended. I looked behind me to see if one might not be coming from behind the kitchen. The fool-bird in the bush crying, "Hoo! hoo! hoo!" all on one note seemed but crying a suitable dirge. Fear hid on the verandah; I could hear him in the creak of a door, in the "pad, pad" of the slave-boy's feet; I could almost have sworn I saw him skulking under the mango tree where were kept the thermometers; and when on Easter Sunday a tornado swept down from the hills, blotting out the vivid green in one pall of grey mist, he was in the shrieking wind and in the shuddering rain.

Never was I more impersonally sorry to leave a man alone, for if I saw my host again I doubt if he would recognise me, but it seemed wicked to leave a fellow white man alone in such a place. If there had been any real danger, of course I should only have been an embarrassment, but at least I was company of his own kind and I kept that haunting fear at bay.

I stayed two days and then I felt go I must. I was also faced with my own carelessness and the casual manner in which I had dropped into the wilderness. Anum mountain was a steep climb of five miles, and beyond that again I had, as far as I could gather, several days' journey in the wilds before I could hope to reach rail-head in German Togo, and I had actually never remembered that I should want a hammock. The Cotton-growing Association didn't possess one, and, like Christian in the "Pilgrim's Progress,"

I "cast about me" what I should do. I could not fancy myself walking in the blazing noonday sun. My host smiled. He did not think it was a matter of any great consequence because he felt sure I could not get through, but he came to my rescue all the same and sent up a couple of labourers to the Basel Mission at Anum to see what they could suggest. The labourers came back with a hammock—rather a dilapidated one—on their heads, and an invitation to luncheon next day.

"It's as far as you'll go," said my friend, "if nothing else stops you; you can't possibly get carriers. Remember, I'll put you up with pleasure on your way back."

But I was not going to face the Volta again by myself, though I did not tell him that. Those black men insulted me by making me fear them.

It was a very hot morning when we started to climb up Anum mountain. The bush on either side was rather thick, and the road was steep and very bad going. It was shaded, luckily, most of the way, and there arose that damp, pleasant smell that comes from moist earth, the rich, sensuous, insidious scent of an orchid that I could not see, or the mouselike smell of the great fruitarian bats that in these daylight hours were hidden among the dense greenery of the roadside. It was a toilsome journey, and my new friend walked beside me, but at last we reached Anum town, a mud-built, native town, bare, hot, dirty, unkempt, and we passed beyond it to the grateful shade once more of the Basel Mission grounds.

CHAPTER XIV
INTO THE WILDS

Anum Mountain—The Basel Mission—A beautiful spot—An old Ashanti raid—A desolate rest-house—Alone and afraid; also hungry—A long night—Jakai—Pekki Blengo—The unspeakable Eveto Range—Underpaid carriers—A beautiful, a wealthy, and a neglected land—Tsito—The churches and the fetish—Difficulties of lodging in a cocoa-store—The lonely country between Tsito and the Border—Doubts of the hammock-boys—The awful road—Butterflies—The Border.

Frankly, my sympathies are not as a rule with the missionaries, certainly not with African missionaries. I have not learned to understand spiritual misery, and of material misery there is none in Africa to be compared with the unutterable woe one meets at every turn in an English city. But one thing I admire in these Swiss and German teachers is the way they have improved the land they have taken possession of. Their women, too, make here their homes and bear their children. "A home," I said as I stepped on to the wide verandah of the Mission Station at Anum; "a home," as I went into the rooms decorated with texts in German and Twi; "a home," as I sat down to the very excellent luncheon provided by the good lady whom most English women would have designated a little scornfully as a *haus-frau*. Most emphatically "a home" when I looked out over the beautiful gardens that were nicely planted with mangoes, bananas, palms, and all manner of pretty shrubs and bright-foliaged trees. It seems to me almost a pity to teach the little negro since he is so much nicer in his untutored state, but since they feel it must be done these Basel Mission people are going the very best way about it by beautifying their own surroundings.

From their verandah over the scented frangipanni and fragrant orange trees you may see far far away the winding Volta like a silver thread at the bottom of the valley, and the great hills that control his course standing up on either side. It is an old station, for in the late sixties the Ashantis raided it, captured the missionary, Mr Ramseyer, his wife and child, and held them in captivity for several years. But times are changed now. The native, even the fierce Ashanti warrior, has learned that it is well for him that the white man should be here, and up in the rest-house on the other side of the mountain a white woman may stay alone in safety.

Why do the powers that be overlook Anum mountain? The rest-house to which my kind friend from Labolabo escorted me after we had lunched at the Basel Mission was shabby and desolate with that desolation that comes where a white man has been and is no longer. No one has ever tried to make a garden, though the larger trees and shrubs have been cleared from about the house and in their stead weeds have sprung up, and the vigour of their growth shows the possibilities, while the beauty of the situation is not to be denied. Away to the north, where not even a native dwells, spreads out the wide extent of the Afram plain, a very paradise for the sportsman, for there are to be found numberless hartebeests, leopards, lions, and even the elephant himself. It lies hundreds, possibly thousands of feet below, and across it winds the narrow streak of the Volta, while to the north the hills stretch out as if they would keep the mighty river for England, barring its passage to the east and to German territory.

And here my friend from Labolabo left me—left me, I think, with some misgivings.

"Come back," he said; "you know I'll be glad to see you. Mind you come back. I know you can't get through."

But I had my own opinion about that.

"What about the carriers Mr Olympia is going to send me to-morrow morning?"

And he laughed. "Those carriers! don't you wish you may get them? I know those carriers black men promise. Why, the missionary said you needn't expect them."

The Basel missionary had said I might get through if I was prepared to wait, and as I said good-bye I was prepared to wait.

The rest-house was on top of a mountain in the clouds, far away from any sign of habitation. The rooms were large, empty, and desolate with a desolation there is no describing. There was a man in charge living in a little house some way off, the dispenser at the empty hospital which was close to the rest-house, and the Basel missionary spoke of him with scorn.

"He was one of my boys," he said; "such a fool I sent him away, and why the Government have him for dispenser here I do not know."

Neither do I, but I suspect he was in a place where he could do the very minimum of harm, for very few people come to Anum mountain. There is a Ju-ju upon it, and my first experience was that I could get no food.

No sooner were we alone than Grant appeared before me mightily aggrieved.

"This bush country no good, Ma. I no can get chop."

I hope I would have felt sorry for him in any case, but it was brought home to me by the fact that he could get no chop for me either.

I had come to the end of my stores and there was not a chicken nor an egg nor bread nor fruit to be bought in the village down the hill. The villagers said they had none, or declined to sell, which came to the same thing. I dined frugally off tea and biscuits, and I presume Grant helped himself to the biscuits—I told him to—tea he hated—and then as the evening drew on I prepared to go to bed.

Oh! but it was lonely, and fear fell upon me. A white mist came softly up, so that I could not see beyond the broad, empty verandahs. I knew the moon was shining by the white light, but I could not see her and I felt shut in and terrified. Where Grant went to I don't know, but he disappeared after providing my frugal evening meal, and I could hear weird sounds that came out of the mist, and none of the familiar chatter and laughter of the carriers to which I had grown accustomed. It was against all my principles to shut myself in, so I left doors and windows wide open and listened for the various awful things that might come out of the bush and up those verandah steps. What I feared I know not, but I feared, feared greatly; the fear that had come upon me at Labolabo worked his wicked will now that I was alone on Anum mountain, and the white mist aided and abetted. I could hear the drip, drip, as of water falling somewhere in the silence; I could hear the cry of a bird out in the bush, but it was the silence that made every rustle so fraught with meaning. It was no good telling myself there was nothing to fear, that the kindly missionaries would never have left me alone if there had been.

I could only remember that on this mountain had raided those fierce Ashanti warriors, that terrible things had been done here, that terrible things might be done again, that if anything happened to me there was no possibility of help, that I was quite powerless. I wondered if a Savage, on these occasions one spells Savage with a very large "S," did come on to the verandah, did come into my bedroom, what should I do. I felt that even a bush-cat would be terrifying, and having got so far I realised that a rabbit would probably send me into hysterics. At the thought of the rabbit my drooping spirits recovered themselves a little, but I spent a very unpleasant night, dozing and listening, till my own heart-beats drowned all other sounds. But I never thought of going back. I don't suppose I should have given up in any case, it is against family tradition, but if I had, there was the Volta behind me, and those preventive service men made it imperative to go on.

But when morning dawned I felt a little better. True, I did not like the thought of tea and biscuits for breakfast, but I thought hopefully of the Basel Mission gardens. I was sure, if I had to stay here, those hospitable people would give me plenty of fruit, and probably a good deal more than that, so I was not quite as depressed as Grant when I dressed and stood on the verandah, looking across the mysterious mist that still shrouded the valley of the Volta.

And before that mist had cleared away, up the steps of the rest-house came the Basel missionary, and at their foot crowded a gang of lightly clad, chattering men and women. My carriers! Mr Olympia had been as good as his word, the missionary kindly came to interpret, and I set out for Pekki Blengo, away in the hills to the east.

It was all hill-country through which we passed; range after range of hills, rich in cocoa and palm oil, while along the track, that we English called a road, might be seen rubber trees scored with knives, so that the milky rubber can be collected. Very little of this rich country is under cultivation, the vegetation is dense and close, and the vivid green is brightened here and there by scarlet poinsettas and flamboyant trees, then at the beginning of the rains one mass of flame-coloured blossom. It was a tangle of greenery, like some great, gorgeous greenhouse, and the native, when he wants a clearing, burns off a small portion and plants cocoa or cassada, yams, bananas, or maize, with enough cotton here and there, between the lines of food-stuffs, to give him yarn for his immediate needs. When the farmer has used up this land, he abandons it to the umbrella trees and other tropical weeds, and with the wastefulness of the native takes up another piece of land, burning and destroying, quite careless of the value of the trees that go to feed the fire. Such reckless destruction is not allowed by the Germans, but a few miles to the east. There a native is encouraged to take up a farm, but he must improve it year by year. Our thrifty neighbours will have no such waste within their borders.

In the course of the morning I arrived at Jakai, and the whole of the village turned out to interview me, and I in my turn took a photograph of as few as I could manage of the inhabitants under the principal tree. That was always the difficulty. When they grasped I was going to take a picture, and there was generally some much-travelled man ready to instruct the others, they all crowded together in one mass in front of the camera—if they did not object altogether, when they ran away—and I always had to wait, and perjure myself, and say the picture was taken long before it was done. But always they were kindly. If I grew afraid at night I always reminded myself of the uniform goodwill of the villages through which I passed; their evident desire that I should be pleased with my surroundings. And at Jakai Grant, with triumph, bought so many eggs that I trembled for my future meals. I foresaw a course of "fly" egg, hard-boiled egg, and egg and breadcrumbs, but after all that was better than tea and biscuits, and when I saw a pine-apple and a bunch of bananas I felt life was going to be endurable again.

At Pekki Blengo, an untidy, disorderly village, where the streets are full of holes and hillocks, strewn with litter and scarred with waterways, Mr Olympia met me, and conducted me to an empty chiefs house, where I might put up for the night. It was a twostoried house of mud, with plenty of air, for there were great holes where the doors and windows would have been, and I slept peacefully once more with the hum of human life all around me again. But I can hardly admire Pekki Blengo. It is like all these villages of the English

Eastern Province. The houses are of mud, the roofs of thatch, and fowls, ducks, pigs, goats, and little happy, naked children alike swarm. That is one comfort so different from travelling in the older lands—these villagers are apparently happy enough. They are kindly and courteous, too, for though a white woman was evidently an extraordinary sight equal in interest to a circus clown, or even an elephant, and they rushed from all quarters to see her, they never pushed or crowded, and they cuffed the children if they seemed likely to worry her.

And beyond Pekki Blengo the road reached its worst. Mr Olympia warned me I should have to walk across the Eveto Range as no hammock-boys could possibly carry me, and I decided therefore that the walking had better be done very early in the morning, and arranged to start at half-past five, as soon as it was light.

The traveller is always allowed the privilege of arranging in Africa. If he does not he will certainly not progress at all, but at the same time it is surprising how seldom his well-arranged plans come off. True to promise my hammock-boys and carriers turned up some time a little before six in the morning, and the carriers, swarming up the verandah, turned over the loads, made a great many remarks that I was incapable of understanding, and one and all departed. Then the hammock-boys apparently urged me to get into the hammock and start, as they were in a hurry to be off and earn the four shillings they were to have for taking me to Ho in German territory. I pointed out, whether they understood I did not know, that I could not stir without my gear, and I went off to interview Mr Olympia, who was sweetly slumbering in his house about a mile away. He, when he was aroused, said they thought I was not giving them enough; that they said they would not carry loads to Ho for one shilling and sixpence and two shillings a load. I said that that was the sum he had fixed. I was perfectly willing to give more; and he set out to interview the Chief, and see if he could get fresh carriers, but he was not very hopeful about getting any that day. I retired to my chiefs house, grew tired of making mental notes of the people and the surrounding country, and got out a pack of cards and solaced myself with one-handed bridge, which may be educational, but is not very exciting. My hammock-boys again pleaded to be taken on, but I was firm. It was useless moving without my gear; and finally when I was about giving up hope Mr Olympia returned. He had found eight men and women who were bound across the Eveto Range to get loads at Tsito. Sixpence, he explained, was the ordinary charge for a load to Tsito, but if I would rise to say ninepence for my heavier loads—he hesitated as if such an enormous expenditure might not commend itself to my purse. But naturally I assented gladly, and off went my loads at sixpence and ninepence a head. For a moment I rejoiced, and as usual began to purr over my excellent management. Not for long though. It was my turn now, and where were my hammock-boys? Inquiry elicited the awful fact that they had gone to their farms and could not be prevailed upon to start till next day; Mr Olympia was sure I could not hope to move before to-morrow morning.

The situation was anything but comfortable. I had had nothing to eat since earliest dawn. I had now not even a chair to sit upon, nor a pack of cards to solace the dull hours. I dare not eat and, worse still, dare not drink. Then I sent word to Mr Olympia that if he would get me a couple of men to carry my hammock I would walk.

I sat on the steps of that house and waited, I walked down the road and waited, and the tropical day grew hotter and hotter, the sun poured down pitilessly, and I was weary with thirst, but still I would not drink the native water. At last, oh triumph, instead of two, eight grinning hammock-boys turned up, and about 1.30 on a blazing tropical afternoon we started. Ten minutes later I was set down at the foot of the unspeakable Eveto Range, and my men gave me to understand by signs they could carry me no longer.

I cannot think that the Eveto Range is perpendicular, but it seemed pretty nearly so. It was thickly wooded, as is all the country, and the road was the merest track between the walls of vegetation, a track that twisted and turned out of the way of the larger obstacles, the smaller ones we negotiated as best we might, holes, and roots, and rocks, and waterways, that made the distance doubly and trebly great. In five minutes I felt done; in ten it was brought home to me forcibly that I was an unutterable fool ever to attempt to travel in Africa. In addition to the roughness there was the steepness of the way to be taken into consideration, and the constant strain of going up, up compelled me again and again to lie down flat on my back to recover sufficient strength and breath to go on. What matter if the view was delightful—it was—when I had neither time, nor strength, nor energy to raise my eyes from the difficulties that beset my feet. But there was nothing to be done except to crawl painfully along with the tropical sun pouring pitilessly down, and not a breath of wind stirring.

And I was dead with thirst. We came across a bunch of bananas, laid beside the track, and my men offered me one by way of refreshment, but I was too done to eat, and I thought what a fool I was not to carry a flask. When I had given up all hope of surviving, and really didn't much care what became of me so long as I died quickly, we reached the top where were native farms with cotton bushes now in full bloom planted among the food-stuffs, and I rested a little and gathered together my energies for the descent. And if the going up was bad, the going down was worse. There were great rocks and boulders that I would never have dared in England, and when I could spare time from my own woes I reflected that the usual charge for taking a load to

Tsito was sixpence, and decided between my own gasps it was the most iniquitous piece of slave-driving I had ever heard of. Twenty pounds, I felt, would never pay me for carrying myself across this awful country, and there were those wretched carriers toiling along for a miserable sixpence, or at most ninepence. I was thoroughly ashamed of myself. And the view was beautiful. Before us, in the evening light, lay the wealthy land where no white man goes, and the beautiful, verdure-clothed hills dappled with shadow and sunshine. The light was going, but, weary as I was, I had to stop and look, for never again might I see a more lovely view.

And at last, just as the darkness was falling, we had crossed the range, and I thankfully and wearily tumbled into my hammock and was carried through the village of Tsito to the trader's store. It was a humble store, presided over by a black man who spoke English, and here they bought cotton and cocoa, and sold kerosene and trade gin, cotton cloths, and the coarsest kinds of tinned fish. I had a letter from Mr Olympia to this black man, and he offered me the hospitality of the cocoa-store; that is to say, a space was cleared among the cocoa and cotton and other impedimenta, my bed and table and bath set up. Grant brought me something to eat—hard-boiled eggs, biscuits, and bananas, with tea to drink. How thankful I was for that tea! I dined with an admiring crowd looking on, and I remembered my repentance on the mountain and sent for my carriers and paid them all double. I still think it was too little, but in excuse it must be remembered that I was alone and hardly dared risk a reputation for immense wealth.

There are difficulties connected with lodging in a cocoa-store, especially when you are surrounded by a population who have never seen a white woman before. I needed a bath, but how to get it I hardly knew, with eyes all over the place, so at last I put out the lights and had it in the dark, and I went to bed in the dark, and as I was going to sleep I heard the audience dispersing, discussing the show at the top of their voices. As I did not understand what they said I did not know whether they had found it satisfactory. At least it was cheap, unless Swanzy's agent charged them.

I was not afraid now, curiously enough, right away from civilisation, entirely at these peoples' mercy. I felt quite safe, and after my hard day I slept like the dead. It is mentally very soothing, I notice, to say to oneself, "Well done!" and our mental attitude has a great effect upon our physical health. At least I found one thing—I had pitied myself most unnecessarily. My exertions had done me no harm, and I never felt in better health than when I waked up next morning in Swanzy's cocoa-room and proceeded to get dressed in the dark. That was necessary, because I knew the sound of my stirring would bring an interested audience to see how the white woman did things. I really don't think the White City rivalled me as a provider of amusement for the people in the eastern district of the Volta and the western district of Togo in the end of April and beginning of May last.

GOING TO HIS FARM, TSITO.

I had picked up a discarded map on the floor of the rest-house at Anum, and here I saw that many of the villages were marked with crosses to show that there was a church, but I saw no church here in Tsito, though I doubt not there was one. What I did see, not only in Tsito but at the entrance to every village I passed through, was a low, thatched shed, under which were the fetish images of the village. These were generally the rough-cut outline in clay or wood of a human figure seated. Sometimes the figure had a dirty rag round it, sometimes a small offering in front of it, and dearly should I have liked to have had a picture, but the people, even Swanzy's agent, objected, and I did not like to run counter to local prejudice. And yet Swanzy's agent is by way of being a Christian, but I dare say Christianity in these parts of Africa, like

Christianity in old-time Britain or Gaul, conforms a good deal to pagan modes of thought.

I met a picturesque gentleman starting out for his farm, and him I photographed after he had been assured that no harm could possibly happen to him, though he begged very anxiously that he might be allowed to go home and put on his best cloth. I think he is a very nice specimen of the African peasant as he is, but I am sure he would be much troubled could he know he was going into a book in his farm clothes.

It was just beginning to get hot as I got back to the store after wandering round the village, and I found Grant and the carriers with all my gear had already started and were nowhere to be seen. It was, perhaps, just as well that it never occurred to Grant that I might be afraid to be left alone with strange black men. But to-day my strange black men were not forthcoming. I had expected them to come gaily because, to celebrate the crossing of the Eveto Range, while I had paid the carriers double, I had given the hammock-boys, who had had a very easy time, a couple of shillings to buy either gin or rum or palm wine, whichever they could get. It stamped me as a fool woman, and now, after a long delay, they came and stood round the hammock without offering to lift it from the ground.

"There is trouble," said the black agent sententiously.

I had come out into the roadway, prepared to get into the hammock.

"What is the matter?"

"They say Ho be far. Four shillings no be enough money to tote hammock to Ho."

I was furious. They had made the agreement. I had given exactly what they asked, but where I had made the mistake was in doing more. Now what was to be done? I did not hesitate for a moment. I marched straight back to the cocoa-store.

"Tell them," I said, "they can go home and I will pay them nothing. I will walk."

Now if either the agent or those hammock-boys had given the thing a moment's thought, they must have seen this was sheer bluff on my part. It would have been a physical impossibility for me to walk, at least I think so; besides, I should have been entirely alone and I had not the faintest notion of the way. However, my performance of yesterday had apparently not impressed them as badly as it had impressed me, and just as I was meditating despairingly what on earth I should do, for I felt to give in would be fatal, into the store came those men bearing the hammock, and it did not need Swanzy's interpreter to tell me, "You get in, Mammy. They go quick."

We were out of the village at once and into the country. It was orchard-bush country, thick grass just growing tall with the beginning of the rains, and clumps of low-growing trees, with an occasional patch of miniature forest that grew so close it shut out the fierce sun overhead and gave a welcome and grateful shade. We passed the preventive service station on the Border—an untidy, thatched hut, presided over by a black man, who looked not unlike a dilapidated, a very dilapidated railway porter who had been in store for some time and got a little moth-eaten—and I concluded we were at the end of British territory; but not yet. The road was bad when we started, and it grew steadily worse till here it was very bad indeed. It became a mere track through the rough, grass country on either side, a track that admitted of but one man walking singly, and my boys dropped the hammock by way of intimating that they could carry me no farther. They could not, I could see that for myself, for not only was the track narrow, but it twisted and turned and doubled on itself, so that a corkscrew is straight in comparison with the road to Ho.

And once more fear fell upon me. I was alone with men who could not understand a word that I said, who could not speak a word that I could understand, and since only in a Gilbertian sense could this track be called a road at all, that it could lead to anywhere seemed impossible. There were no farms, no villages, not a sign of habitation. A fool-bird called cynically, "Hoo! hoo! hoo!" and I hesitated whether I would rather these eight men walked in front of me or behind me. I decided they should walk in front, and they laughingly obeyed, and we walked on through the heat. Many-coloured butterflies, large as small birds, flitted across the track. Never have I seen such beautiful butterflies, blue as gentian, or as turquoise with a brilliancy the turquoise lacks; purple, red, yellow, and white were they, and it was only the utter hopelessness of keeping them prevented my making any attempt to catch them. Evidently I was not as afraid as I thought I was because I could reflect upon the desirability of those butterflies in a collection. But I was afraid. Occasionally people, men or women, in twos or threes, came along with loads upon their heads, and I tried to speak to them and ask them if this really was the road to Ho, but I could make no one understand and they passed on, turning to stare with wonder at the stranger. There were silk-cotton trees and shea-butter trees and many another unknown tree, but it seemed I had come right out into the wilds beyond human ken or occupation, and I had to assure myself again and again that these carriers were decent peasants, just earning a little, something beyond what came from cocoa or palm oil, with wives—probably many wives—and children, and the strange white woman was worth a good deal more to them safely delivered at her destination than in any way else. We came to a river, and by a merciful interposition of Providence it was dry, and we were able to ignore the slippery, moss-grown tree-trunk that did duty as bridge, and, scrambling down into its bed, cross easily to the other side, and there, in the midst of a shady clump of trees, was Grant with all the carriers.

So it was the road to Ho after all, and, as usual, I had worried myself most unnecessarily. I sat down on my precious black box that contained all my money, and Grant got out a tumbler, squeezed the last orange I possessed into it, filled it up from the sparklet bottle, and I was ready to laugh at my fears and face the world once more.

Again we went along the tortuous path, and then suddenly the Border!

CHAPTER XV
CROSSING THE BORDER

German roads—German villages—The lovely valley of Ho—The kindly German welcome—German hospitality—An ideal woman colonist—Pink roses—The way it rains in Togo—An unfortunate cripple—Vain regrets—Sodden pillows—A German rest-house—A meal under difficulties—Travelling by night—The weirdness of it—The sounds of the night—The fireflies—A long long journey—Palime by night—More German hospitality—Rail-head.

There was nothing to mark the border between the Gold Coast Colony and Togo. The country on the one side was as the country on the other, orchard-bush country with high grass and clumps of trees and shrubs; the lowering sky was the same, the fierce sun the same, only there was a road at last.

The Germans make roads as the Romans made them, that their conquering legions might pass, and here, in this remote corner of the earth, where neither Englishman nor German comes, is a road, the like of which I did not find in the Gold Coast Colony. It is hard and smooth as a garden-path, it is broad enough for two carts or two hammocks to pass abreast, it runs straight as a die, on either side the bushes and grass are kept neatly trimmed away, and deep waterways are cut so that the heavy rainfall may not spoil the road.

After a short time we came to a preventive station, neat and pretty as a station on the Volta, higher praise I cannot give it, and beyond that was a village; a village that was a precursor of all the villages that were to come. As a Briton I write it with the deepest regret, but the difference between an English village and a German village is as the difference between the model village of Edensor and the grimy town of Hanley in the Black Country. Here, in this first little village on the Togo side, all the ground between the houses was smoothed and swept, the houses themselves looked trim and neat, great, beautiful, spreading shade-trees of the order *ficus elasticus* were planted at regular intervals in the main street, and underneath them were ranged logs, so that the people who lounge away the heat of the day in the shade may have seats. Even the goats and the sheep had a neater look, which perhaps is no wonder, for here is no filthy litter or offal among which they may lie.

As I passed on my wonder increased. Here was exactly the same country, exactly the same natives, and all the difference between order and neatness and slatternly untidiness.

TREES IN GERMAN VILLAGE ON THE WAY TO HO.

I went on through this charming country till I found myself looking across a lovely valley at a house set high on a hill, the Commissioner's house at Ho at last. I went down into the valley, along a road that was bordered with flamboyant trees, all full of flame-coloured blossom, and then suddenly the curtain of my hammock was whisked up, and there stood before me a bearded white man, dressed in a white duck suit with a little red badge in his white helmet—the Commissioner, he told me in his halting English, at Ho.

Now I had come into that country without a letter or a credential of any sort, a foreigner, speaking not one word of the language, and I wondered what sort of reception I should meet with. I tried to explain that I was looking for a rest-house, but he waved my remarks aside with a smile, made me understand that his wife was up in the house on the hill, and that if I would go there she could speak English, and would make me welcome. And so I went on through country, lovely as the country round Anum mountain, only in the British colony there is this great difference—there the land is exactly as Nature made it, bar the little spoiling that man has done, innocent of roads, and exceedingly difficult to traverse, while here in German territory everything is being carried out on some well-thought-out plan. Ho was a station straggling over hill and valley, with high hills clothed with greenery near at hand, high hills fading into the blue distance, and valleys that cried out to the Creator in glad thankfulness that such beauty should be theirs. The road up to the Commissioner's bungalow was steep, steep as the Eveto Range, but it had been graded so that it was easy of ascent as a path in Hyde Park. Every tree had been planted or left standing with thought, not only for its own beauty but for the view that lies beyond; flamboyant, mango, palm, frangipanni, that the natives call forget-me-not, all have a reason for their existence, all add to the beauty and charm of the scene. And when I got to the top of the hill I was at the prettiest of brown bungalows, and down the steps of the verandah came a rosy-cheeked, pretty girl, ready to welcome the stranger.

"Of course you stay with us," she said in the kindness of her hospitable heart, though there was certainly no of course about it.

She took me in and gave me coffee, and as we sat eating cakes, home-made German cakes, I asked her, "You have not been out very long?" because of the bright colour of her cheeks.

"Oh, not long," she said, "only a year and two months. But it is so nice we are asking the Government to let us stay two years."

"And you do not find it dull?"

"Oh no, I love it. The time goes so quick, so quick. There is so much to do."

And then her husband came and added his welcome to hers, and paid off my carriers in approved German official style, and they took me in to "evening bread," and I found to my intense surprise they had wreathed my place at table with pink roses. Never have I had such a pretty compliment, or such a pretty welcome, and only the night before I had been dining off hard-boiled eggs and biscuits in Swanzy's cocoa-house at Tsito.

Bed after dinner, and next morning my hostess took me round, and showed me everything there was to be seen, and told me how she passed her time. She looked after the house, she saw to the food, she went for rides on her bicycle, and she worked in the garden. It was the merry heart that went all the day, and I will venture to say that that pretty girl, with her bright, smiling face and her bright, charming manners, interested in this new country to which she had come, keen on her husband's work, was an asset to the nation to which she belonged; worth more to it than a dozen fine ladies who pride themselves on not being *haus-frau*. And as for the Commissioner, if I may judge, he was not only a strong man, but an artist. He had the advantage over an English Commissioner that his tour extended over eighteen months, instead of a year, and that he always came back to the same place. His bungalow looked a home; round it grew up a tropical garden, and behind he had planted a grove of broad-leaved teak trees, and already they were so tall the pathway through the grove was a leafy tunnel just flecked with golden sunshine, that told of the heat outside.

Those Germans were good to me. I feel I can never be grateful enough for such a warm welcome, and always, for the sake of those two there in the outlands, shall I think kindly of the people of the Fatherland.

They helped me to take photographs; the Commissioner mended my camera for me, and he got me more carriers, and told me that they were engaged to take me on thirty miles to Palime for the sum of two shillings a piece, that it could be done in one day if I chose, indeed it must be done in one day unless I stayed in the rest-house at Neve, and he warned me that I carried about with me a great sum of money, and asked if I were sure of my boy. I did not think it was likely Grant would rob me at this stage of the proceedings, but I suddenly realised with a little uncomfortable feeling what implicit trust I was putting in him; and then they gave fresh instructions for my comfort. It would rain, they said it always rained in Togo at this season in the afternoon; and I evidently did not realise how it rained, so they tied up my camera in American cloth and instructed me to put my Burberry on at the first drop of rain. Then with many good wishes we parted, and I set off on the road to Palime.

The road was most excellent, and anyone who has travelled for miles along a track that is really little better than a hunter's trail can understand the delights of smooth and easy going. We passed through villages where the villagers all turned up to see the show, but I fancied, it may have been only fancy, that the people were not as lightheartedly happy as in English territory, and whenever we came to a stream my men stopped and begged in pantomime that they might be allowed to bathe. I should like to have bathed myself, so I assented cheerfully, and the result was that we did not get over the ground very quickly. One of them spoke a little, a very little Twi, the language of the Fantis and Ashantis, and Grant spoke a little, and that was my only means of communication, lost of course when he was not with me, but they were most excellent men and went on and on untiringly.

Presently the clouds began to gather, a great relief, because the sun had been very hot, a few drops of rain fell, and I, remembering instructions, flew out of my hammock and put on my Burberry. By the time it was on the few drops were many drops, and by the time I was in my hammock again, the water was coming down as if it had been poured out of a bucket. Such sheets of rain fairly made me gasp. Now, my hammock was old. I had forgotten the need of a hammock when I started up the Volta, and finding this elderly one at Anum, marked "P.W.D." Public Works Department, and there being nobody to say me nay, I commandeered it. Now, far be it from me to revile a friend who carried me over many a weary mile of road, but there is no disguising the fact, the poor old hammock was not in the first bloom of youth, and the canopy was about as much use against a rainstorm as so much mosquito-netting. The water simply poured through it. Now the canvas of which the hammock was made, of course, held water, so did the Burberry, the water trickled down my neck, and, worse still, carried as I was, with my feet slightly raised, trickled down my skirts, and the gallant Burberry held it like a bucket. When the water rose up to my waist, icy-cold water, I got out and walked.

The sky was heavily overcast, and it was raining as if it had never had a chance to rain before, and never expected to have a chance to rain again, so I walked on, hatless, because I did not mind about my hair getting wet. I thought to myself, "when the sun comes out, it will dry me," and I looked at the string of dejected-looking carriers tailing out behind with all their loads covered with banana leaves. And I walked, and I walked, and I walked, and there seemed no prospect of the rain stopping; apparently it proposed to go on to doomsday, or at least the end of the rainy season. An hour passed, two hours, three, my pillows were simply sodden masses, my hammock was a wisp of wet canvas, and I was weary to death; then a village came into view, a little neat German village, and the people came out to look at me with interest, though they had certainly seen a white woman before. I always think of that village with regret. A man passed along through the mud, working his way in a sitting posture, and having on his hands a sort of wooden clog. So very very seldom have I seen misery in Africa that I was struck as I used to be struck when first I came to England, and I put my hand in my pocket for my purse, but all my money with the exception of threepence was in my box, and that threepence I bestowed upon him. Now there remains with me the regret that I did not give him more, for never have I seen such delight on any man's face. He held it out, he called all his friends to look, he bowed obeisance before me again and again. I was truly ashamed of so much gratitude for so small a gift, and while I was debating how I could get at my box to make it a little more, he clattered away, as happy apparently as if someone had left him a fortune. But I always think of it sadly. Why didn't I manage to give him two shillings. It would have meant nothing to me, and so much to him.

But now I was very tired, and when the rest-house was pointed out to me, I hailed it with delight. I have seen many weird rest-houses on my travels, but that was the most primitive of them all. A mud floor was raised a little above the surrounding ground, and over it was a deep thatch, a couple of tiny windowless rooms were made with mud walls, and just outside them was a table, made by the simple process of sticking upright stakes into the ground and laying rough boards across them; two chairs alongside the table were also fixtures, but I sat down wearily, and Grant promptly produced a pack of cards, and went away to make tea.

Bridge was not a success; I was so wet and cold, but the tea came quickly along with a boiled egg and biscuits and mangoes, for the Germans it appears, after their thorough fashion, always insist that wood and water shall be ready in their rest-houses. I was sorry for the carriers, wet and shivering, and I was sorrier for my own servant, for the rain was still coming down pitilessly. I suggested he should have some tea to warm him, but he did not like tea, and the other egg he also rejected, quite rightly I decided when I tried to partake of the specimen he brought for me. But the tea was most refreshing, and I was prepared to try and understand what the carriers wanted. Briefly, they wanted to stop here. Though I could not understand their tongue, I could understand that.

"They say Palime be far, Ma," said Grant.

Yes, I reckoned Palime must be about fifteen miles, but I looked at the dismal house and decided it was an impossible place to stay. I would rather walk that fifteen miles. I looked at my bedding roll, and decided it must be wet through and through, and then I got into that dripping and uninviting hammock, among the sodden pillows, and gave the order to go on. I was wet through, and I thought I could hold out if we got to Palime as quickly as possible, but I knew we could not possibly do it under five hours, probably longer. However, it was not as hard on me as on the men who had to walk with loads on their heads. Of course I was foolish. I ought either to have changed in one of those dismal-looking little mud rooms, or to have filled my hot-water bottle—I always carried one to be ready for the chill I never got—with hot water and wrapped myself up in a rug; but I foolishly forgot all these precautions, and my remembrance of that tramp to Palime is of a struggle against bitter cold and wet and weariness. It was weird, too, passing along the bush in the dark. Grant and the carriers dropped behind, the rain stopped, and the hammock-boys lighted a smoky lantern which gleamed on the wet road ahead, and was reflected in the pools of water that lay there, and made my two front boys throw gigantic shadows on the bush as they passed along. Strange sounds, too, came out of the bush; sometimes a leopard cried, sometimes one of the great fruitarian bats bewailed itself like a woman in pain, there was the splash, splash of the men's feet in the roadway, the deep croak of the African bull-frog, there was the running of water, a drip, drip from the trees and bushes by the roadside, and always other sounds, unexplained, perhaps unexplainable, that one hears in the night. Sometimes tom-toms were beating, sometimes we passed through a village and a few lights appeared, and my men shouted greetings I suppose, but they might have been maledictions. It is an experience I shall never forget, that of being carried along, practically helpless, and hearing my men, whom I could not understand, exchange shouts that I could not understand with people that I could not see. It was hot I dare say, but I was wet to the skin and bitter cold, and I know the night after the rain was beautiful, but I was too tired and too uncomfortable to appreciate it. Then the fireflies came out, like glowing sparks, and again and again I thought we were approaching the lights of a town only to look again and see they were fireflies.

Such a long journey it was. It seemed years since I had left Ho that morning, æons since I had unhappily struggled across the Eveto Range, but I remembered with satisfaction I *had* crossed the Eveto Range, and so I concluded in time I should reach Palime, but it seemed a long night, and I was very cold.

At last, though it was wrapped in darkness, I saw we had entered a town; we passed up a wide roadway, and finally got into a yard, and my men began banging on a doorway, and saying over and over again, "Swanzy's."

The German Commissioner had suggested I should go to Swanzy's; and was it possible we had really arrived? It seemed we had.

I can never get over the feeling of shyness when I go up to a total stranger's house and practically demand hospitality. True, I had in my pocket a telegram from Mr Percy Shaw, one of Swanzy's directors, asking his agents to give me that hospitality, but still I felt dreadfully shy as I waited there in the yard for some sign of life from out of the dark building. It came at last, and in English too.

"Who is dere?" said a voice, and my heart sank. I thought it must be a negro, since I knew the agent was a German, and thought he would be sure to hail in his own tongue. Somehow I felt I could not have stood a negro that night. Prejudices are very strong when one is tired.

But I was wrong. The agent was a German, and down long flights of stairs he came in his dressing-gown, welcoming me, and presently was doing all he could for my comfort. He roused out an unwilling cook, he got cocoa and wine, South-Australian wine to my surprise, and hot cakes, and bread, and fruit, and then when I was refreshed, my baggage not yet having come in, he solemnly conducted me to my bedroom, and presented me with a couple of blankets and a very Brodbignag pair of slippers. I was far more tired than when I had'crossed the Eveto Range, and I undressed, got into bed, wrapped myself up in those warm blankets, and slept the sleep of the woman who knows she has arrived at rail-head, and that her difficult travelling is over.

CHAPTER XVI
ONE OF THE CURSES OF THE DARK CONTINENT

The neat little town of Palime—The market—The breakfast—A luxury for the well-to-do—Mount Klutow—The German Sleeping Sickness Camp—The German's consideration for the hammock-boys—Misahohe, a beautiful road, well-shaded—A kindly welcome—The little boys that were cured—Dr von Raven, a devotee to science—The town of the sleeping sickness patients—"Last year strong man, this year finish"—Extreme poverty and self-denial—A ghastly, horrible, lingering and insidious disease—Dr von Raven's message to the English people.

Palime is the neatest of little towns, set at the foot of some softly rounded hills. Not hills clothed with dense bush such as I had come across farther west, but hills covered with grass, emerald in the brilliant sunshine, with just here and there a tree to give it a park-like appearance. And the town, it is hardly necessary to say, was spotlessly neat and tidy. All the streets were swept and garnished, and all the fences were whole, for if a German puts up a picket fence, he intends it for a permanency, and not for a fuel supply for the nearest huts. That the streets were neat was perhaps a little surprising, for every morning, beginning at dawn, in those streets there was held a market in which all manner of goods, native and European, were exposed for sale, spread out on the ground or on stalls. I looked with interest to see if I could notice any difference between the native under English and under German rule in the markets, and I came to the conclusion that there was none whatever. Here, at rail-head, both native and European goods were bought and sold, and here too the people took their alfresco meals. The native of West Africa usually starts the morning with a little porridge, made of cassada, which is really the same root from which comes our tapioca, but his tapioca is so thin you can drink it, and it looks and smells rather like water starch. It was being made and served out "all hot" at a copper a gourd, the customer providing his own gourd, and the porridge being in a goodsized earthen pot fixed on three stones over a little fire of sticks, or else the fire was built inside another pot out of which one side and the top had been knocked. Porridge of course is not very staying, so a little later on good ladies make their appearance who fry maize-meal balls in palm oil, and sell them for two a "copper," the local name for a *pfennig*, which is not copper at all, but nickel. Very appetising indeed look these balls. The little flat earthenware pan on the fire is full of boiling palm oil, and the seller mixes very carefully the maize meal, water, a little salt, and some native pepper, till it is smooth like batter, such as a cook would make a pancake of, then it is dropped into the boiling oil, and the result, in a minute or so, is a round, brown ball, which looks and smells delicious. Sometimes trade is brisk, and they are bought straight out of the pan, but when it slacks they are taken out and heaped up on a calabash. I conclude that it is only the aristocracy who indulge in such luxuries, for I am told that the average wage of a labourer in Palime here is ninepence a day, but judging by what I saw, there must have been a good many of the aristocracy in Palime. After all, the woman from the time she is a tiny child is always self-supporting, so in a community where every man and woman is self-supporting, I conclude that many luxuries are attainable that would not be possible when one man has to provide for many.

PORRIDGE SELLERS IN THE MARKET, PALIME.

The butchers' shops presided over as they are on the Gold Coast by Hausas are not inviting, and tend to induce strong vegetarian views in anyone who looks upon them, and the amount of very highly smelling stink-fish makes the vegetarian regime very narrow. But there are other things beside foodstuffs for sale; from every railing flutter gay cloths from Manchester, or its rival on the Coast, Keta, and there were several women selling very nice earthenware pots, that attracted me very much. They were the commonest household utensils of the native woman; she uses the smaller ones as plates and dishes, and the larger ones for water, for washing, or for storage. The big ones were terribly expensive and cost a whole sixpence, while a penny brought me a big store of small ones. I thought how very quaint and pretty my balcony at home would look with plants growing in these pots from such a far corner of the earth, and so I bought largely, even though I knew I should have to engage a couple of extra carriers for them, and my host applauded my taste.

That young German was very kindly. I showed him my telegram, but he laughed at it, and gave me to understand that of course I was welcome anyhow, though again I can certainly see no of course about it. Why should he, in the kindness of his heart, put himself out for me, a total stranger, who did not even belong to his nation? Still he did.

I was bent on going on to Mount Klutow, the German Sleeping Sickness Camp, and he said he had never seen it, though it was only a short distance away, so he would get carriers and come with me. Accordingly we got carriers, paying them threepence extra because it was Sunday, and went up to Mount Klutow. They were very good carriers, but since I have heard so much about the German's inconsiderateness to the native, I must put it on record that when we came to a steep part of the road, and it was very steep, though a most excellent road, that German not only got out and walked himself, but expected me to do the same. I did of course, but many and many a time have I made my men carry me over far worse places, and many an Englishman have I seen doing likewise.

Again I must put it on record that these German roads are most excellent. They are smooth and wide, well-rolled and hard, and they are shady, a great boon in such a climate. Every native tree that is suitable has been allowed to stand, and others have been planted, shapely, dark-green mangoes and broad-leaved teak, and since all undergrowth has been cleared away, the road seems winding through a beautiful park, while there is absolutely no mosquito. During all my stay in German territory I never slept under a mosquito curtain, and I never saw that abomination, a mosquito-proof room. The Germans evidently think it is easier to do away with the mosquito.

Misahohe is a little Government station, set on the side of the mountain up which we were climbing. It looks from a distance something like a Swiss chalet, and the view from there is as magnificent as that from Anum mountain itself, only here there are white men connected, I think, with the German medical station to see and appreciate its beauties. On and on went the beautiful road; but even the Germans have not yet succeeded in getting rid of the tsetse fly, and so though the roads are good, there are as yet no horses. We met great carts of trade goods going to Kpando, fifteen miles away, and they were drawn and pushed their slow, slow journey by panting, struggling Kroo boys. Strongly as I should object to carrying a load on my head, I really think it would be worse to turn the wheels of a laden cart, spoke by spoke, while you slowly worked it up-hill.

At Mount Klutow, the German Sleeping Sickness Camp, there is no timber, and the first impression is of barrenness. We went up and up, and I, who had not yet recovered from my long day's journey to Palime, was exceedingly thankful when my escort allowed me to lie in my hammock till we arrived at a plateau surrounded by low hills. It was really the top of the mountain. There was a poor-looking European bungalow, a very German wooden kiosk on the other side of the road, and a winding road, with on either side of it little brown native huts built of clay, and thatched. It is just a poor-looking native village, with the huts built rather farther apart than the native seems to like his huts when he can choose, and none of the usual shelter trees which he likes about his village. After the magnificent tropical scenery we had just passed through it looked dreary in the extreme, but the young man who came out of the bungalow and made us most kindly welcome, Dr von Raven, the doctor in charge, explained that this barrenness was the very reason of its existence. They wanted a place that the cool winds swept, and they wanted a place that gave no harbour to the *glossina pal palis*, the tsetse fly that conveys the disease. Mount Klutow was ideal.

I had hesitated a little about visiting a doctor and asking him for information. I had no claim, no letters of introduction, and I should not have been surprised if he had paid no attention to me, but, on the contrary, Dr von Raven was kindness itself. He took us to the little kiosk and sent for wine and cakes and beer, so that we might be refreshed after our hot journey, though it was hardly hot here. The good things were brought by two small boys, and the doctor put his hand first on one shoulder and then on the other, and turned the little laughing black faces for me to see.

"Sleeping sickness," said he. "Cured," and he gave them a friendly cuff and let them go. He knew very little English, and I knew no German, and Mr Fesen's, even though he was agent for an English firm, was of the scantiest; so that it was a process of difficulty to collect information, and it was only done by the infinite kindness and patience of the two Germans. Dr von Raven produced papers and showed me statistics, and so by degrees I learned all there is to be known, and then he took me round and showed me the patients.

Many men in Africa count themselves exiles, but never saw I more clearly the attributes of exile than in Dr von Raven. Comforts he had none, and his house was bare almost to poverty. Here he had lived for two and a half years without going home, and here he intended to live till some experiments he had in hand were complete. A devotee to science truly, but a cheerful, intensely interested one, with nothing of the martyr about him. Very few white people he must have seen, and he said himself he had only been down to the nearest town of Palime three times in two years, but he looked far better in health than many a man I have seen who has been on the Coast only as many months.

KROO BOYS DRAWING CART ON THE WAY TO MESMORIE.

From the doctor's house there curves a road about a kilometre in length, and off this are the houses of the sleeping sickness patients. Two and two they are built, facing each other, two rooms in each house and plenty of space between. They are built of mud, with holes for doors and windows, and the roofs are of grass—native huts of the most primitive description. Each patient has a room, and each is allowed one relative to attend him. Thus a husband may have a wife, a mother her daughter, and between them they have an allowance of sevenpence a day for food, ample in a country where the usual wage for a day labourer is ninepence. There are one hundred and fifty-five patients in all, and besides them there are a few soldiers for dignity, because the neighbouring chiefs would think very lightly of a man who had not evidences of power behind him, and so whenever the doctor passes they come tumbling out of the guard-room to salute him. There are also a certain number of labourers, because though many of the sick are quite capable of waiting on themselves, it would never do for them to go beyond the confines of the camp, and possibly, or probably, infect the flies that abound just where wood and water are to be had.

Of course there is a market where the women meet and chat and buy their provisions; there are cookhouses and all the attributes of a rather poor native village, but a village where the people are among the surroundings to which they have been accustomed all their lives and in which they are more thoroughly at home than in a hospital. Part of the bareness may be attributed to economy, but the effect is greatly heightened by the absence of all vegetation. Anything that might afford shelter for the flies or shut out the strong, health-giving breezes that blow right across the plateau is strictly forbidden. And here were people in all stages of the disease—those who had just come in, who to the ordinary eye appeared to have nothing wrong with them, great, strong, healthy-looking men, men of thews and sinews who had been completely cured, and those who were past all help and were lying waiting for death.

"You would like to see them?" asked the doctor.

I said I would, and I would like to take a photograph or two if I might. My stock of plates was getting woefully scarce.

"Yes," he said, and we went down the roadway.

A man was borne out of one of the huts and laid on the ground in the brilliant sunshine. He was wasted to skin and bone, his eyes were sunken and half-open, showing the whites, his skeleton limbs lay helpless, and his head fell forward like a baby's. The doctor pointed to him pitifully.

"Last year," he said, "strong man like this," indicating the men who bore him; "this year—finish."

"He will die?"

"Oh, he will die—soon."

DYING OF SLEEPING SICKNESS.

And the great brawny savages who carried the stretcher, stark but for a loin cloth and a necklace, with their hair cut into cock's combs, had come there with sleeping sickness and were cured. They brought them out of all the huts to show the visitor—women in the last stages after epilepsy had set in, with weary eyes, worn faces, and contracted limbs, happy little children with swollen glands, a woman with atoxyl blindness who was cured, a man with atoxyl blindness who, in spite of all, will die. They were there in all stages of the disease, in all stages of recovery. Some looked as if there was nothing the matter with them, but the enlarged glands in the neck could always be felt. The doctor did not seem very hopeful. "We could cure it," he said; "it is quite curable if we could only get the cases early enough. Not 2 per cent, of the flies are infected, and of course every man who is bitten by an infected fly does not necessarily contract the disease."

It comes on very insidiously. Three weeks it takes to develop, and then the patient has a little fever every evening. In the morning his temperature is down again, only to rise once more in the evening. Sometimes he will have a day without a rise, sometimes three or four, but you would find, were you to look, the parasites in the blood. After three or four months the glands of the neck begin to swell, and this is the time when the natives recognise the danger and excise the glands. But swollen glands are not always caused by sleeping sickness, and, in that case, if the wounds heal properly, the patient recovers; but if the parasites are in the blood then such rough surgery only causes unnecessary suffering without in any way retarding the progress of the disease. Slowly it progresses, very slowly. Sometimes it takes three or four months before nervous symptoms come on, sometimes it may be twelve months, and after that the case is hopeless. Not all the physicians in the world in the present state of medical knowledge could cure it. In Europeans—and something like sixty Europeans are known to have contracted the disease—very often immediately after the bite of the fly, symptoms have been noticed on the skin, red swellings, but in the black man apparently the skin is not affected.

The treatment is of the simplest, but the doctor only arrived at it after careful experiment. After having ascertained by examination of the blood that the patient has sleeping sickness he weighs the patient and gives him five centigrams per kilogram of his own weight of arsenophenylycin. This is divided into two portions and given on two consecutive days, and the treatment is finished. Of course the patient is carefully watched and his blood tested, and if at the end of ten days the parasites are still found, the dose is repeated. Sometimes it is found that the toxin has no effect, and then the doctor resorts to atoxyl, which he administers the same way every two days, with ten days between the doses. This has one grave drawback, for sometimes in conjunction with sleeping sickness it causes blindness. Out of eighty-five cases that have taken atoxyl since 1908 five have gone blind. I saw there one young man cured and stone-blind, and one woman also cured and but just able to see men "as trees walking." Apparently there was nothing wrong with their eyes, but the blank look of the blind told that they could not see.

At first this camp here up among the hills was looked upon with suspicion by the natives, and they resisted all efforts to bring them to it. They feared, as they have always feared, all German thoroughgoing methods. But gradually, as is only natural, a good thing makes its own reputation, and the natives who were before so fearful come long distances to seek help where they know only help can be found.

SLEEPING SICKNESS AFTER NERVOUS SYMPTOMS HAVE SET IN.

After we had walked all round the camp and got well soaked with the ordinary Togo afternoon shower, of which none of us took any notice, we went back to the kiosk for more refreshment, and here we found waiting us one of the Roman Catholic Fathers from Palime. He was a fair-bearded man in a white helmet and a long, white-cotton *soutane*, which somehow, even in this country of few clothes, gave the appear-ence of extreme poverty and self-denial. He had come up on a bicycle and had a great deal to say about the sleeping sickness. A day or two before he had been travelling two days west of Palime and he was asked by a native if he could speak English, and, when he assented, was taken to see a sick man. The man was a stranger to the people round and could only make himself understood in pigeon English. He told the Father he lived six days away, in British territory, and as he talked he perpetually took snuff. "Why," asked the Father, "do you take snuff when you talk to me?" Because, the man explained, he had the sickness, and unless he took the strong, pungent snuff into his nostrils he could not talk, his head would fall forward, and he would become drowsy at once. This, he went on to say, was his reason for being here, so far from his home. He had heard there was a doctor here who could cure the sickness, and he was journeying to him as fast as he could. It is sad to think after such faith that he had probably left it too late.

"It is very difficult, indeed," said the doctor, "to be sure of a cure." The patient is discharged as cured and bound over to come back every six months for examination, and if each time his blood is examined it is free from parasites, all is well. He is certainly cured. But he has gone back to his home in an infected district, and if after six months or twelve months the parasite is again found, who is to say whether he has been re-infected or whether there has been a recrudescence of the old disorder? Occasionally, says the doctor, it is impossible to find the parasite in the blood, while the patient undoubtedly dies of sleeping sickness; the parasite is in the brain.

Since 1908 there have been four hundred cases through the doctor's hands. Of these 19 per cent, have died of sleeping sickness, 67 per cent, have been sent away as cured, and about 3 per cent, have died of other causes. Only ten of those sent away as cured have failed to present themselves for re-examination, and in this land where every journey must be made on foot, and food probably carried for the journey, it speaks very well, I think, for both doctor and patients that so many have come back to him. He is far kinder, probably, than the natives would be to each other—too kind for his own convenience, for the natives fear his laboratory, and will not come there at night, because when a patient is dying and past all other help he has him brought there to die. "Why?" I asked. "I may be able to help a little," he said. "But how kind!" He shrugged his shoulders with a little smile. "It is nothing, it is doctor," and he waved the thought aside as if I were making too much of it.

The disease comes, so says Dr von Raven, from west to east, and was first noticed in the Gambia in 1901. As long ago as 1802 a Dr Winterbottom described the sleeping sickness, and in 1850 a slavetrader noticed the swelling of the glands and refused to take slaves so afflicted. Undoubtedly cases of sleeping sickness must have been imported to the West Indies or America, but owing to the absence of the *glossina palpalis* to act as host the disease did not spread. That it is a ghastly, horrible, lingering, and insidious disease, that every man who has it where the *glossina palpalis* abounds is a danger to the community among whom he dwells, no one can doubt. They say that after a certain time the natives of a district may acquire immunity, but as this immunity comes only after severe suffering, it is perhaps better to stop the spread of the disease. The Germans have no hesitation in restricting the movements of the native if he is likely to become a public danger, but the British Government is very loath to interfere with a man's rights, even though it be the right to spread disease and death. Dr von Raven and the English Dr Horne met in conference a few months ago with the object of urging upon their respective Governments the absolute necessity for allowing no man to cross the Volta unless he have a certificate from a medical man that he is free from sleeping sickness. They contend, probably rightly, that a little trouble now would ensure the non-spread of the disease and assist materially in stamping it out. The Volta is a natural barrier; there are only two or three well-known crossing places where the people pass to and fro; and here they think a man might well be called upon to present his certificate. Against this is urged the undoubted fact that large numbers of the people are at no time affected, and, therefore, it would be going to a great deal of trouble and expense to effect a small thing. But is it a small thing?

"You write," said the doctor as he bid me farewell; "you write?"

I said I did a little.

"Then tell the English people," said he, "how necessary it is to stamp out this disease while it is yet small."

And so to the best of my ability I give his message, the message of a man who is denying himself all things that go to make life pleasant, for the sake of curing this disease, and if that sacrifice is worth while, and he says it is well worth while, then I think it should be well worth the while of us people, who are responsible for these dark children we govern, to put upon them, even at cost to themselves and us, such restrictions as may help to save in the future even 2 per cent, of the population from a ghastly and lingering death.

CHAPTER XVII
GERMAN VERSUS ENGLISH METHODS

Lome, the capital of Togo—A bad situation but the best laid-out town on the Coast—Avenues of trees—Promising gardens—The simple plan by which the Germans ensure the making of the roads—The prisoner who feared being "leff"—The disappointed lifer—The A.D.C.'s kindness—The very desirable prison garb—The energetic Englishman—How to make a road—Building a reputation.

People who sigh, "I am such a bad traveller," as if it were something to be proud of, and complain of the hardships of a railway journey, should come upon the railway after they have had several days in a canoe, some hard walking, and some days' hammock journeying, and then they would view it in quite a different light. I felt it was the height of luxury when I stepped into a first-class railway carriage on the little narrow gauge railway, that goes from Palime to Lome, the capital of Togo.

My host had insisted on telegraphing to Swanzy's there.

"They meet you. More comfortable."

Undoubtedly it would be more comfortable, but I wondered what I had done that I should merit so much consideration for my comfort from men who were not only total strangers, but belonged to a nation that has not the reputation for putting itself out for women. I can only say that no one has been kinder to me than those Germans of Togo, and for their sakes I have a very soft corner in my heart for all their nation, and when we English do not like them I can only think it is because of some misunderstanding that a little better knowledge on both sides would clear away.

You do not see the country well from a railway train even though the stoppages are many. I have a far better idea of the country between the English border and Palime than of the country between Palime and Lome. I was the only first-class passenger; the white men travelled second class, and all the coloured people third, that is in big, empty, covered trucks where they took their food, their babies, their bedding, their baggage, and in fact seemed to make themselves quite as comfortable as if they were at home.

And at Lome a young German from Messrs Swanzy's met me with a cart and carriers for my gear, and carried me off and installed me at their fine house on the sea-front as if I had every right to be there, which I certainly had not.

Lome is the most charming town I have seen in West Africa. It is neat and tidy and clean, it is beautifully laid out, and the buildings are such as would do credit to any nation. Very evident it is that the German does not consider himself an exile, but counts himself lucky to possess so fine a country, and is bent on making the best of it. For Lome has certainly been made the very best of. Only fifteen years ago did the Germans move their capital from Little Pope in the east to Lome in the west of their colony, not a great distance, for the whole sea-board is only thirty-five miles in length, and all that length is, I believe, swamp. Lome is almost surrounded by swamp; its very streets are rescued from it, but with German thoroughness those streets are well-laid-out, the roads well-made and well-kept, and are planted with trees, palms, flamboyant, and the handsome *ficus elasticus*. Here is a picture of a street in Lome, and the trees are only four years old, but already they stretch across the road and make a pleasant shade. The gardens and the trees of Lome made a great impression on me. Any fences one sees are neat, but as a rule they do not have many fences, only round every bungalow is a well-laid-out, well-kept, tropical garden; if it is only just made you know it will be good in the future because of the promise fulfilled in the garden beside it.

A STREET IN LOME.

All the Government bungalows look like young palaces, and are built to hold two families, the higher-class man having the choice of the flats, and generally taking the upper. Indeed I could find no words to express my admiration for this German capital which compared so very favourably with the English capital I had left but a short time before.

When I had talked to the Commissioner at Ho about the magnificent roads, I had hinted at the forced labour which is talked of so openly in the English colony as being a sin of the Germans. But he denied it.

"How do you make your roads then?" I asked.

"There is a tax of six shillings a head or else a fortnight's labour a year. It is right. If we have no roads how can we have trade?" and I, thinking of the 25 per cent, of the cocoa harvest left up the Afram river because "we no be fit to tote," quite agreed.

Every English village has some sort of tax by which the roads are kept in order, why object if that tax is paid in the most useful sort of kind, namely labour.

Very very wisely it seems to me have the Germans laid the foundations of their colony, and though it has not paid in the past, it is paying now and in the future it will pay well.

But a certain set of people were not quite as happy as those in the English towns, and that was the prisoners working in the streets. They had iron collars round their necks and were chained together two and two, and though they were by no means depressed, they were not as cheery as the English prisoners. The English negro prisoner is unique. His punishment has been devised by people at home who do not understand the negro and his limitations, and the difficulty of adequately punishing is one of the difficulties of administration in an English colony.

"How do you keep your villages so neat?" I asked the Germans.

"If they are not neat we fine them."

"But if they do not pay the fine?"

"Then we beat them."

And though it may sound rather brutal, I am inclined to think that is the form of teaching the negro thoroughly understands. He is not yet educated up to understanding the disgrace of going to prison, and regards it somewhat in the light of a pleasant change from the ordinary routine.

The German prisoner is clad in his own rags, the garb an ordinary working-man usually wears. The English prisoner is at the expense of the Government clad in a neat white suit ornamented with a broad arrow. He can hardly bring himself to believe that this is meant for a disgrace, and rather admires himself I fancy in his new costume. Many many are the tales told of the prisoner and his non-realisation of the punishment meted out to him. Once a party of three or four were coming along a street in Freetown, under the charge of a warder, and they stopped to talk to someone. Then they went on again, but one of the party lingered behind to finish his gossip.

The warder looked back. They were still in earnest conversation.

"No. 14," he called, warningly.

No. 14 paid no attention.

"No. 14," a little more peremptorily.

Still No. 14 was interested in his friend.

"No. 14," called the warder sternly, as one who was threatening the worst penalties of the law, "if you no come at once, I leff you, No. 14."

And No. 14 with the dire prospect of being "leff" to his own devices, shut out of paradise in fact, ran to join the others.

There is another story current in Accra about an unfortunate prisoner who got eight months extra. He had been "leff," and, finding himself shut out, promptly broke into prison; what was a poor man to do? At any rate, the authorities gave him an extra eight months, so I suspect all parties were entirely satisfied.

Then there was the man who was in for life, and was so thoroughly well-behaved that after sixteen years the Government commuted his sentence and released him. Do you think that prisoner was pleased? He was in a most terrible state of mind, and the mournful petition went up—What had he done to be so treated? He had served the Government faithfully for sixteen years, and now they were turning him away for absolutely no fault whatever.

He prayed them to reconsider their decision and restore him to the place he had so ably filled!

The fact of the matter is, the negro is very much better for a strong hand over him. He is a child, and like a child should have his hours of labour and his hours of play apportioned to him. The firm hand is what he requires and appreciates. What he may develop into in the future I do not know, with his mighty strength, his fine development, and his superb health; if he had but a mind to match it he must overrun the earth. Luckily for us he has not as yet a mind to match it, he is a child, with a child's wild and unrestrained desires, and like a child it is well for him that some stronger mind should guide his ways. So he thoroughly appreciates prison discipline, but it never occurs to him that it is any disgrace. Even when he has reached a higher standing than that of the peasant, it is hard to make him understand that there is anything disgraceful in going to prison.

Not so very long ago there was a black barrister in one of the West-African capitals who had been home to England. He was naturally a man of some education and standing. Now the Governor's A.D.C. had been for some little time inspector of prisoners. There was a dinner-party at Government House, and what was this young man's astonishment to have his hand seized and shaken very warmly by the black barrister who was a guest.

"I have to thank you," said he, "for your great kindness to my mother while she was in prison, when I was in England last year."

Clearly, then, it seems that the Germans are on the right track when they do not dress their prisoners in any special garb. If you come to think of it, a white suit marked with a broad arrow is quite as smart and a good deal cheaper than a red cloth marked with a blue broom, and the black man naturally feels some pride in swaggering round in it.

A good sound beating is of course the correct thing, and though a good sound beating is not legal in English territory, luckily, say I very luckily—for the negro does not understand leniency, he regards it as a sign of weakness—it is many a time administered *sub rosa*, and the inferior respects the kindly man who is his master, who if he do wrong will have no hesitation in having him laid out and a round dozen administered. If English administration was not hampered by the well-meaning foolishness of folks at home, I venture to think that native towns would be cleaner and West-African health would be better. Because much as I admire the Germans and the wonderful fixed plan on which they have built up their colony, I have known Englishmen who could get just as good results if their hands had not been tied. And occasionally one meets or hears of a man who will not allow his hands to be tied.

In a certain district by the Volta there are excellent roads much appreciated by the natives. Now these roads were extra vile and likely to remain so before Government could be prevailed upon to stir up the local chiefs to a sense of their duty. But there was an officer in that district who thoroughly understood how to deal with the black man, and he was far enough away from headquarters to make sure of a free hand. He found the making of those roads simple enough. He bought a few dozen native hoes and set a sentry on the road to be made with a rifle over his shoulder and a watch upon his wrist. His orders were to stop every man who passed, put a hoe into his hand, and force him to work upon that road for half an hour by the watch. History sayeth not what happened if he rebelled, but of course he did not rebel. Once, so says rumour, this mighty coloniser came to a place where the roads were worse than usual, which from my experience is saying they were very bad indeed, and he sent for the Chief. The Chief said he could not make his people come to work—the English had destroyed his power.

"All right," said the energetic Englishman, "the fine is £5. If they are not in in half an hour it'll be £10, and I'll bring 'em in in handcuffs." He began to collect them—with the handcuffs—but the second fine was not necessary. They were both illegal, but, as I have said, he was far away from headquarters, and he made those roads. The native bore no malice. It was exactly the treatment he understood. There was a rude justice in it. It was patent to every eye that the road was bad. It was common sense that the man who used it should mend it, and as long as that official was in the country there were in his district roads and bridges as good as any in German Togo; and bridges as a rule are conspicuous by their absence in English territory. Also, as the Government never sends a man back to the same place, this man's good work is all falling back into disrepair, for it is hardly to be expected that Government will be lucky enough to get another man who will dare set its methods at defiance.

Lome, like Accra, has made an effort to get the better of the fierce surf that makes landing so difficult all along the African coast, and they, instead of a useless breakwater, have built a great bridge out into deep water, and at the end of this bridge a large wharf pier or quay, high above the waves, where passengers and goods can be lifted by cranes, and the men can walk the half-mile to the shore dry-shod, or the goods can be taken by train right to the very doors of the warehouses for which they are intended. This cost the much less sum of £100,000. It was highly successful, and a great source of pride to all Togo till a tremendous hurricane a week or so after I had left, swept away the bridge part and left Lome cut off from communication with the rest of the coast, for so successful had this great bridge been they had no surf boats. Still, in spite of that disaster, I think the Germans have managed better than the English, for the bridge even after the necessary repairs have been done will have cost scarcely £150,000, much less than Accra's breakwater, and of course there is no necessity for the sand-pump.

I feel it is ungracious to abuse my own nation and not to recognise all they have done for the negro—all they have done in the way of colonisation, but after that journey across the little-known part of the Gold Coast into the little-known part of German Togo, I can but see that there is something much to be admired in the thorough German methods. Particularly would I commend the manner in which they conserve the trees and preserve the natural beauties of the country. A beauty-spot to them is a beauty-spot, whether it be in the Fatherland or in remote West Africa, while England seems indifferent if the beautiful place be not within the narrow seas. Possibly she has no eyes; possibly she is only calm in her self-conceit, certain of her position, while Germany is building—building herself a reputation.

CHAPTER XVIII
KETA ON THE SAND

The safety of the seashore—Why they do not plant trees in English territory—The D.C.'s prayer—Quittah or Keta—The Bremen Sisters—The value of fresh air as a preventive of fever—A polygamous household—The Awuna people—The backsliding clerk of the Bremen Mission—Incongruity of antimacassars and polygamy—Naming the child—"Laughing at last" and "Not love made you"—Forms of marriage—The cost of a wife—How to poison an enemy—Loving and dutiful children—The staple industry of the place—Trading women—The heat of Keta.

Having got into Lome the question was how to get out of it. I wanted to go to Keta, twenty-seven miles away in British territory, and my idea was to go by sea as I could do it in three hours at the very most, and Elder Dempster, having very kindly franked me on their steamers, it would cost me nothing save the tips to the surf boats that landed me; but there was one great thing against that—my hosts told me that very often the surf was so bad it was impossible to land at Keta. The head of Swanzy's had a man under him at Keta, and when he went to inspect he invariably went overland. That decided me. I too must go overland.

But carriers were by no means cheap. I had got hammock-boys to carry me the thirty miles from Ho to Palime for two shillings, and here for twenty-seven miles along the shore I paid my hammock-boys six shillings and sixpence and my carriers five shillings and sixpence, so that my pots were adding to their original price considerably.

So on a fine, hot morning in May I was, with my train of carriers, on the road once more. First the going was down between groves of palms by the Governor's palace, which is a palace indeed, and must have cost a small fortune. A very brief walk brought us to the Border, and then the contrast was once more marked. The English villages were untidy and filthy, with a filth that was emphasised now that I had seen what could be done by a little method and orderliness; those Coast villages remain in my mind as a mixture of pigs, and children, and stagnant water, and all manner of litter and untidiness. One saving grace they had was that they were set among the nice clean sand of the seashore that absorbed as much as possible all the dirt and moisture, and we passed along through groves of cocoa-nut palms that lent a certain charm and picturesqueness to the scene. I am never lonely beside the sea; the murmur of its waves is company, and I cannot explain it, but I am never afraid. I do not know why, but I could not walk in a forest by myself, yet I could walk for miles along the seashore and never fear, though I suppose many deeds of violence have been done along these shores; but they have been done on the sand, and the waters have swept over them, and washed all memory of them away.

Soon it was evident that we were travelling along almost as narrow a way as that which led along the shore to Half Assinie. There was a lagoon on the right hand, and the sea on the left, and the numerous villages drew their sustenance from the sea and from the cocoa-nut palms in which they were embowered.

All the hot long day we travelled, and at last, towards evening, on either side of the road, we came upon fine shade-trees of an order of *ficus*, planted, it is hardly needful to say, by the Danes who owned this place over thirty years ago. It makes such a wonderful difference, this tree-planting, that I have preached it wherever I went. I met one young D.C. who agreed with me heartily, but explained to me the difficulties of the job in English territory.

I had suggested they might get trees from the agricultural stations that Government is beginning to dot over the country, and he said it was quite possible. In fact they had planted three hundred the year before. The place I was in was rather barren-looking, so I asked where they were. He shrugged his shoulders and pointed to the native sheep and goats; they are only to be distinguished by their tails, and a certain perkiness about the goats.

"But," said I, surprised, "if you plant trees, you should certainly protect them."

"How?" said he.

"Barbed wire," was my idea.

"And where are we to get the money for barbed wire? We put cactus all round those three hundred trees we planted, and then the medical officer got on to us because the cactus held water and became a breeding place for mosquitoes, and so we had to take it away, and I don't believe six of those trees are alive now. You see it is too disheartening."

Another thing that is very disheartening is the fact that tours, as they call a term of service among the English, last twelve months, and that a man at the end of a tour goes away for five months, and very often never again returns to the same place, so that he has no permanent interest in its welfare.

"Give peace in my time, oh Lord," they declare is the prayer of the West-African D.C., and can we wonder? A man is not likely to stir up strife in a place if he is not going to remain long enough to show that he has stirred it up in a good cause. Fancy a German D.C. explaining his failure to have proper shade-trees by the fact that the native sheep and goats had eaten them!

The English have decided that Keta shall be called Quittah, which means nothing at all, but the native name is, and I imagine will be for a long time to come, Keta, which means "On the sand," and on the sand the town literally is. It is simply built on a narrow sand-bank between the ocean and a great lagoon which stretches some days' journey into the interior, and at Keta, at its widest, is never more than a quarter of a mile in extent.

I appealed to the D.C. for quarters, and he very kindly placed me with the Bremen Mission Sisters, and asked me to dinner every night. I feel I must have been an awful nuisance to that D.C., and I am most grateful for his kindness, and still more grateful for his introduction to those kindly mission Sisters.

"Deaconesses" they called themselves; and they had apparently vowed themselves to the service of the heathen as absolutely as any nun, and wore simple little cotton dresses with white net caps. Sister Minna, who had been out for ten long years, going home I think in that time twice, spoke the vernacular like a native, and Sister Connie was learning it. They kept a girls' school where some three hundred girls, ranging from three to thirteen, learned to read, and write, and sew, and sum, and I was introduced to quite a new phase of African life, for never before had I been able to come so closely in touch with the native.

Again I have to put it on record that I have absolutely no sympathy with missionaries. I cannot see the necessity for missions to the heathen; as yet there should be no crumbs to fall from the children's table while the children of Europe are in such a shameful state as many of them are, far worse than any heathen I have ever seen in Africa. But that did not prevent me admiring very much these Sisters, especially Sister Minna. It was a pity her services were lost to Germany, and given to these heathen, who, I am bound to say, loved and respected her deeply.

But Keta was hot. Never in my life have I lived in such a hot place, and the first night they put me to sleep in their best bedroom, in which was erected a magnificent mosquito-proof room, also the window that looked on the back verandah was covered carefully with coloured cretonne to ensure privacy. In spite of all their kindness I spent a terrible night; the want of air nearly killed me, and I arose in the morning weary to death, and begging that I might be allowed to sleep in the garden. There there was a little more air, but the ants, tiny ones that could get through the meshes of my mosquito curtains, walked over me and made life unbearable. Then I put up a prayer that I might be allowed to sleep on the verandah. The good Sisters demurred. It was, in their opinion, rather public; but what was I to do? Sleep I felt I must get, and so every night Grant came over and put up my camp-bed on the verandah, or rather balcony, and every night I slept the comfortable, refreshing sleep of the fresh-air lover, and if a storm of rain came up, as it did not infrequently, this being the beginning of the rainy season, I simply arose and dragged my bed inside, and waited till it was over. I admit this had its drawbacks, but it was better than sleeping inside. The Sisters were perpetually making remarks on my healthy colour, and contrasting it with their own pale faces, and their not infrequent attacks of fever with my apparent immunity, and they came to the same conclusion that I did, that it was insured by my love of fresh air. Why they did not do likewise I do not know, but I suspect they thought it was not quite proper; not the first time in this world that women have suffered from their notions of propriety.

Under the guidance of Sister Minna I began a series of calls, visiting first one of the head chiefs, who had about sixty wives. Some dwelt in little houses off his compound, some were scattered over the town, and some were away in the country. It was the first time I had really been introduced into a polygamous household with understanding eyes, and I went with interest. It is approaching the vital points of life from an entirely different angle.

The Chief received us most graciously. He was a big man, old, with a bald head on which was a horrid red scar, got, he explained, in a big fight. He said he was very pleased to see me, spoke for a moment to one of his attendants, and then presented me with a couple of florins, and wished me well. After all, that was certainly a most substantial sign of goodwill. Then I called upon his wives, young, old, and middle-aged, and I don't even now understand how he managed to have so many without interfering seriously with the natural distribution of men and women. Of course his descendants are many, and many are the complications, for I have seen a married woman, the grand-daughter of the Chief, nursing on her knee her little great-aunt, his daughter, and well spanking her too if she did not come to school quick enough.

One of his old wives had broken her leg, and we visited her; she had a room in his house, and was lying on her bed on the floor, while beside her sat another wife who had come to see how she was getting on.

"If I were a wife," said I, from the outlook of a monogamous country, "I should not call upon another wife a man chose to take, even if she were sick."

"I don't know," said kind-hearted Sister Minna. "I have lived so long in a country like this that I think I should. It is only kind."

And we went from one household to another, and were received most graciously, and generally Sister Minna was given some small sum of money to entertain me. Sometimes it was sixpence, sometimes it was a shilling, sometimes it even rose as high as two shillings, and she was instructed to buy chickens and bananas that I might be well fed. Also they can never tell a white person's age, and many a time she was asked, because I was short, whether I was not a child.

Altogether I was most agreeably struck with these Awuna people, and found there was even something to be said for the polygamous system. I have always, from my youth upwards, admired the woman who worked and made a place for herself in the world, and here were certainly some of my ideals carried out, for every woman in this community was selfsupporting for the greater part of her life, and not only did she support herself, but her children as well. It was in fact not much of a catch to marry a chief; of course, being a rich man, he probably gave her a little more capital to work upon in the beginning, but she had to pay him back, and work all the same.

We visited another household, the home of a clerk in the Bremen Mission Factory, a gentleman who wore a tweed suit and a high collar, and who once had been a pillar of the mission church. He had four wives, and he lived inside a compound with small houses round it, and his house, the big house, on one side. Each wife had her own little home, consisting of two rooms and a kitchen place; the wife without children was the farthest away from him, and the last wife, just married, had a room next his. His sitting-room was quite gorgeous, furnished European fashion with cane chairs, and settee, coloured cushions, an ordinary lamp with a green shade, and a rack, such as one sees on old-fashioned ships, hung with red and green wineglasses. I don't know why I should have felt that antimacassars and tablecloths were out of place with polygamy, but I did, especially as the wives' houses were bare, native houses, where the women squatted on the floor, their bedrooms were dark and dismal hot places, with any amount of girdle beads hanging against the walls. For clothes are but a new fashion in Keta, and the time is not far off when a woman went clothed solely in girdle beads, and so still it is the fashion to have many different girdle beads, though now that they wear cloths over them they are not to be seen except upon the little girls who still very wisely are allowed to go stark. Each woman's children, not only in this house, but in the Chief's house, ran in and out of the other wives' houses in very friendly fashion, and they most of them bore English names—Grace, Rosina, and Elizabeth. And the names, when they are not English, are very curious and well worth remembering. A couple had been married for many years, and at last the longed-for child came. "Laughing at last," they called it. "Come only" is another name. "A cry in my house"—where so long there had been silence. "Every man and his," meaning with pride, "this is mine, I want nothing more." But they are not always pleased. "God gives bad things"—a girl has been born and they have been waiting for a boy. "A word is near my heart," sounds rather tender, but "I forgive you" must have another meaning, and the child would surely not be as well loved as the one its mother called "Sweet thing." Then again girls do not always marry the man they love or would choose, and they will perhaps call their child "Not love made you," but on the whole I think pleasant names predominate, and many a child is called "So is God," "God gives good things," or merely "Thanks." Often too a child is called after the day of the week upon which it is born.

"What day were you born?" asked the Chief of me.

"Wednesday," I said.

"Then your name is Aquwo," said he.

Marriage in a country like this has a somewhat different status from what it does, say in England. What a woman wants most of all is children; motherhood is the ideal, and the unmarried woman with a child is a far more enviable person than the married woman without, and even in this land, where motherhood is everything, there was in every household that I visited an unhappy woman without children, because vice has been rampant along the Coast for hundreds of years. You may know her at once by her sad face, for not only is she deeply grieved, but everyone despises her, as they do not despise the woman who has had a child without being married. Of course parents prefer their daughters to be chaste, and if a man marries what the Sister described as a "good" girl, he will probably give her a pair of handsome bracelets to mark his appreciation of the fact, but if on the other hand a daughter, without being married, suddenly presents the household with an addition, they are not more vexed than if the daughter in civilised lands failed to pass her examination, outran her allowance, or perhaps got herself too much talked about with the best-looking ineligible in the neighbourhood. It is a natural thing for a girl to do, and at any rate a child is always an asset.

COMPOUND OF A HOUSE IN KETA.

There is one binding form of marriage that is absolutely indissoluble. If the man and woman, in the presence of witnesses, drink a drop or two of each other's blood, nothing can part them; they are bound for ever, a binding which tells more heavily upon the woman than the man, because he is always free to marry as many wives as he likes, while she is bound only to him, and whatever he does, no one, after such a ceremony, would give her shelter should she wish to leave him. All other marriages are quite easily dissolved, and very often the partings occasion but little heart-burnings on either side. The great desire of everyone is children, and once that is attained, the object of the union is accomplished, wherefore I fancy it is very seldom couples, or rather women, take the trouble to bind themselves so indissolubly. The most respectable form of marriage is for a man to take a girl and seclude her with an old woman to look after her for from five to nine months after marriage. She does no work, but gives herself up to the luxury and enjoyment of the petted, spoiled wife. Her brothers and sisters and her friends come and see her, but she does not pass outside the threshold, and being thus kept from the strong sunlight, she becomes appreciably lighter in colour, and is of course so much the more beautiful. He may take several women after this fashion, and all the marriages are equally binding, but of course this means that he must have a little money. Another kind of marriage is when the man simply gives the woman presents of cloths, and provides her with a house. It is equally binding but is not considered so respectful; there is something of the difference we see between the hasty arrangement in a registry office and the solemn ceremony at St George's, Hanover Square.

One thing is certain, that when an Awuna man asks a girl to marry him, she will most certainly say "No." Formerly the parents were always asked, and they invariably said "No," and then the man had to ask again and again, and to reason away their objections to him as a suitor. Now, as women are getting freer under English rule, the girl herself is asked, and she makes a practice of saying "No" at least two or three times, in order to be able to tell him afterwards she did not want him. Even after they are Christians, says Sister Minna, the women find it very hard to give up this fiction that they do not want to marry, and the girl finds it very difficult to say "Yes" in church.

She likes to pretend that she does not want the man. As a rule this is, I believe, true enough. There is no trust or love between the sexes; you never see men and women together. A woman only wants a man in order that she may have children, and one would do quite as well as another.

After marriage the woman has a free time for a little. She does not have to begin cooking her husband's meals at once, and this also holds good after the first baby is born. A man is considered by public opinion a great churl if he does not get somebody to wait on his wife and fetch her water from the well at this time. After the second baby they are not so particular, and a woman must just make her own arrangements and manage as best she may. It is a woman's pride to bear children, and to the man they are a source of wealth, for the boys must work for the father for a time at least, and the girls are always sold in marriage, for a wife costs at least five or six pounds.

With all due deference to these kindly missionaries, I cannot think that Christianity has made much progress, for these Awuna people have the reputation of being great poisoners. One of the Chief's wives offered me beer, stuff that looked and tasted like thin treacle, and she tasted it first to show me, said the Sister, that it was quite safe; but also she explained they insert a potent poison under the thumb nail, drink first to show that the draft is innocuous, and then offer the gourd to the intended victim, having just allowed the tip of the thumb nail to dip beneath the liquid.

The early morning is the correct time to do the most important things. Thus if a man wants a girl in marriage he appears at her parents' house at the uncomfortable hour of four o'clock in the morning, and asks her hand. The morning after the Chief had given me a dash, I sent Grant round early, not at four o'clock I fear, when in the Tropics it is quite dark, with a box of biscuits and two boxes of chocolates and the next morning early he sent me his ring as a sign that he had received my dash and was pleased. If by any chance they cannot come and thank you in the morning, they say, "To-morrow morning, when the cock crows, I shall thank you again." They use rather an amusing proverb for thanking; where we should say, "I have not words to thank you," they say, "The hen does not thank the dunghill," because here in these villages, where they do not provide food for the fowls, the dunghill provides everything. Sister Minna once received a very large present of ducks and yams from a man, so she used this proverb in thanking him, as one he would thoroughly understand. Quick came the response, "Oh please do not say so. I am the hen, and you are the dunghill," which does not sound very complimentary translated into English.

It was delightful staying here at the Mission House, and seeing quite a new side of African life, seeing it as it were from the inside. Every day at seven o'clock in the morning the little girls came to school, and I could hear the monotonous chant of their learning, as I sat working on the verandah. Somewhere about nine school was out and it was time for the second breakfast. The second breakfast was provided by the little markets that were held in the school grounds, where about a dozen women or young girls came with food-stuffs to sell at a farthing, or a copper, for they use either English or German money, a portion. They were rather appetising I thought, and quite a decent little breakfast could be bought for a penny. There were maize-meal balls fried in palm oil, a sort of pancake also made of maize meal and eaten with a piece of cocoa-nut, bananas, split sections of pine-apple, mangoes, little balls of boiled rice served on a plantain leaf, and pieces of the eternal stink-fish. Every woman appears to be a born trader, and I have seen a little girl coming to school with a platter on her head, on which were arranged neatly cut sections of pine-apple, She had managed to acquire a copper or two, and began her career as a trader by selling to the children for their school breakfast. She will continue that career into her married life, and till she is an old old woman past all work, when her children will look after her, for they are most dutiful children, and Christian or heathen never neglect their parents, especially their mother.

Old maids of course you never see, and it is considered much more natural, as I suppose it is, that a woman should have a child by a man whom she has met just casually, than that she should live an old maid. There was a good missionary woman who took a little girl into her household and guarded her most carefully. The only time that girl was out of her sight was once or twice a week for half an hour when she went to fetch water from the well. Presently that girl was the mother to a fine, lusty boy, and the missionary's wife was told and believed that she did not know the father. He was a man she had met casually going to the well.

When they asked me, as they often did, how my husband was, I always explained that he was very well, and had gone on a journey; it saved a lot of trouble, but it amused me to find that Sister Minna, when she was among strangers, always did the same. She explained that once on her way to Lome she stopped her hammock and spoke to a woman. This woman brought up a man, who asked her how her husband was, and in her innocence she explained she had none. The man promptly asked her to marry him, and as she demurred, the ten or twelve standing round asked her to choose among them which man she would have for a husband. The situation was difficult. Finally she got out of it by explaining that she was here to care for their children, and if she had to cook her husband's dinner it would take up too much of her time. Of course in Keta they now know her, and appreciate her, and respect her eccentricities if they do not understand them, but if she goes to a strange place she is careful to hide the fact that she has not a husband somewhere in the background. It is embarrassing to be single.

She is a firm believer in the good that the missions are doing; I am only a firm believer in the good that a woman like Sister Minna could not help doing in any land.

Keta is the place whence come all the cloths of the Guinea Coast, and again and again in a compound, in a little, sheltered dark corner, you may come across a man working his little loom, always a man, it is not women's work, and often by his side another winding the yarn he will use, and the product of their looms goes away, away to far Palime and Kpando, and all along the

Coast, and up the railway line to Kumasi, and into the heart of the rubber country beyond.

But here, being an enterprising people, they are beginning to do their own weaving, and have imported, I am told, men from Keta to show them the best way.

WEAVING AND WINDING YARN, KETA.

I shall not soon forget Keta. If I shut my eyes I can see it now. The bare hot sand with the burning hot sun pouring pitilessly down upon it; the graceful cocoa-nut palms; the great *ficus* trees that stand in rows outside the little Danish fort that is so white that it makes your eyes blink in the glare; the flamboyant tree, all red blossom, that grows beside it. Some Goth of a D.C. took the guns from the walls, and stood them upside down in the earth in a row leading down to the beach, and subsequent Commissioners, making the best of a bad job, have painted them carefully with tar to keep them from rusting. At the wells the little naked girls with beads round their middles draw the water, and in the streets, making the best of every little patch of shade, though they have not initiate enough to plant for themselves, are the women sitting always with some trifle to sell, early-morning porridge, or maize-meal balls, or portions of pine-apple, or native sweets made from imported sugar. Once I went into a chiefs house and wanted to photograph the people at work under the shade of the central tree in the courtyard. He sent word to say he would like to be photographed too, and as there was nothing particularly striking or objectionable about his shirt and trousers, I agreed.

He kept me waiting till the light was almost gone, and then he appeared in a tourist cap, a light-grey coat, a red tie, a pink shirt, khaki breeches, violent green socks pulled up over the ends of his breeches, and a pair of red-and-yellow carpet slippers. I sent the plate home, but have been unable to discover that photograph anywhere, and I think in all probability the plate could not stand him. So I did not get the people at work. The market is held on a bare piece of ground close to the lagoon, and whenever there is a high tide it is half under water, and the Chief calls upon the people to bring sand from the seashore to raise the ground, and after about six hundred calabashes have been spilled, it looks as if someone had scattered a handful of sand there. Indeed, though Keta has existed for many years, it looks as if at any moment an extra high tide might break away into the lagoon behind, and the whole teeming population, for whose being there I can see no possible reason, might be swept into the sea.

It was hotter in Keta than any other place I visited along the Coast, as there are no cool sea breezes for all they are so close to the sea. The sand-bank on which it is built runs almost north and south, and the prevailing wind, being from the south, blows always over hot-baked sand instead of over the cool sea. But yet I enjoyed life in that Mission House very much. It was a new piece of the world to me, and kind Sister Minna told me many things about the native mind. When first she came she had tried to do without beating the children, tried to explain to them that it was a shame that a girl should be beaten, but they would have none of her ways. All they thought was that she was afraid of them, the children despised her, and the school was pandemonium. Now she has thoroughly grasped their limitations, and when a girl does wrong she beats her, and they respect and love her, and send their children to her to be corrected.

"I have beaten thirty to-day," she would say with a sigh, as we sat down to dinner, or if we were going to the Commissioner's there was generally one in prison who had to be released before we could go. Sometimes, if she were specially bad, a girl was kept in prison all day and all night, in addition to her beating. Once in the compound opposite I saw a little stark-naked girl about thirteen stand screaming apparently without any cause. The Sisters stood it for about half an hour, then I saw them stealing across the road; they entered the compound, and promptly captured the small sinner. Her aunt, who was the owner of the compound, had apparently given her up as hopeless, and she looked on with interest. I had thought the captive's lungs must have given out long before, but as they crossed the road she put on a fresh spurt, and she yelled still more heartrendingly when she was beaten. But the next day she came trippingly along the verandah, confident, and happy, and apparently all the better for the correction she had received the day before. I do not know what her sin was. Probably she had not obeyed her aunt when she told her to rub the beads. Beads are bought in strings in Germany or England, and then every bead has to be rubbed smooth with water on a stone. It must be a dull job, but the women and children are largely occupied in doing it; the stones you see in every compound are worn hollow, and the palms of the woman's hands are worn quite hard. But it is part of a woman's education and she must do it just as a man must do the weaving.

CORNER OF MARKET PLACE, KETA.

The day came at last when I had to go, and I sat on the beach, surrounded by my goods and chattels, waiting for the surf boat that was to take me to the ship. Grant was bidding regretful farewells to the many friends he had made, and I was bidding my kind Sisters good-bye. Then I was hustled into a boat in a man's arms, hastily we dashed through the surf, and presently I was on board the *Bathurst* bound for Addah at the mouth of the Volta River.

CHIEFS' DAUGHTERS SELLING BEANS, MARKET, KETU

CHAPTER XIX
FACING DEATH

The Spanish nuns—One of the loneliest settlements in West Africa—Hospitality and swamp—A capable English woman—A big future in store for Addah—The mosquitoes of Addah—The glorious skies—Difficulties of getting away—A tremendous tornado—The bar steamer—The boiling bar—"We've had enough!"—Would rather be drowned in the open—The dismantled ship—Everybody stark—The gallant engineer—On the French steamer bound for Accra.

At Addah, at the mouth of the Volta, a place that exists solely for the transport, there is the very worst surf on all this surf-bound coast. There is a big native town a few miles up the river, but here at its entrance live the handful of Europeans, either right on the beach or on the banks of the river, over a mile away, with a great swamp between. The river is wide at its mouth, and the miles of swamp lend to the country an air at once weird and austere.

"Enter not here," cries the surf; "enter not here." But when its dangers have been dared, and the white man has set foot on the Dark Continent, the swamp takes up the refrain in another key, more sullenly threatening.

"In spite of warning you have crossed the outworks. Now, see how you like the swamp and the mosquito, the steaming heat and the blazing sun." And men come still, as they came three or four hundred years ago.

But I, for one, did not much like the landing. The Captain of the *Bathurst* explained that he had had no intention of calling at Addah, but hearing that there was a white woman on the beach wanting to go, he of his courtesy had decided to take her, and he wanted to be off as he wished to discharge cargo at Pram-Pram before it grew dark. And here, for once, on board an African steamer I found the women passengers largely outnumbering the men, for they had on board a number of nuns who had been exiled from San Paul de Loanda. They were Spanish, French, and German Sisters in the costume of their order; gentle, kindly women with faces that bore evident marks of an indoor life in the Tropics, a mark that cannot be mistaken. They had been very very frightened at first, and they were still very seasick, but the sailormen had made them most kindly welcome, for their sakes were staunch Monarchists when Portugal was spoken of, and they brought them the captain's cat to play with, and looked with deepest admiration on their wonderful embroidery. Never was so much sewing before seen on an African steamer.

I unwittingly added to their woes, for the surf was bad at Addah.

"We'll whistle and the bar steamer will come out for you," said the captain, and the steamer gave vent to the most heartrending wails.

In the distance I could see a most furious white surf, a palm or two cutting the sky line, and a speck or two that were probably bungalows, but it was a typical African shore and I didn't like the look of it at all. It is bad enough to go to a place uninvited, not to know where you are going to be put up, but when to that is added a bad surf, you wish—well, you wish it was well over. The ship rolled sickeningly in the swell; the Sisters, first one and then another, disappeared, to come back with faces in all shades of green whiteness, and the ruddy-faced captain paced the deck with an impatience that he in vain tried to control, and I felt an unutterable brute. If I had been seasick it would have crowned things; luckily for myself I am not given that way. At intervals the *Bathurst* let off shrieks, plaintive and angry, and we went to lunch. I felt I might as well have luncheon, a luncheon to which I really had a right.

"You'll have to come on with us to Pram-Pram," said the captain; "the beach is evidently too bad."

But presently, after luncheon, we saw a surf boat making its way towards us, and the captain through the glasses proclaimed, "Custom's boat. No white man. The surf is very bad."

When the boat same alongside, the black Custom officer said the captain was right. The surf was bad. They had rather hesitated about coming out, but the bar steamer in the river could not come out till to-morrow.

"Will you land," said the captain, "or shall we take you on?"

It seemed a pity to pass Addah, now I had come so near, and if the Customs could get through I did not see why I should not, so I got into the mammy-chair and was lowered into the surf boat with my servant and my gear. A surf boat is about five feet deep, and this time, as no one had expected a white woman to land, no chair had been provided, so I was obliged to balance myself on one of the narrow planks that ran across the boat and served as seats, and of course my feet dangled uncomfortably. Also, as we approached it, the surf looked most threatening. We were going straight into a furiously boiling sea with white, foam-lashed waves that flung themselves high into the air. I did not like the look of it at all, but as we were bound to go through it, I whisked myself round on my seat so that I sat with my back to the thing I was afraid of. Then the Custom-house officer, a black man, edged his way close beside me, and stretching out his hand put it on my arm. I did not like it. I object to being touched by black men, so I promptly shook it off, and as promptly the boat was apparently flung crash against a stone wall; she had really hit the beach, and over I went backwards and head first into the bottom of the boat. The man's help had been kindly meant; he would have held me in my place. But there is no time for apologies when a surf boat reaches the beach. Before I had realised what was happening, two Kroo boys had dived to the bottom of the boat, seized me without any ceremony whatever, and raced me up to the shore, where they put me down in all the blazing sun of an African afternoon, without even a helmet or an umbrella to protect my head. Grant followed with the helmet, and I endeavoured to smooth my ruffled plumes. At least, I had landed in safety, and the thing was now to find the Commissioner and see what he would do for me. We were on a beach where apparently was not even a boat, only the forlorn remains of the wreck of an iron steamer rapidly coming to its last end. The shore, rising to a height of about six or eight feet, was all sand with a little sparse, coarse grass upon it. We climbed up the yielding bank, and then I saw a native town, Beachtown, on my right, and on my left three or four bungalows built after the English fashion, on high posts rising out of cement platforms. Those bungalows at Beachtown, Addah, are perhaps the forlornest places on all the West-African coast. The wild surf is in front of them, the coarse grass all around them, and behind is a great swamp. Brave, brave, it seemed to me, must be the men and women who lived here and kept their health. The strong sea breeze would be healthgiving, but the deadly monotony of life must be something too terrible. But here the doctor, who was going home by the next steamer, had his wife, and the doctor who had just come out had brought his bride; two women, and I was told there was a third at the transport station. The Commissioner came forward, and I looked at him doubtfully. I had thought I should have known him and I didn't.

"You have forgotten me?"

Yes; I certainly ought to know him, but—it came on me with a flash, and I spoke my thoughts. "Ah, but you have grown a beard since I met you."

He laughed and blushed.

"I've just come off trek and I've lost my razors."

It was so like Africa. The dishevelled woman from the sea met the unkempt man from the bush, and we foregathered.

They were awfully good to me. Packed they were already with two more people than the bungalows were intended to hold, and so they considered what they should do for me, and while they were considering, hearing I had had luncheon, they gave me coffee and other drinks and offered cigarettes, and then they wrote to the transport company and asked them if they would take in a stray woman.

The kindness of these people in Africa! Can I ever repay it? I know, of course, I never can. The head of Swanzy's transport and his pretty wife sent over to say they would be delighted to have me, and I was to come at once and consider myself at home. And, moreover, they had sent a cart for me, drawn by three Kroo boys.

I have said many hard things about the English women in West Africa. I had begun to think, after my visit to Accra, that only the nursing Sisters were worthy of the name of capable women; but, when I went to Addah, my drooping hopes revived. For I met there, in Mrs Dyson, the transport officer's wife, a woman, charming, pretty, and young, who yet thought it not beneath her dignity to look after her husband's house, to see that he lived well here in the wilderness, and who enjoyed herself and made the very best of life.

And Addah, I must admit, takes a deal of making the best of. It has been settled for long years. In Beachtown you may see old guns; in Big Addah, a native town six miles up the Volta, you may see more of them lying about the rough, uncared-for streets, and you may see here a clump of tamarind trees that evidently mark the spot where once the fort has been. Not one stone of it remains. The authorities say that these "old shells of forts" are not worth preserving, and the natives have taken them literally at their word, and incorporated the very stones in their own buildings.

I am sorry, for Addah at the mouth of the great river must have been a great slaving station once; trade must have come down the river in the past, even as it does now, as it will do, doubled and trebled, in the future.

The house I stayed in was close on the river, and my bedroom opened out on to a verandah that overlooked it. In the shipbuilding yard below perpetually rings the clang of iron on the anvil, for always there are ships to be built or repaired; and there, grown into a great cotton tree in that yard, may be seen the heavy chains that the slavers of oldtime used to hold their ships to the shore. The slavers have gone, the past is dead; but, knowing that wonderful river, I do not mind prophesying that, in spite of that dangerous surf, in spite of those threatening swamps, there is a big future in store for that lonely outpost of the Empire. That sixty-five miles of unimpeded waterway that lies between it and Akuse is not to be lightly disregarded, and the rich country goes far beyond that.

But, at present, there is not much to see at Addah. There is the swamp, apparently miles of it, there is a great, wide, mangrove-fringed river, and there are the never-to-be-forgotten mosquitoes. The mosquitoes of Addah are the sort that make you feel you should go about armed, and that made me feel for once that a mosquito-proof house was an actual necessity. One thing, there is always a strong breeze blowing at Addah, and my hostess was always very particular to have her wire-netting swept down carefully every day so that every scrap of air that could come in did so, and I conclude it was owing to this that I did not feel the air so vitiated and oppressive as I have in other houses. I hope one of the next public works of the Gold Coast will be to fill in that swamp, and so rid the place of those terrible mosquitoes. One solace the white people have, if there are mosquitoes, there is no undergrowth, and so there are no tsetse flies, and they can keep horses. My hostess's two solitary amusements—because she was a smiling, happy-faced girl she made the best of them—were to ride along the beach and to play tennis after it had grown cool in the evening, as it always does in Africa before the sun goes down. And those sunsets across the swamp, too, were something to wonder at. Purple and red and gold were they. Every night the sun died in a glory over swamp and heath; every morning he rose golden and red across the wide river, as if he would say that if Addah had naught else to recommend it there was always the eternal beauty of the skies.

THE WHARF AT ADDAH.

But having got there it was rather difficult to get away.

The *Sapele*, they said, should come and take me back to Sekondi or, at least, to Accra, but the *Sapele* did not come, and if my hosts had not been the kindest in the world I should have begun to feel uncomfortable. I would gladly have gone overland, but carriers were not, even though some of my precious pots had been broken in the surf, and so my loads were reduced.

But every day there was no steamer, till at last a German steamer was signalled, and the bar steamer, a steamer of 350 tons, which usually lay at the little wharf just outside my bedroom window alongside the shipbuilding yard, prepared to go out. All my gear was carried down and put on board, and then suddenly the captain appeared on the verandah and pointed out to us two waiting women a threatening dark cloud that was gathering all across the eastern sky.

He shook his head, "I dare not go out till that is over." And so we stood and waited and watched the storm gather.

It was a magnificent sight. The inky sky was reflected in an inky river, an ominous hush was over everything, one felt afraid to breathe, and the halfnaked workmen in the yard dropped their tools and fled to shelter. The household parrot gave one loud shriek, and the harsh sound of his call cut into the stillness like a knife.

From the distance we could hear the roaring of the surf, as if it were gathering strength, and then the grasses in the swamp to the west bent before a puff of air that broke on the stillness. There was another puff, another, and then the storm was upon us in all its spendour. Never have I seen such a storm. Though it was only four o'clock in the afternoon, it was dark as night, and the lightning cut across like jagged flame, there came immediately the crash of thunder, and then a mighty roaring wind, a wind that swept everything before it, that bent the few trees almost to the ground, that stripped them of their leaves as if they had been feathers shaken out of a bag, that beat the placid river into foam, and tore great sheets of corrugated iron from the roofs of the buildings and tossed them about the yard as if they had been so many strips of muslin.

The bar steamer's captain had gone at the first sign to see that his moorings were safe, and we two women stood on the verandah and watched the fury of the elements, while my hostess wondered where her husband was, and hoped and prayed he was not out in it. The inky blackness was all over the sky now, the wind was shrieking so as to deaden all other sounds, and the only thing we could hear above it was the crash of the thunder. And then I looked at the horizon away to the south-west. There, about a mile away as the crow flies, was the shore, and there against the inky darkness of the sky I could see tossed high into the air great sheets of foam. The surf on that shore must have been terrific. I would have given a good deal to go and see it, but, before I could make up my mind to start, down came the rain in torrents, the horizon was blotted out, the road through the swamp was running like a mill race, and it looked as if it would be no light task to beat my way through wind and rain to the shore.

And when the storm was subsiding back came the bar steamer's captain.

"No going out to-day," said he; "I wouldn't dare risk the bar. Look at the surf!" and he pointed across the swamp to where we could again see the great white clouds of foam rising against the horizon. "To-morrow," he said, "very early"; and he went away, and my host, soaked through and through, came back and told us what the storm had looked like from Beachtown.

The next morning was simply glorious. The world was fresh and clean and newly washed, and the river, from my window, looked like a brightly polished mirror.

"It'll be a bad bar, though," said my host, shaking his head. "Better stay."

It was very kind of him, but I felt I had trespassed on their kindness long enough; besides, there were other parts of the Coast I wished to see, and I felt I must take this opportunity of getting out of Addah. What was a bad bar? I had faced the surf before. So I bid them farewell, with many grateful thanks, and went on board, and in all the glory of the morning we set off down the river.

I was the only white passenger on board, and was allowed to stand on the bridge beside the wheel. Behind me was a little house wherein I might have taken shelter, but I thought I might as well see all there was to be seen; besides, I held my camera in my hand and proposed to take photographs of this "bad bar."

The mouth of the Volta is utterly lonely looking. A long sandpit ran out on the right hand, whereon grew a solitary bush, blighted, for there was not a sign of a leaf upon it, and to the left was also sand, with a few scattered palms. I fancy there must have been a native hut or two, though I do not remember them, for I remember the captain saying, "We have to make our own marks. When you get a hut in line with a certain tree you know you are in the channel." I was glad to hear there was a channel, for to my uninitiated eyes we seemed heading for a wild waste of boiling water, worse than anything I had ever conceived of, and yet I was not unaccustomed to surf, and had faced it before now in a surf boat. Never again shall I face surf with equanimity. I tried to carry out my programme, but I fear I must have been too upset to withdraw the slides, for I got no photographs. Presently we appeared to be right in the middle of the swirl. The waves rose up like mountains on either side, and towards us would come a great smooth green hill of water which towered far above our heads and then, breaking, swept right over us with a tremendous crash. I can see now the sunlight on that hill; it made it look like green glass, and then, when the foam came, there were all the colours of the rainbow. Again and again the two men at the wheel were flung off, their cloths seemed to be ripped from them as if they had been their shells, and the ship trembled from stem to stern and stood still. I thought, "Is this a bad bar? I'm afraid, I'm afraid," but as the captain came scrambling to the wheel to take the place of the men who had been thrown off I did not quite like to say anything. It is extraordinary how hard it is to make one believe there really is anything to fear, and I should hate to be a nuisance at a critical moment, so I said to the captain—he and I and the German engineer were the only white people on board: "It's magnificent."

He was holding on to the wheel by my side and a naked black man, stripped by the ruthless water, was holding on to it on the other, and I could see the moisture on his strained face. Was it sweat or sea water?

"Magnificent!" said he. "Don't you see we can't stand it? We've had enough!"

So that was it. We were going down. At least, not exactly going down, but the water was battering us to pieces. I learned then that what I was afraid of was fear, for now I was not afraid. It had come, then, I thought. This was the end of the life where sometimes I had been so intensely happy and sometimes I had been so intensely miserable that I had wanted to die. Not so very long ago, and now I was going to die. Presently those waters that were soaking me through and through would wash over me once for all and I was not even afraid. I thought nothing for those few moments, except how strange that it was all over. I wondered if I had better go into the little house behind me, but no, I saw I was not in the way of the men at the wheel. I could hear the crashing of broken wood all round me, and I thought if I were to be drowned I would rather be drowned in the open. Why I held on to my camera I do not know. That, I think, was purely mechanical. The waves beat on the ship from all quarters, and so apparently held her steady, and I might just as well hold on to the camera as to anything else. I certainly never expected to use it again. Crash, crash, crash came the tons of water, there was a ripping of broken wood, and a human wail that told me that crew and black passengers had realised their danger. Crash, crash, crash. It seemed to me the time was going very slowly, and then suddenly the ship seemed to give a leap forward, and instead of the waves crashing on to us we were riding over them, and the captain seized me by the arm.

"Come inside. You're wet to the skin."

"But———"

"We're all right. But, my God, you'll never be nearer to it."

And then I looked around me to see the havoc that the bar had wrought. The bulwarks were swept away, the boats were smashed, the great crane for working cargo was smashed and useless, the galley was swept overboard, the top of the engine-house was broken in, and, transformation scene, every solitary creature on board that little ship, with the exception of the captain and me, was stark. Custom-house officers had stripped off their uniforms, clerks who had come to tally cargo in all the glory of immaculate shirts and high-starched collars were nude, and the black men who worked the ship had got rid of their few rags as superfluous. Everyone had made ready to face the surf.

"Much good would it have done 'em," opined the captain; "no living thing could have got ashore in that sea."

Then up came the chief engineer, a German; his face was scalded and his eyes were bloodshot, and it was to him we all owed our lives.

The waves had beaten in the top of the engine-room, and the water had poured in till it was flush with the fires; a gauge blew out—I am not sure if I express myself quite rightly, but the place was full of scalding steam, and all those educated negro engineers fled, but the white man stuck to his job.

"I tink it finish," said he, "when I see the water come close close to the fires, but I say, 'well, as well dis vay as any oder,' so I stick to do my job, an' I not see, I do it by feel."

And we all three shook hands, and the captain and engineer had a glass of whisky, and though it was so early in the morning, never did I think it was more needed. I had been but an onlooker. On them had fallen the burden and heat of the day.

And then came boats, bringing on board the captains of the French and German steamers that lay in the roadstead, far out, because the surf was so bad.

They had been watching us. They thought we were gone, but though they had out their boats they confessed they would have been powerless to aid. No boat could have lived in such a sea, and the captain declared that though he was swept bare of all food nothing would induce him to go back. It would be certain death.

We looked a rather forlorn wreck, but the German captain came to the rescue with a seaman-like goodwill, lending men to work the cargo in place of the broken-down crane, and giving food to the hungry ones. He had come from Lome, and he brought news that the hurricane of the night before had swept away the bridge that had been the pride and delight of the people of Togo, and that never for many a long year had there been such a storm along the Guinea Coast. He had been unable to get his papers and had come away without them. He would take me if I liked, but he must go back to Lome.

But I was rather feeling I had had enough of the sea, and so I turned to the Frenchman. He was just as kind and courteous. His ship was small, he said, and he was not going to Sekondi, but I might tranship at Accra if I liked. The captain of the bar steamer advised my going on board at once, for his ship was in a state of confusion, and also he was going to tranship cargo.

Then Grant took a hand in the proceedings. Whether he had stripped I don't know, for I did not see him, but he presented himself before me in a very wet and damp condition.

"Medicine chest gone, Ma."

Now, the medicine chest was my soldier brother's, the pride of my heart. I had proposed to bring it back to him and show him that the only time it had been used in this unhealthy climate was when the carrier had inadvertantly got cascara for his pneumonia. Well, it was gone, and there was nothing more to be said. Its pristine beauty had been lost in the rains in Togo. Grant departed, but presently he was on the bridge again.

"Pots be all bruck, Ma."

"Oh, Grant!" I had got them so far only to lose them in the end. Grant was like one of Job's comforters. He seemed to take a huge delight in announcing to me fresh disasters. My things were all done up small for carrying on men's heads, and the sea had played havoc with them. The bucket was gone; the kettle, an old and tried servant, was gone; the water-bottle was gone, so was the lantern; the chop box had been burst open, and the plates and cups smashed; while the knives and forks had been washed overboard, and the majority of my boots, for some reason or other, had followed. After Grant had made about his tenth journey, announcing fresh disasters, I said:

"Oh, never mind, Grant. We must make the best of it; I'm rather surprised we are not gone ourselves," and with a grin he saw to the handing of the remains of my goods into the boat, and getting them on board the steamer.

That steamer was tiny. I looked at the cabin assigned me, and determined if I had to sit up all night I would not occupy it, and then I had my precious black box brought on deck, and proceeded to count the damage. It was locked and it was supposed to be air-tight and water-tight. I can't say about the air-tight, but water-tight it certainly was not, for every single thing in that box was soaked through and through. I took them out one by one; then, as no one said me nay, I tied them on to the taffrail, and let my garments flutter out in the breeze and the sunshine. There were four French women on board, bound from the French Congo to Konakri, and they took great interest and helped me with suggestions and advice, but I must say I was glad that I was bound for Sekondi, where my kind friend the nursing Sister was keeping fresh garments for me. As for my poor little typewriter, it was so drenched with water that, though I stood it out in the sun, I foresaw its career in West Africa was over.

As the sun was setting, came on board the captain of the bar steamer to bid me God-speed. We had never met till the day before, but that morning we had faced death together, and it made a bond.

"Go back to-night?" said he; "not if I know it. Not for a week, if that surf doesn't go down. I couldn't face it."

I wanted him to stay and dine, because I knew he had nothing, but he told me how good the German had been, and said he did not like leaving his own ship after dark; so we said "good-bye" with, I hope, mutual respect, and, after dinner, I began to consider how I should spend the night. I knew my own bedding must be rather wet, but I knew, also, the camp-bed would be all right, and I told Grant to bring it up on deck and make it up with bedding from the Frenchman's bunk.

"They no give you cabin, Ma," said he, surprised.

Nothing would induce a child of Nature to sleep in the open as long as he can find any sort of a cuddy-hole to stew in. I was a little afraid of what the French captain might say, but he took my eccentricity calmly enough.

"Ah, zat your bed? Ah, zat is good idea"; and left me to a night rolling beneath the stars, when I tossed and dreamed and woke with a start, thinking that the great green hills of water were about to overwhelm me; and as about twenty times more terrified of the dream than I had been of the reality.

Next morning found us outside Accra, a long way outside, because the surf was bad, and I found to my dismay there was no mail in yet, and I must land, for there was no cargo for the *Gergovia*, and she wanted to go on her way.

I found the landing terrible. I can frankly say I have never been so frightened, and I had no nerve left to stand up against the fear. But it was done. I saw my friend in Accra, and again recounted with delight my travels. For the first time I began to feel I had done something, and I felt it still more when the people in Schenk & Barber's, a great trading firm, held up their hands and declared that I had done a wonderful thing to cross by Krobo Hill at night. I had done well, then, I kept saying to myself, I had accomplished something; but I must admit I was most utterly done. When the mail steamer arrived, the port officer made it his business to see me off to the ship himself; we were drenched to the skin as we rounded the breakwater, and I was so nervous when the mammy-chair came dangling overhead from the ship's deck, that I hear he reported I was the worst traveller he had ever been on board with. Then, in addition to my woes, instead of being able to sit and chat and tell my adventures comfortably to the friends I met, I was, for the first time for many a long year, most violently seasick.

But, when I went to bed, I slept dreamlessly, and when I awakened we were rising to the swell outside Sekondi, and I felt that even if I had to face the surf again I should be among friends presently, and there was a feeling of satisfaction in the thought that I had at least seen something of the most beautiful river in the world, and some unknown country in the east of the Colony.

Always there is that in life, for, good or evil, nothing can take away what we have done. We have it with us, good or bad, for ever. Not Omnipotence can alter the past.

CHAPTER XX
WITH A COMPANION

The kindness of Sekondi—Swanzy's to the rescue—A journey to Dixcove—With a nursing Sister—The rainy season and wet feet—Engineering a steep hill in the dark—Rains and brilliant fireflies—The P.W.D. man's taste in colours—The need of a woman in West Africa—Crossing the Whin River—My fresh-air theory confirmed.

Sekondi, from the nursing Sister outwards, was as it always has been, awfully good to me, and I felt as if I were come home. I had the kindest offers of help from all sides, and the railway company took my damaged goods in hand and did their level best to repair damages. I was bound for the goldfields and Ashanti, but I had still uneasily in my remembrance that little bit of coast to the west of Sekondi that I had left unvisited. If I had not written so much already about the carrier difficulties, I might really write a book, that to me would be quite interesting, about that day's journey to Dixcove. Swanzy's transport came to the rescue and provided me with carriers, a most kindly gift, for which I am for ever grateful, and I took with me a young nursing Sister who was anxious to see something of bush travel.

There is always a fascination about the shore, the palm trees and the yellow sand and the blue sky and bluer sea, but now the difficulties were being added to daily and hourly, because it was the beginning of the rainy season, and all the little rivers had "broken out," and to cross from one bank to another when a river is flooded, even if it is only a little one, is as a rule no easy matter. To my great amusement I found my companion had a great objection to getting her feet wet. I am afraid I laughed most unsympathetically.

"You can't," I decided, and I fear she thought me a brute, "travel in the rainy season in Africa and hope to keep dry"; and I exhorted her not to mind if the water were up to her ankles, but to wade through. She brought home to me difficulties of travel that I had never thought of before. It had never occurred to me to worry as to whether I was likely to get wet before; a little water or a little discomfort never seemed to matter. The seat of the canoe I was sitting in broke and let me down into the waist-deep puddle of water in the bottom, and somehow it seemed a less thing to me than that her feet should get wet did to her. She was a nice, good-looking girl, pleasant and smiling, but I decided that never again as long as I lived would I travel with another woman. I know my own shortcomings, but I never know where another woman will break out.

And we went along that coast, where, two hundred years ago, quaint, gossipy old Bosman had found so much of beauty and interest. Tacorady Fort was deserted in his day. It is overgrown and forgotten now. Boutry is on a high hill, the place of the old fort only marked by a thick clump of trees, dark-green against the sky line; but it was getting dark when we reached Boutry, there was a river to cross, and I was obsessed with a sense of my responsibilities, such as I had never felt when I had only my own skin to look after, and I was very thankful that a doctor who was going to Dixcove had overtaken us. If I damaged my travelling companion in any way, I felt that he at least could share responsibility. We crossed the river, and the darkness fell, pitchy, black darkness; it rained in a businesslike way as it does in the Tropics, and there was a high hill to climb. It was a very steep hill, with a very shocking track that did duty as a road, and my companion expressed her utter inability to get up it. I was perfectly sure that our Kroo hammock-boys could never get us up it, and I was inclined to despair; then that doctor came to our aid. He had four Mendi boys, the best carriers on the Coast, and we put them on to my companion's hammock, and gaily she went off. She knew nothing of the dangers of the way. I did, but I did not feel it necessary to enlighten her. I don't know what the doctor did, but I put on my Burberry and instructed two of my carriers that they must help me over the road. It was a road. When I came back over it in the light, three days later, I wondered how on earth we had tackled it in the dark; still more did I wonder how a heavily laden hammock—for she was a strapping young woman, a good deal bigger than I am—had been engineered up and down it. But Mendi carriers are wonderful, and there was a certain charm in walking there in the night. When the rain stopped, the fireflies came out, and the gloom beneath the trees was lightened by thousands of brilliant sparks of fire. I don't know whether fireflies are more brilliant after rain, but I remember them most distinctly on those two wet nights when I was travelling, once on my way to Dixcove and once on the way to Palime.

Up the hill we went and down the hill, along the sands, across the shallows of a river just breaking out—and the lantern light gleamed wetly on the sand—through little sleepy villages and across more hilly country, and at last, just as the moon was rising stormily in the clouded sky, we were opposite a long flight of wide steps, and knew we had reached Dixcove.

There was one white man, a P.W.D. man, in Dixcove, and a surprised man was he. Actually, two women had come out of the night and flung themselves upon him. Of course, we had brought servants and provisions and beds, so it was only a question of providing quarters. Now I smile when I think of it. We crossed the courtyard, we climbed the stairs, we entered the modern house that was built on top of the little fort, and out of a sort of whirlpool a modified disorder emerged, when we found ourselves, two men and two women, by the light of a fluttering, chimneyless Hinkson lamp, all assembled in the room that two camp-beds proclaimed the women's bedroom, and we all partook of a little whisky to warm ourselves while we waited for dinner. The P.W.D. man was fluttered and, I think, pleased, for at least our coming broke the monotony, and the nursing Sister undertook the commissariat and interviewed his cook. Altogether we made a cheerful little week-end party in that romote corner of the earth, and when it rained, as rain it did most of the time, we played bridge as if we had been in London.

Dixcove is a pretty little place, literally a cove, and the fort is built on high ground on a neck of land that forms the head of the cove. Round it grow many orange groves, and altogether it is a desirable and delightful spot, but it must be very lonely for the only white man who was there. He had just repainted the bungalow on top of the fort, and whether he had used up the odds and ends of paints, or whether this was his taste, or whether he had desired something to cheer him, or whether he was actuated by the same spirit that seems to move impressionist painters, I do not know, but when I got up next morning and walked on the bastion, that bungalow fairly took my breath away. It was painted whole-heartedly a violent Reckitt's blue; the uprights and the other posts that criss-crossed across it were a bright vivid green, and they were all picked out in pink. There was the little white fort set in the midst of tropical greenery, everything beautiful, with the bungalow on top setting the discordant note. It was pitiful, but at the same time the effect was so comic that the nursing Sister and I laughed till we cried, and then our host came out and could not understand what we were laughing about. We came to the charitable conclusion he must be colour-blind.

The two men wanted us to stay. They said it was more comfortable, and when I compared the luncheon the doctor gave us to the meals we had when I provided the eatables and the nursing Sister gave her attention to the cuisine, I must say I agreed with them, and resolved once again to proclaim the absolute necessity for having women in West Africa. But she had to go back to her work, and I had to go on my travels, and so, like the general who marched his army up the hill and marched it down again, presently I was on my way back. And not a moment too soon. It was raining when we started, and our host and the doctor pressed us to stay, but I had not been on the Coast all this time without knowing very well what that rain would mean. The rivers that had been trickles when we set out would be roaring torrents now, and I knew in a little time they would be impassable; then the only thing would be to go back to Sekondi by surf boat, and I had had enough of the surf to last me for many a long day. Besides, our provisions were getting low. We started early; we had less to carry, for we had eaten most of the provisions, and we had more men, for we brought back most of the doctor's following, but still it took us all we knew to get across those rivers, and the Whin River was nearly too much for us. It had been bad when we came, now the sea was racing across the sands, the flooded, muddy water of the river was rushing to meet it, and the two black men who were working a surf boat as a ferry came and asked an exorbitant sum to take us across. My headman demurred and said we wouldn't go. I left it to him, and the bargaining was conducted in the usual slatternly Coast English at the top of their voices. I must confess, as my companion and I sat on the sand and watched the wild waters, I wondered what we would do if we did not cross, for Dixcove was fully fourteen miles behind us. Down came the price by slow degrees, in approved fashion, till at last it appeared I, my companion, our goods, chattels, hammocks, and our followers, numbering fully twenty men, were to be taken across for the sum of two shillings and sixpence. I sent the gear first, and then some of the men, and finally the nursing Sister and I went. Unfortunately there was not room in the boat for the two last men, and I could not help being amused when the ferryman came to be paid, and the men all clustered round vehemently demanding that I should do no such thing till their two companions were also brought over. Not a scrap of faith had they in the ferryman keeping his word, so I had to sit down on the sand among the short, coarse grass and the long stalks of the wandering bean, and wait till those two men were fetched, when I paid up, and we went on to Sekondi.

The journey was short; it is hardly worth recording, hardly worth remembering, but for those wonderful fireflies, and for another thing that bears strongly on my theory regarding health in West Africa.

The nursing Sister I took with me was a tall, goodlooking girl, considerably younger than I am, and she looked as if she ought to have been very much stronger. She had barely been on the Coast a short three months, but she had already had one or two goes of fever, a thing I have never had, and she did not like it. She was very careful of herself, and she abominated the climate. At night I noticed she shut herself away from all chance of draughts, drawing curtains and shutting doors so as to insure herself against chill. When we started on our journey she was not well, "the climate was not agreeing with her," and they were beginning to think she "could not stand it." We spent a day in the open and we got somewhat wet. When night came we shared a room and she wanted to close, at least, a shutter. Partly that was to have privacy and partly to keep away draughts. Then I brutally put down my foot.

I considered it dangerous to be shut in in Africa, and as I was engineering that expedition I thought I ought to have my way. One thing I did not insist upon, I did not have the windows open all round, but I had them wide on two sides, so that a thorough draught might blow through the room. My bed I put right in it, but I allowed her to put hers in the most sheltered part of the room she could find, and, of course, I could not prevent her wrapping her head in a blanket.

She put in those two nights in fear and trembling, I know, but she went back to Sekondi in far better health than she had left it. That she acknowledged herself, but she does not like Africa; the charm of it had passed her by, and I wonder very much if she will complete her term of service.

CHAPTER XXI
THE WEST-AFRICAN GOLDFIELDS

A first adventure—Tarkwa—Once more Swanzy to the rescue—Women thoroughly contented, independent, and well-to-do—The agricultural wealth of the land—The best bungalow in West Africa—Crusade against the trees—Burnt in the furnaces—Prestea—The sick women—A ghastly hill—Eduaprim—A capable fellow-countrywoman—"Dollying" for gold—Obuasi—Beautiful gardens—75 per cent.—The sensible African snail.

I was born and brought up on the goldfields. My first adventure—I don't remember it—was when my nurse, a strapping young emigrant from the Emerald Isle, lost me and herself upon the ranges, and the camp turned out to search, lest the warden's precious baby and her remarkably pretty nurse should spend an unhappy night in the bush. As a small girl, I watched the men wash the gold in their cradles, and I dirtied my pinafore when the rain turned the mullock heaps into slimy mud. As I grew older, I escorted strangers from the Old Country who wanted to go down the deep mines of Ballarat. I watched, perforce, the fluctuations of the share market, and men who knew told me that the rise and fall had very often nothing whatever to do with the output of gold; so that I grew up with the firmly fixed idea—it is still rather firmly fixed—that the most uninteresting industry in the world was goldmining.

Wherefore was I not a bit keen on going to the gold mines of West Africa, and I only went to Tarkwa because I felt it would never do to come away not having seen an industry which I am told is going up by leaps and bounds. The question was, where could I go for quarters? There are no hotels as yet, and once more I am deeply indebted to Messrs Swanzy and their agent in the mining centre of the Gold Coast. He put me up and entertained me right royally, and not only did he show me round Tarkwa, but he saw to it that I should have every chance to see some of the other mines, Prestea and Eduaprim.

SHOPS IN NATIVE TOWN, TARKWA.

Tarkwa is set in what we in Australia should call a gully, and the high hills rise up on either side, while the road, along which straggles the European town, runs at the bottom of the gully. For there are several towns in Tarkwa. There is the European town where are all the stores, the railway station, and the houses of the Government officials, and in this town there is some attempt at beautifying the place; some trees have been planted along the roadside, grass grows on the hillsides, whether by the grace of God or the grace of the town council I know not, and round most of the bungalows there is generally a sort of garden, and notably in one or two, where there are white women who have accompanied their husbands, quite promising beginnings of tropical gardens.

There is the native town, bare and ugly, without a scrap of green, just streets cutting each other at right angles, and small houses, roofed with corrugated iron or thatch, and holding a teeming and mixed population that the mines gather together, and then every mine has its own village for its workers; for the labour difficulty has reached quite an acute stage in the goldfields, and the mines often import labour from the north, which they install in little villages, that are known by the name of the mine where the men work, and are generally ruled over by a white officer appointed by the mine. These villages, too, are about as bare and ugly as anything well could be that is surrounded by the glorious green hills and has the blue sky of Africa over it.

Tarkwa gives the impression of a busy, thriving centre; trains rush along the gully and the hills echo their shrill whistles, the roadways are thronged with people, and the stores set out their goods in that open fashion that is half-eastern, so that the hesitating buyer may hesitate no longer but buy the richest thing in sight. In all my travels I never saw such gorgeously arrayed mammies as here. The black ladies' cloths, their blouses, and the silken kerchiefs with which they covered their heads, all gave the impression of having been carefully studied, and my host assured me they had. Many of them are rich, and in this comfortable country they are all of them self-supporting wives. They sell their wares, or march about the streets, happy, contented, important people, very sure of themselves. Let no one run away with the impression that these women are in any way down-trodden. They look very much the reverse. We may not approve of polygamy, but I am bound to say these women of Tarkwa were no down-trodden slaves. They looked like women who had exactly what they wanted, and, curiously enough whenever I think of thoroughly contented, thoroughly independent, well-to-do women, I think of those women in the goldmining centre of West Africa.

My host told me they spent, comparatively speaking, enormous sums on their personal adornment, were exceedingly particular as to the shade and pattern of their cloths, and were decided that everything, cloth, blouse, and head kerchief, should tone properly. They lay in a large store of clothes too, and when Mr Crockett wrote the other day of "The Lady of the Hundred Dresses," he might have been thinking of one of these Fanti women. The reason of this prosperity is of course easy to trace. The negro does not like working underground, for which few people I think will blame him, therefore high wages have to be paid, and these high wages have to be spent, and are spent lavishly, much to the advantage of these women traders.

STREET IN NATIVE TOWN, TARKWA.

Because Tarkwa is a great centre of industry, Government have very wisely made it one of their agricultural stations, and there, set on a hill, and running down into rich alluvial flats, are gardens wherein grow many of the plants that will in the future contribute largely to the industrial development of the Colony. There is a rubber plantation, a great grove of dark trees already in bearing, plantations of bananas, pine-apples, hemp, and palm trees, and the director, set in his lonely little bungalow on the hilltop, rejoices over the wealth and fertility of the land, which he declares is not in her gold, but in her agricultural products which as yet we are but dimly realising, and then he mourns openly because the Government will not let him bring out his wife. "She would be ready to start in an hour if I might send for her," he sighed, "and I would want nothing more. But I mayn't. Oh, think of the dreary days. And I could work so much better if she were here. I should want nothing else."

And I sympathised. Think of the dreary days for him, and the still more dreary days for her, for at least he has his work. It would surely I think pay the Government to give a bonus to the woman who proved that she could see her year out without complaint, and who was to her husband what a woman ought to be, a help and a comfort.

Another thing in Tarkwa I shall never forget is Messrs Swanzy's bungalow, where I stayed for nearly a fortnight. My host had superintended the building of it himself, and it was ideal for a West-African bungalow. It was built of cement raised on arches above the ground; floors and walls were of cement. There was a very wide verandah that served as a sitting-room and dining-room, and the bedrooms, though they were divided from each other by stout walls of cement, were only shut off from the verandah by Venetian screens that could be folded right away. They did not begin till a foot above the floor, and ended six feet above it, consequently there was always a thorough draught of air, and Messrs Swanzy's bungalow at Tarkwa is about the only house I know in West Africa where one can sleep with as much comfort as if in the open air. Needless to say, they are not so foolish as to go in for mosquito-proof netting. They keep the mosquitoes down by keeping the place round neat and tidy, and though the verandah is enclosed with glass, it is done in such fashion that the windows may be thrown right open and do not hinder the free passage of air. Flies and mosquitoes there were, but that, when I was there, was attributed to the presence of the town rubbish tip on the next vacant allotment, and my host hoped to get it taken away. Why the Government had a town rubbish tip close to the handsomest bungalow in the Colony, I do not pretend to say. It was just one of those things that are always striking you as incongruous in West Africa. My host used to fret and fume at every evil fly that came through his windows, and, when I left, was threatening to stand a gang of Hausas round that tip with orders to kick anyone who desired to deposit any more rubbish there.

RUBBER PLANTATION, TARKWA.

It is hardly necessary to say there had been at the same time a great crusade against the trees in Tarkwa. But a short time ago the whole place had been dense forest, very difficult to work, and after the usual fashion of the English everyone set to work to demolish the forest trees as if they were the greatest enemies to civilisation. The mines, of course, I believe burn something like a hundred trees a day, and the softwood trees are no good to them. What their furnaces require are the splendid mahogany, the still harder kaku, a beautiful wood that is harder than anything but iron, and indeed any good hard-wood tree; the worth of the wood is no business of theirs. They consider the wealth of Africa lies beneath the soil, and they must get it out; wherefore into their furnaces goes everything burnable, even though the figured mahogany may be worth £1 a foot, and the tree be worth £1000. It is a pity, it is a grievous pity, but Tarkwa is certainly prosperous, and I suppose one cannot make omelettes, and look for chickens. Only I cannot help remembering that never in our time, nor in our children's time, nor their children's time, will the hills of Tarkwa be covered with such trees as she has ruthlessly consigned to the flames. Even the soft-wood trees such as the cotton, that might have added beauty to the slopes, have gone because an energetic doctor waged war upon them as shelterers of the mosquito, and the hill-sides lie in the blazing sun for close on twelve hours of a tropical day. Oh for a sensible, artistic German to come and see to the beautifying of Tarkwa, for never saw I a place that could lend itself more readily to the hand of an artist.

But if Tarkwa is being ruthlessly treated, what shall I say of beautiful Prestea, which lies but a short railway journey right away in the heart of the hills. Prestea is a great mine, so large that the whole of the one hundred and eighty white people who make up the white town are employed upon it. It is so hilly that there are hardly any paths, and the people seem to move about on trolleys, winding in and out of the hills, and, it was reported once, one of the unhealthiest places in West Africa. The doctor very kindly gave me hospitality, and we promptly agreed to disagree on every subject. I hate to be ungracious to people who have been kind to me, but with all the will in the world I have to keep my own opinion, and my opinion was diametrically opposed to the doctor's. The nursing Sister who ran the hospital, a nice-looking, capable, sensible Scotch woman, whom it did my heart good to meet, was one of the few I have met who put the sickness of the average English woman in West Africa down to the same causes as I did.

"They come from a class who have nothing to think of, and when they have nothing to do they naturally fall sick," said she. "Every woman on this camp has been sent home this year."

I debated with her whether I should give my opinion of the climate to the world in my book. It meant I was up against every doctor in the place, who ought to know better than I, a stranger, and a sojourner.

"If you don't," said she, "someone else will come along presently and do it."

That decided me. I am doing it.

STREET IN OLD NATIVE TOWN, PRESTEA.

This nursing Sister, while she had to have the hospital mosquito-proof, in deference to the doctor's opinion, sternly declined to have any such abomination anywhere near her little bungalow, and so the cool, fresh night air blew in through her great windows, and we had an extensive view of the glorious hillsides, all clothed in emerald green, and if a clammy white mist wrapped us close when we waked in the early morning so that we could not see beyond our own verandahs, the rolling away of that mist was a gorgeous sight, ever to be remembered.

Needless to say, the doctor's house was carefully enclosed in mosquito-proof wire, and I dined in an oppressive atmosphere that nearly drove me distracted. The bungalow was set high on a hilltop, in the middle of a garden that should one day be beautiful, but he has of course cut down every native tree, and owing to the mosquito-proof wire we got no benefit from the cool breeze that was blowing outside. He took me to see the new native village he was building, a place that left an impression of corrugated iron and hard-baked clay. Trees, of course, and all vegetation were taboo, but I am bound in justice to say that the old village, a place teeming with inhabitants, drawn from all corners of West Africa, attracted by the lust for gold, was just as bare and ugly, and a good deal more unkempt.

He took me out, and pointed out to me the principal hill in the centre of Prestea, on which are the mining manager's and other officials' houses, and he pointed it out with pride.

"There's a nice clean hill for you."

The sun glared down fiercely on corrugated-iron roofs, the soil of the hill looked like a raw, red scar, and there was not so much as a blade of grass to be seen. I did not wonder that the unfortunate women of Prestea had gone home sick if they had been compelled to live in such a place.

I said, "It's a horrible place. I never saw a beautiful place more utterly spoiled."

He looked at me with surprise, and his surprise was thoroughly genuine. "Why, what's the matter? It's nice and clean."

I pointed to the beautiful hills all round.

"Mosquitoes," said he, with a little snort for my ignorance.

"But you want some shade?"

He shook his head doubtfully.

"You can't have trees. The boys would leave pots under them. Breeding places for mosquitoes."

He was my host, so I did not like to say all I felt.

"I'd rather die of fever than sunstroke any day," was the way it finally came out.

"My dear lady," he said judicially, as one who was correcting a long-standing error, "no one dies of fever in Africa."

"Exactly what I always maintain," said I; "you, with your ghastly hills are arranging for them to die of sunstroke."

But he only reiterated that they could not have the trees, because the boys would leave pots and pans under them, and so turn them into mosquito traps. Personally, I didn't arrive at the logic of that, because it has never seemed to me to require trees for boys to leave pots about. The theory was, I suppose, that they would not walk out into the hot sun, while they might be tempted to do work and make litter under shade-trees. And again I did not wonder that there were no women save the nursing Sister in Prestea. To live on that hill and keep one's health would have been next door to impossible.

"It doesn't matter," said the doctor, "we don't want women in West Africa. I keep my wife at home. It isn't a white man's country."

PRESTEA, A MINING CAMP.

But I'm bound to say that they very often arrange it shall not be a white man's and emphatically not a white woman's country. It suits somebody's plan that the country should have an evil reputation.

Goldfields, too, must never be judged in the same category as one judges the ordinary settlements in a country. When I was a tiny child I learned to discriminate, and to know that "diggers" must not be judged by the rules that guide the conduct of ordinary men. The population of a goldfield are a wild and reckless lot, and they lead wild and utterly reckless lives, and die in places where other people manage to live happily enough.

When the gold first "broke out" in Victoria, my father was Gold Commissioner on the Buckland River, among the mountains in the north-eastern district, and I have heard him tell how the men used to die like flies of "colonial" fever, and the theory was that there was some emanation from the dense vegetation that was all around them. Nowadays the Buckland is one of the healthiest spots in a very healthy country, and no one ever gets fever of any sort there. Now I do not wish to say that West Africa is one of the healthiest countries in the world, but I do say that men very very often work their own undoing.

"You should see Tarkwa," said a man to me, who was much of my way of thinking, "when an alcoholic wave has passed over it!"

Eduaprim was another mine I went to see from Tarkwa. But it was in direct contrast to Prestea, though it too was in the heart of the forest country. No railway led to it; I had to go by hammock, and so I got my first taste of forest travelling, and enjoyed it immensely.

It is a solitary mine about nine miles from Tarkwa, and I started off early in the morning, and noticed as I went that the industry is, for good or ill, clearing the forests of West Africa, opening up the dark places, even as it did in my country over fifty years ago. Along the hillsides we went to Eduaprim, past mines and clearings for mining villages; sometimes the road was cut, a narrow track on the side of the hill, with the land rising up on one side and falling sheer on the other, sometimes a little river had to be bridged, and the road went on tunnel-like through the forest that must disappear before the furnaces, but at last I arrived at the top of the hill, and on it, commanding a wonderful view over the surrounding country, stood a bungalow, in a garden that looked over the tops of range upon range of high hills. I saw a storm come sweeping across the country, break and divide at the hilltop upon which I stood, and pass on, veiling the green hills in mist, which rolled away from the hills behind, leaving them smiling and washed and clean under a blue sky. If for no other sight than that, that journey into the hills was worth making.

ON THE WAY TO EDUAPRIM.

The wife of the manager of the mine was a fellow-countrywoman of mine. She liked West Africa, kept her health there, and felt towards it very much as I did. No one likes great heat. The unchanging temperature is rather difficult to bear for one unaccustomed to it, but she thought it might be managed by a woman interested in her work and her husband, and as for the other discomforts—like me, she smiled at them. "The people who grumble should live in Australia," said she, "and do their own work, cooking, washing, scrubbing. Do it for a week with the temperature averaging 100 degrees in the shade, and they wouldn't grumble at West Africa, and wouldn't dream of being sick." And yet this contented woman must have led a very lonely life. Some wandering man connected with the mines, or a stray Commissioner, would come to see her occasionally, and the news of the world would come on men's heads from Tarkwa. And, of course, I suppose there was always the mine, which was her husband's livelihood. They took me into the bush behind the bungalow and showed me a great mahogany tree they had cut down, and then they showed me what I had seen many and many a time in my life before, but never in Africa—men washing the sand for gold. They were "dollying" it first, that is crushing the hard stone in iron vessels and then washing it, and the "show," I could see for myself, was very good.

I lingered in Eduaprim; the charm of talking with a woman who found joy in making a home in the wilderness was not to be lightly foregone, and I only went when I remembered that it was the rainy season, the roads were bad, and Tarkwa was away over those forbidding hills.

And from Tarkwa I went up the line to Obuasi.

This railway line that runs from Sekondi to Kumasi, the capital of Ashanti, is a wonderful specimen of its class. Every day sees some improvement made, but, being a reasonable being, I cannot help wondering what sort of engineers laid it out. It presents no engineering difficulties, but it was extremely costly, and meanders round and round like a corkscrew. They are engaged now in straightening it, but still they say that when the guard wants a light for his pipe all he has to do is to lean out of his van and get it from the engine. It was laid through dense forest, but the forest is going rapidly, the trees being used up for fuel. In the early days, too, these trees were a menace, for again and again, when a fierce tornado swept across the land, the line would be blocked by fallen trees, a casualty that grows less and less frequent as the forest recedes. When first the line was opened they tell me all passengers were notified that they must bring food and bedding, as the company could not guarantee their being taken to their destination. There is also the story of the distracted but pious negro station-master, who telegraphed to headquarters, "Train lost, but by God's help hope to find it." It is a single line of 168 miles, so I conclude his trust in the Deity was not misplaced.

Obuasi, on the borders of Ashanti, is the great mine of West Africa, a mine that pays, I think, something like 75 per cent, on its original shares, and even at their present value pays 12 per cent. It is enough to set everyone looking for gold in West Africa.

And like Prestea, Obuasi is the mine, and the mine only. There are, I think, between eighty and one hundred white men, all, save the few Government officials and storekeepers, in some way or another connected with the mine, and the place at night looks like a jewel set in the midst of the hills, for it is lighted by electricity. Every comfort of civilisation seems to be here, save and except the white woman, who is conspicuous by her absence. "We want no white women," seems to be the general opinion; an opinion, I deeply regret to say, warranted by my experience of the average English woman who goes to West Africa.

BRIDGE ON THE WAY TO EDUAPRIM.

The place is all hill and valley, European bungalows built on the hills, embowered generally in charming gardens such as one sees seldom in the Colony, and the native villages—for there are about five thousand black men on the books of the mine—in the valleys. There are miles of little tramway railways too, handling about 35,000 tons a month, more, they tell me, than the Government railway does, and the mine pays Government a royalty of £25,000 a year.

Obuasi is a fascinating, beautiful place; I should have liked to have spent a month there, but it is not savagery. It is as civilised in many ways as London itself. I stayed in the mining manager's bungalow, and am very grateful to him for his hospitality, and the manager's bungalow is a most palatial place, set on the top of a high hill in the midst of a beautiful garden. Palm and mango and grape-fruit trees, flamboyant, palms, dahlias, corallita, crotons, and roses, the most beautiful roses in the world, red, white, yellow, pink, everywhere; a perfect glory of roses is his garden, and the view from the verandah is delightful. His wide and spacious rooms are panelled with the most beautiful native woods, and looking at it with the eyes of a passer-by, I could see nothing but interest in the life of the man who had put in a year there. He will object strongly, I know, to my writing in praise of anything West-African, and say what can I know about it in a brief tour. True enough, what can I know? But at least I have seen many lands, and I am capable of making comparisons.

Every man I met here pointed out to me the evils of life in Africa.

"You make the very worst of it," said I, and proceeded to tell the story of a bridge party in a Coast town that began at three o'clock on Friday afternoon and ended up at ten o'clock on Monday morning.

"And if those men have fever," said I, feeling I had clinched my argument, "they will set it down to the beastly climate."

"So it is," said my opponent emphatically; "we could always do that sort of thing in Buluwayo."

I thereby got the deepest respect for the climate of Buluwayo, and a most doubtful estimate of the character of the pioneer Englishman. Perhaps I look on these things with a woman's narrow outlook, but I'm not a bit sorry for the men who cannot dissipate without paying for it in Africa. I heartily wish them plenty of fever.

The manager took me on a trolley along one of these little lines, right away into the hills. This was a new form of progression. A seat for two people was fixed on a platform and pushed along the line, uphill or on the flat, by three or four negroes, and fairly flew by its own weight downhill. It was a delightful mode of progression, and as we flew along, Xi my host, while pointing out the sights, endeavoured to convert me, not to the faith that West Africa was unfit for the white woman, that would have been impossible, but that the mining industry was a very great one and most useful to the Colony. And here he succeeded.

DOLLYING FOR GOLD, EDI APRIM.

I admired the forests and regretted their going, but he showed me the farms that had taken their place. Bananas and maize and cassada, said he truly enough, were far more valuable to the people than the great, dark forests they had cleared away—ten people could live now where one had lived before; and so we rolled on till we came to the Justice mine, where all the hillside seemed to be worked, a mine that has been paying £10,000 a month for the last three years. Truly, it is a wonderful place, that Obuasi mine with its nine shafts, an industry in the heart of savage Africa. They pay £11,000 a week in wages, and when I was thinking how closely in touch it was with civilisation, the manager told me how the chiefs had just raised a great agitation against the mine because it worked on Friday, their sacred day. They complained that the snails were so shocked at this act of sacrilege that they were actually leaving the district. Now the snails in Ashanti are very important people, boundaries are always calculated with reference to them, and if a chief can prove that his men are in the habit of gathering snails over a certain area, it is proof positive that he holds jurisdiction over that land. That the snails should leave the district shocked would be a national calamity. The African snail looks like an enormous whelk, he haunts the Ashanti forest, and is at his best just at the commencement of the rains, when he begins to grow fat and succulent, but is not yet too gross and slimy. He is hunted for assiduously, and all along the forest paths may be seen men, laden with sticks on which are impaled snails drawn from their shells, dried, and smoked. Luckily also these African snails appear to be very sensible, and when it was put to them that the mines could not possibly stop working on a Friday, but a small monetary tribute would be paid to them regularly through the principal chief, they amiably consented at once to stay and meet their final end, as a self-respecting snail should, by impalement on a stick.

VIEW IN OBUASI.

CHAPTER XXII
A NEW TRADING CENTRE

The siege of Kumasi—The Governor in 1900—The rebellion—The friendlies under the walls of the fort—The Ashanti warrior of ten years ago and the trader of to-day—The chances of the people in the fort—The retreat—The gallant men who conducted it—The men who were left behind—The rescue—Kumasi of to-day—The trade that comes to Kumasi as the trade of Britain came to London in the days of Augustus—The Chief Commissioner—The men needed to rule West Africa.

And when I had been to Obuasi nothing remained but to go up the line and see Kumasi and go as far beyond as the time at my disposal would allow.

I wonder if English-speaking people have forgotten yet the siege of Kumasi. For me, I shall never forget, and it stands out specially in my mind because I know some of the actors, and now I have seen the fort where the little tragedy took place; for, put it what way you will, it was a tragedy, for though the principals escaped, some with well-merited honour, the minor actors died, died like flies, and no man knoweth even their names.

It was dark when I reached Kumasi and got out on to the platform and was met by the kind cantonment magistrate, put into a hammock, and carried up to the fort, and was there received by the Chief Commissioner and his pretty bride, one of the two white women who make Kumasi their home, I had seen many forts, old forts along the Coast, but this fort was put up in 1896, and in 1900 its inmates were fighting for their lives. In it were shut up the Governor, his wife, two or three unfortunate Basel missionary women, a handful of troops, and all the other white people in the place. Standing on the verandah overlooking the town to-day, with a piano playing soft music and a dining-table within reach set out with damask and cut-glass and flowers and silver, it is hard to believe that those times are only ten years back. I have heard men talk of those days, and they are reticent; there are always things it seems they think they had better not tell, and I gather that the then Governor was not very much beloved, and that no one put much faith in him. The rebellion started somewhere to the north, and by the time it reached Kumasi it was too late to fly, for it was a good eight days' hard march to the Coast through dense forest. The nearest possible safety outside that fort lay beyond the River Prah, at least three or four days' march away. Every white man and many of the black who were not Ashantis had taken refuge in the fort, which was crowded to suffocation, and outside, in front of the fort, camped the friendlies, safe to a certain extent under the white man's guns, but dying slowly because the white man could not give what he had not got himself—food; and here they died, died of disease and hunger and wounds, and the reek of their dying poisoned the air so that the white man, starving behind his high walls of cement, was like to have his end accelerated by those who stood by him.

And out beyond, where the English town now stands, with broad streets planted with palms and mangoes and *ficus*, were the encampments of fierce Ashanti warriors, their cloths wound round their middles, their hair brushed fiercely back from their foreheads, their powder-flasks and bullet-bags slung across their shoulders, and their long Danes in their hands, the locks carefully covered with a shield of pigskin. The same man, very often the very same individual, walks about the streets of Kumasi to-day, and if he wears a tourist cap and a shirt, torn, ragged, and dirty, he is at least a peaceful citizen, and ten years hence he will probably, like the Creoles in Sierra Leone, be talking of "going home." But it was ghastly in the fort then. It was small and it was crowded to suffocation. The nearest help was at Cape Coast, nigh on 200 miles away, and between lay the dense forest that no man lightly dared. The Ashanti too was the warrior of the Coast, and the difficulty was even to get carriers who would help to move a force against him. Shut up in the fort there they looked out and waited for help and waited for death that ever seemed coming closer and closer.

Kumasi is set in a hollow, and round it, pressing in on every side, was the great forest. Away to the south went the road to Cape Coast, but it was but a track kept open with the greatest difficulty, and hidden in the depths of the forest on either hand were these same warriors. Truly the chances of the people in the fort seemed small, small indeed. And day after day passed and there was no sign of help. Provisions were getting low, ammunition was running short, and from the Ashanti no mercy could be expected. It was war to the death. Any man or woman who fell into their hands could expect nothing but torture. I gather that his advisers would have had the Governor start for the Coast at once on the outbreak of hostilities, but he could not make up his mind, and lingered and lingered, hoping for the help that did not, that could not come. No one has ever had a word of praise for that Governor, though very gallantly the men under him came out of it. Starvation and death stared them all in the face; the gallant little garrison, heavily handicapped as it was, could certainly hold out but little longer, and the penalty of conquest was death—death, ghastly and horrible.

At last the Governor gave in and they started, a forlorn little company, for the River Prah, which had generally set a bound to Ashanti raids. The Governor's wife was carried in a hammock, but the Basel missionary women, who had escaped with only the clothes they stood up in, walked, for the hammock-boys were too weak to carry them, and they had to tramp through mud and swamp. The soldiers did their best to protect the forlorn company, the friendlies crowded after, a tumultuous, disorderly crew fleeing before their enemies, and those same enemies hung on their flanks, scrambled through the forest, ruthlessly cut off any stragglers, and poured volleys from their long Danes into the retreating company. Knowing the forest, I wonder that one man ever escaped alive to tell the tale; that the principal actors did, only shows that the Ashanti was not the practised warrior the Coast had always counted him. Had those Ashantis been the lean Pathan from the hills of northern India, not a solitary man would have lived to tell the tale, and the retreat from Kumasi would have taken its place with some of those pitiful stories of the Afghan Border. But one thing the Ashanti is not, he is not a good marksman. He blazes away with his long Dane, content to make a terrific row without making quite sure that every bullet has reached its billet. And so, thanks to the bad marksmanship of the Ashantis, that little company got through.

But let no man think I am in any way disparaging the men who fought here, who by their gallantry brought the Governor and his wife through. Major Armitage and his comrades were brave men of whom England may well be proud, men worthy to take their places beside Blake and Hawkins and all the gallant Britons whose names are inscribed on the roll of fame; they fought against desperate odds, they were cruelly hampered by the helpless people under their care, and they stuck beside them, though by so doing they risked not only death, but death by ghastly torture. Some of them died, some of them got through—they are with us still, young men, men in the prime of life—and when we tell our children tales of the way England won her colonies, we may well tell how that little company left the fort of Kumasi, every man who was wise with cyanide of potassium in his pocket, and fought his way down to the Prah.

But even though they went south they were not going to abandon Kumasi, which had been won at the cost of so much blood, and in that fort were left behind three white men and a company of native soldiers. All in good time the relief must come, and till then they must hold it.

A verandah hangs round the fort nowadays that the piping times of peace have come, but still upstairs in the rooms above are the platforms for the gun-carriages, and I climbed up on them and walked along the verandahs and wondered how those men must have felt who had looked out from the self-same place ten years ago. If no help came, if waiting were unduly prolonged, they would die, die like rats in a hole, and the men in their companies were dying daily. They were faithful, those dark soldiers of the Empire, but they were dying, dying of disease and hunger, and their officers could not help them, for were they not slowly dying themselves? Rumours there were of the relief force, but they were only rumours, and the spectres of disease and starvation grew daily. Could they hold out? Could they hold out? The tale has been told again and again, and will probably be told yet again in English story, and at last when they had well-nigh given up to despair they heard the sound of English guns, so different from the explosions of the long Danes, and presently there was the call of the bugles, and out into the open trotted a little fox terrier, the advance guard of the men who had come to save Kumasi.

And now the change. Kumasi has a train from the coast port of Sekondi every day, it has a population that exceeds that of the capital of the Gold Coast itself, every day the forest is receding and in the streets are growing up great buildings that mark only the beginning of a trade that is already making the wise wonder how it was when wealth lay on the ground for the picking up, England, who had it all within her grasp, was amiable enough to allow the greater portion of this wonderful land to fall to the lot of the French and Germans.

The forest used to close Kumasi in on every side. It is set in a hollow, and the tall trees and luxuriant green in the days that I have just spoken of threatened to overwhelm it. Now that sensation has passed away. Whatever Kumasi may be in the future, to-day it is a busy centre of life and trade. Where the fetish tree stood, the ground beneath its branches soaked with human blood and strewn with human bones, is now the centre of the town where the great buildings of the merchant princes of West Africa are rising. They are fine, but they are a blot on the landscape for all that. The nation that prides itself on being the colonising nation of the earth never makes any preparation for the expansion of its territory or the growth of its trade, so here in this conquered country, bought at the cost of so much sweat and blood, the authorities are allowing to go up, in the very heart of the town buildings, very handsome buildings without doubt, so close together that in a tropical land where fresh air is life itself they are preparing to take toll of the health of the unfortunates who will have to dwell and work there. But beyond that one grave mistake Kumasi promises to be a very pretty place as well as a very important one. Its wide, red roads, smooth and well-kept, are planted with trees, mangoes and palms; its bungalows are set well apart, surrounded by trees and shrubs and lawns, their red-brown roofs and verandahs toning picturesquely with the prevailing green.

CHIEF RAISED IN HIS HAMMOCK CHAIR.

Curious it is when one thinks of its history to see the white painted sign-posts on which are recorded the names of the streets. There is "Kingsway" for one, and "Stewart-avenue," after the man who deeply loved the country, for another, and there are at least two great roads that lead away to the fruitful country in the north, roads that push their way through the dense forest and must even compel the admiration of our friends the Germans, those champion road-makers. And down those roads comes all the wonderful trade of Kumasi, not as the trade of London, of course, but as the trade of London was, perhaps, when Augustus ruled at Rome. The trade of the world comes to London nowadays, the trade of the back-country came to London then, and so does the trade of all the country round come to the Ashanti capital. Its streets are thronged with all manner of peoples, dark, of course, for the ruling whites are but an inconsiderable handful, and only the Chief Commissioner and one missionary have been daring enough to bring their wives.

Ashanti is a conquered country, and it seems to me it has got just the right sort of Government, a Government most exactly suited to the requirements of the negro in his present state of advancement. What a negro community requires is a benevolent despotism, but as a rule the British Government, with its feeling for the rights of the individual, does not see its way to give it such a Government. But Ashanti was conquered at great cost, wherefore as yet England has still to think of the rights of the white men who dwell there as against the rights of the black man, and the result to me, an onlooker, appears to be most satisfactory for both white and black. Of course, such a Government requires to administrate not only excellent men, not only honest and trustworthy men, but men who have the interests of the country at heart, and who devote themselves to it, and such men she has got in the Chief Commissioner, Mr Fuller, and the subordinates chosen by him. Only an onlooker am I, a woman, a passer-by, but as a passer-by I could not but be struck by the difference between the feeling in the Gold Coast Colony and the feeling in Ashanti. The whole tone of thought was different. Everywhere on the Gold Coast men met me with the question, "What did I think of this poisonous country? Wasn't it a rotten place?" and they seemed bitterly disappointed if I did not confirm their worst blame.

CHIEF OF NKWANTA.

But in Ashanti it was different. The very clerks in the mercantile houses had some good word to say for the country, and were anxious that I should appreciate it and speak well of it, and this I can but set down to the example and guidance of such men as the Chief Commissioner and the men he chooses to serve under him. Had the rest of West Africa always had such broad-minded, clever, interested men at the head of affairs, I think we should have heard a great deal less about its unhealthiness and a great deal more about the productiveness of the country. Since I have seen German methods I am more than thankful that I have been to Ashanti and learned that my own country is quite equal to doing as well, if not beating them at their own methods. The Ashanti himself, the truculent warrior of ten years ago, has under the paternal and sympathetic Government of this Chief Commissioner become a man of peace. If he has not beaten his long Dane gun into a ploughshare he has at least taken very kindly to trade and is pleased, nay eager that the white man should dwell in his country. He stalks about Kumasi in his brightly coloured, toga-like cloth still, very sure that he is a man of great importance among the tribes, and his chiefs march through the streets in chairs on men's heads, with tom-toms beating, immense gaily coloured umbrellas twirling, their silken' cloths a brilliant spot in the brilliant sunshine, their rich gold ornaments marking them off from the common herd, and all their people who are not Christian still give them unquestioned devotion. But Kumasi, as I said, is the centre of a great trade, and the native town, which is alongside but quite apart from the European town, is packed with shops, shops that are really very much in the nature of stalls, for there are no fronts to them, and the goods are exposed to the street, where all manner of things that are attractive to the native are set out.

And here one gathers what is attractive to the native. First and foremost, perhaps, are the necessities of life, the things that the white man has made absolute necessaries. First among them, I think, would be kerosene and bread, so everywhere, in market-place and shop, or even just outside a house, you may see ordinary wine and whisky bottles full of kerosene, and rows and rows of loaves of bread. Then there comes men's clothing—hideous shirts and uglier trousers, tourist caps that are the last cry in hooliganism, and boots, buttoned and shiny, that would make an angel weep. Alas! and alas! The Ashanti in his native state, very sure of himself, has a certain dignity about him even as must have had the old Roman. You might not have liked the old Roman, probably you would not unless he chose to make himself pleasant, but you could not but recognise the fact that he was no nonentity, and so it is with the Ashanti till he puts on European garments. Then how are the mighty fallen! for like all negroes, in the garb of civilisation, he is commonplace when he is not grotesque. What they are to wear I cannot say, but the better-class among them seem to realise this, for I have often heard it said, not only in Ashanti but in other parts of the Coast: "The Chief may not wear European clothes."

CHIEF COMMISSIONER AND HIS WIFE, KUMASI.

And beside clothes in the native shops are hurricane lanterns, ordinary cheap kerosene lamps, and sewing machines which the men work far more often then the women, accordions, mouth harmoniums, and cotton goods in the strange and weird patterns that Manchester thinks most likely to attract the native eye. I have seen brooms and brushes and dustpans printed in brilliant purple on a blue ground, and I have seen the outspread fingers of a great hand in scarlet on a black ground. But mostly there is nothing of very great interest in these shops, just European goods of the commonest, cheapest description supplied apparently with the view of educating the native eye in all that is ugliest and most reprehensible in civilisation.

There are horses in Kumasi, for the forest and undergrowth have been cleared away sufficiently to destroy the tsetse fly, and so most evenings, when the heat of the day has passed, the Chief Commissioner and his wife go for a ride, and on occasions many of the soldiermen play polo and hold race-meetings, but as yet there is no wheeled traffic in the streets. Most of the goods are carried on men's heads, and the roadways are crowded. There are women with loads on their heads and generally children on their backs, walking as if the world belonged to them, though in truth they are little better than their husbands' slaves. There are soldiers all in khaki, with little green caps like condensed fezes, lor the place is a great military camp and the black soldier swaggers through the street; there are policemen in blue uniforms with red fezes, their feet bare like those of the soldiers, and their legs bound in dark-blue putties; and there are black men from all corners of West Africa. There are the Kroo boys, those labourers of the Coast, with the dark-blue freedom mark tattooed on their foreheads, never carrying anything on their heads, but pushing and pulling heavily laden carts, in gangs that vary from four to a dozen, and their clothing is the cast-off clothing of the white man; there are Hausas and Wangaras, than whom no man can carry heavier loads, and they wear not a flowing cloth like the Ashanti, but a long, shirt-like garment not unlike the smock of the country labourer. It is narrower and longer, but is usually decorated with the same elaborate needlework about the neck and shoulders; if their legs are not bare they wear Arab trousers, full above and tight about their feet, and the flapping of their heelless slippers makes a clack-clack as they walk. There are Yorubas, dressed much the same, only with little caps like a child's Dutch bonnet, and there are even men from the far north, with blue turbans and the lower part of their faces veiled. Far beyond the dense forest lies their home, away possibly in French territory, but the trade is coming to this new city of the Batouri, and they wander down with the cattle or horses. For all the cattle and horses come down through the forest, driven hastily and fast because of the deadly tsetse, and many must perish by the way. A herd of the humped, long-horned cattle come wearily through the streets. Whatever they may have been once, there is no spirit left in them now, for they have come down that long road from the north; they have fed sparely by the way, and they are destined for the feeding of the population that are swarming into Kumasi to work the mines in the south.

GREAT FETISH CHIEF, KUMASI.

Three towns are here in Kumasi: the European quarter, the Ashanti town, and the Mohammedan town or *zonga*. Here all the carrying trade that is not done by Government is arranged for—by a woman. Here the houses are small and unattractive, nondescript native huts built by people who are only sojourners in the land, come but to make money, ready to return to their own land in the north the moment it is made. And they sit by the roadside with little things to sell. Food-stuffs often, balls of kenki white as snow, yams and cassada, which is the root of which we make tapioca, cobs of Indian corn, and, of course, stink-fish that comes all the way from the Coast and is highly prized as a food, and does not appear to induce ptomaine poisoning in African stomachs. Some of these dainties are set out on brass trays made in Birmingham; others on wooden platters and on plates delicately woven in various patterns of grass dyed in many colours. But most things they have they are ready to sell, for the negro has great trading instincts, and that trading instinct it is that has made him so easy to hold once he is conquered.

Kumasi is peaceful enough now, and the only reminder of the bad days of ten years back is the fort just above the native town, but it looks down now across a smooth green lawn, on which are some great, shady trees, where chiefs assembled whom I photographed. One was a great fetish chief with gold ornaments upon his head and upon his feet, and knowledge of enough magic, had this been the fifteenth century instead of the twentieth, to drive the white man and all his following back to the sea from whence he came; but it is the twentieth, and he is wise enough to know it, and he flings all the weight of his authority into the scales with the British raj. But at the gate of the fort still stands a guard of black soldiers in all the glory of scarlet and yellow which stands for gold, for the Chief Commissioner lives here, and in a land where a chief is of such importance it is necessary to keep up a certain amount of state, and the Chief Commissioner ruling over this country and receiving obeisance from the chiefs, clad in their gorgeous silken cloths, laden with golden jewellery, men looked up to by their followers as half-divine, must feel something like a Roman proconsul of old carrying the eagles into savage lands, and yet allowing those savages as far as possible to govern themselves by their own laws. Africa has always been the unknown land, but now at last the light is being let into dark places, the French have regenerated Dahomey, and the railway comes to Kumasi. I sat on that verandah and thought of the old days that were only ten years back, and learned much from the Commissioner, and I felt that civilisation was coming by leaps and bounds to Ashanti, and if it be true, as old tradition has it, that a house to be firmly built must have a living man beneath its foundation stone, then must the future of Kumasi be assured, for its foundations were well and truly laid in rivers of human blood.

CROSSING THE OFIN RIVER, ASHANTI.

CHAPTER XXIII
IN THE HEART OF THE RUBBER COUNTRY

Bound for Sunyani—The awe-inspiring-forest—The road through the forest—The people upon that road—Ofinsu and an Ashanti house—Rather a public bedroom—Potsikrom—A night of fear—Sandflies—Attractive black babies—A great show at Bechem—A most important person—The Hausa who went in fear of his life—Coronation night at Tanosu—A teetotal party—The medical officer's views on trees—Beyond the road—Sunyani.

I talked to the Commissioner, and those talks with him made me want to go somewhere out into the wilds. Kumasi was beginning to look strangely civilised to me. It was a great trading-centre, and presently it would be as well known, it seemed to me, as Alexandria or Cairo, or at the other end of the Continent, Buluwayo. I should like to have gone into the Northern Territories, but the rainy season was upon us, and if that did not daunt me—and it would not have done so—I had to consider the time. I ought to be back in London. I had intended to be away for six months, and now it was close on eight since I had come out of the mouth of the Mersey.

"Go to Sunyani," said the Chief Commissioner, "and go on to Odumase, where the rising began at the beginning of the century. You will be the first white woman to go there, and I think you will find it worth your while."

So I interviewed the head of the transport service, and by his kindness was supplied with seventeen carriers, and one hot day in June started north.

They had doubts, these kind friends of mine, about my capabilities as a traveller, at least they feared that something might happen to me while I was in their country, and they told me that a medical officer was starting north for Sunyam that day and would go with me.

I looked up the medical officer and found him in the midst of packages that he was taking with him beyond civilisation to last for a year. He was most courteous, but it seemed to me that he felt the presence of a woman a responsibility, and I was so sure of myself, hated to be counted a nuisance, that when he said he had intended to go only as far as Sansu that night, I expressed my intention of going on to Ofinsu, and hinted that he might catch me up next morning if he could.

So by myself I set out into the heart of the rubber country north of Kumasi. I was fairly beyond civilisation now. Ten years ago this country was in open rebellion against English rule, and even now there are no European stores there; there is no bread, no kerosene, no gin—those first necessities of an oncoming civilisation; it was simply the wild heart of the rubber country, unchanged for hundreds of years. It has been known, but it has not been lightly visited. It has been a country to be shunned and talked of with bated breath as "the land of darkness." The desert might be dared, the surf might be ventured, the black man might be defied, but the gloom of the forest the white man feared and entered not except upon compulsion. The Nile has given up its secrets, the Sahara yields to cultivation, but still in Africa are there places where the all-conquering white man is dwarfed, and one of them is the great forest that lies north of the capital of Ashanti.

PATH IN THE FOREST, ASHANTI.

Here we know not the meaning of the word forest. England's forests are delightful woods where the deer dwell in peace, where the rabbits scutter through the fern and undergrowth, and where the children may go for a summer's holiday; in Australia are trees close-growing and tall; but in West Africa the forest has a life and being of its own. It is not a thing of yesterday or of ten years back or of fifty years. Those mighty trees that dwarf all other trees in the world have taken hundreds of years to their growth. When a slight young girl came to the throne of England, capturing a nation's chivalry by her youth and innocence, the mahogany and kaku and odoum trees were old and staid monarchs of the forest. When the first of the Georges came over from Hanover, unwelcome, but the nation's last hope, they were young and slim but already tall trees stretching up their crowns to the brilliant sunlight that is above the gloom, and now at last, when the fifth of that name reigns over them, at last is their sanctuary invaded and the seclusion that is theirs shall be theirs no longer. For already the axe is laid to their roots, and through the awe-inspiring forest runs a narrow roadway kept clear by what must be almost superhuman labour, and along that roadway, the beginning of the end, the sign that marks the peaceful conquest of the savage, that marks also the downfall of the forest though it is not even whispered among the trees that scorn them yet, flows a perpetual stream of traffic, men, women, and children. Backwards and forwards from the north to Kumasi and the sea they come, and they bear on their heads, going north, corrugated iron and cotton goods, kerosene, and flour, and chairs, all the trifles that the advance of civilisation makes absolute necessaries; and coming down they bring all in their season, hides, and heavy cakes of rubber, and sticks of dried snails, and all the other articles of native produce that a certain peace has made marketable along the way or in the markets of Kumasi.

The spell was upon me the moment I left the town. That road is like nothing else in the world. The hammock and the carriers were dwarfed by the great roots and buttresses of the trees to tiny, crawling ants, and overhead was a narrow strip of blue sky where the sunlight might be seen, but only at noon did that sunlight reach the roadway below. We travelled in a shadow pleasant in that heat; and on either side, close on either side, were the great trees. Looking down the road I could see them straight as a die, tall pillars, white and brown; ahead of me and close at hand the mighty buttresses that supported those pillars rose up to the height of perhaps ten men before the tree was fairly started, a tall trunk with branches that began to spread, it seemed to me, hundreds of feet above the ground. And between those tree-trunks was all manner of undergrowth, and all were bound and matted together with thickly growing creepers and vines. It was impossible to step an inch from that cleared path. There would be no getting lost in the bush, for it would be almost impossible for the unpractised hand to get into the bush. There is nothing to be seen but the brown, winding roadway, the dense green of the undergrowth, and the trunks of the trees tall and straight as Nelson's column and brown or white against the prevailing green. And there are all shades of green, from that so pale that it is almost golden to that so dark it is almost black, but never a flower breaks the monotony, the monotony that is not monotony but dignity, and the flowers of an English spring or an autumn in Australia would but cheapen the forest of the Gold

Coast. There must have been orchids, for sometimes as I passed their rich, sensuous smell would come to my nostrils, but I only knew they were there by my sense of smell just as sometimes I smelt a strong smell of mice, and knew, though I could not see them, that somewhere in the depths of the gloom were hidden away a great colony of fruitarian bats that would not come out into the daylight.

RUBBER CARRIERS IN POTSINROM.

When there was a village there was, of course, a clearing, and on the first day I passed several villages until at last I came to Ofinsu, where I had arranged to spend the night. Ofinsu is on the banks of a river, and the road comes out of the forest and passes broadly between two rows of mud-walled houses with steeply pitched, high-thatched roofs, and my carriers raced along and stopped opposite a small wooden door in a mud wall and rapped hard.

For the first time on my travels I had really excellent carriers. They were Krepis from beyond the German border, slight, dark men with slim wrists and ankles, and crosses cut as tribal marks on each cheek, and they were cheerful, smiling, willing. When I remembered my before-time tribulations I could hardly believe these were actually carriers who were going along so steadily and well, who were always up before me in the morning, and in as soon as I was at night, who never lingered, never grumbled, never complained, but were simply ideal servants such as I had never had before in my life save perhaps for a day, as when I went to Palime from Ho, and such as I shall count myself extremely lucky if I ever have again.

"We *have* got good carriers," the transport officer had said, "though you don't seem to believe it"; and he proved his words, for never have I travelled more comfortably than I did on that one hundred and sixty miles to Sunyani and back.

The knocking at the little door brought a black lady with a shaven head and a blue cloth wrapped round her middle. She was a woman past all beauty, and very little was left to the imagination, but she threw open the door and indicated that we were to enter, and she looked at me very curiously. Never before had a white woman come to Ofinsu.

I entered, and this was my first introduction to an Ashanti house, a house that seems to me singularly suited to the climate and people. It is passing away, they tell me, and I for one am sorry.

We went into a courtyard open to the sky, and round it, raised at least two feet from the ground, were the rooms, I suppose I must call them, but though there was a roof overhead and walls on three sides, walls without windows, the fourth side was open to the central courtyard. When I entered the place was crowded; Hausas or Wangaras—I never could tell one from the other—were settled down on the platforms, and their loads—long bundles made up for carrying on the head—were all over the place. I said nothing. I am generally for the superiority of the white man and exact all the deference that is my due, but clearly these people were here first, and it seemed to me they had it by right, only how I was to bathe and sleep in a house where everything was so public among such a crowd I did not know.

HEADMAN IN FRONT OF AUTHOR'S BEDROOM, OFINSU.

But my hostess had other views. No sooner had I entered than she began clearing out the former guests, and in less than a quarter of an hour the place that had seemed so crowded was empty, swept and garnished for my accommodation. My bed was put up on one platform, my table and chair on another. "Get table quick and chair, so can play cards," Grant instructed my headman, and behind, through a little door that may be seen in the picture, was a place that answered for a kitchen, and a cup of tea was quickly produced for my comfort. It was weird going to sleep there in the open, but it was very, very delightful. I rigged up in the corner of one of the rooms—I have no other names for them—with ground sheet and rugs, a little shelter where I could have my bath in comfort, but I undressed without a qualm and went to bed and slept the sleep of the woman who has been in the open air the livelong day and who, happily for herself, can indulge her taste and sleep in the open air all night.

I took a picture of my open-air bedroom with my valuable headman and two small children who belonged to the household I had invaded in the foreground. But that was before I went to bed at night. At earliest dawn, before the dawn in fact, my headman was at my bedside wanting to pack up and start.

That night's lodging cost me one shilling and threepence. The headman told me one shilling was enough, so I bestowed the extra threepence as a dash on the shaven old woman who had done all for me that my servants could not do, and she seemed so delighted that I was left wondering what the Wangaras who had given place to me had paid.

Just as the sun was rising we crossed the Ofin River, and I found there assembled the entire population of the village to look at the strange sight—a perfectly courteous, polite people who never crushed or crowded though they looked their fill. I can only hope I was a success as a show, for certainly I attracted a great deal of attention, but of course I had no means of knowing whether I came up to expectations. It took some time to get my goods and followers across the river in the crank canoe which is only used in the rainy season, for usually the Ofin River can be waded, and while I waited on the farther shore I looked with interest at the other people who were waiting for their loads to be ferried across.

The men were Hausas or Wangaras, some wearing turbans, some with shaven heads, and clad in long, straight, shirt-like garments, while the women excited my deepest compassion. They may have been the men's wives, I know not; but by whatever name they were called they were slaves if ever I saw slaves. They had very little on besides a dirty, earthen-coloured cloth hitched round their loins, their dark faces were brutalised and depressed with that speechless depression that hardly realises its own woes, and their dusty hair that looked as if it had not been washed for years was generally twisted into short, thick, dusty looking plaits that were pressed downwards by the weight of the load they one and all carried. They carried children, too, on their backs, tiny babies that must have been born on the journey, or lusty youngsters that were a load in themselves. But a Hausa will carry an enormous load himself—sometimes up to 240 lbs.—so it is not likely he will have much consideration for his women. It may be, of course, that their looks belied them, but it seemed to me that they cared little whether Fate drowned them there in the swirling brown waters of the river or brought them safely through to the other side to tramp on, footsore, tired, weary, heartsick—if these creatures who looked like dumb beasts had life enough in them to be heartsick—to their destination three months away in the north.

FOREST PATH IN ASHANTI.

They waited there as I passed, and they looked at me dully and without interest; presently their loads would be brought across and they would be on the march again, and I went on pitying to Potsikrom.

The forest was getting denser and denser. There were fewer towns and clearings on this day—nothing but the great trees and the narrow ribbon of road with the strip of blue sky far, far away. It was very awe-inspiring, the forest. I should have been unspeakably terrified to pass through it alone, but my chattering men took away all sense of loneliness. There was not much to see, but yet the eternal trees had a most wonderful charm. It was like being in some lofty cathedral where the very air was pulsating with the thought of great and unseen things beyond the comprehension of the puny mortals who dared rashly to venture within the precincts. No wonder the Ashanti gave human sacrifices. Sacrifice, we all know, is the basis of all faith, and what lesser thing than a man could be offered in so great a sanctuary?

And that afternoon we came to Potsikrom, a little village deep in the forest.

The rest-house was a mud building with a thatch roof somewhat dilapidated, and built not after the comfortable, suitable Ashanti fashion, but after the European fashion, possibly in deference to some foolish European who probably regarded all the country as "poisonous." That is to say, it was divided into two rooms with holes in the clay, very small holes for windows, and, saving grace, a door at each side of one of the rooms. In the corner of one of these impossible rooms I saw, to my surprise, a camp-bed put up, and for the moment thought it was mine. Then I saw a suit of striped pyjamas which certainly were not mine, and realised it must belong to the medical officer whom I had left at Kumasi the day before. His boys had stolen a march ahead, and, thinking to do better than the white woman, had put up his bed in what they considered the most desirable place, thinking doubtless that possession was nine points of the law.

I certainly didn't desire that corner, but I felt my authority must be maintained, and so I asked:

"Who that bed belong to?"

"Massa," said a grinning boy.

"Take it down," said I.

Up came the Chief's clerk. All these Ashanti chiefs now have a clerk who can write a little English and so communicate for them with Government, and the clerk, interested as he was to see a white woman, was very certain in his own mind that the white man was the more important person. He probably regarded me as his wife come on ahead, and said that the Chief had another house for me.

I didn't like that rest-house, but pride has suffered pain since the beginning of the world, so I distinctly declared my intention of staying there and ordered them to clear out the medical officer's bed forthwith.

My boys were very anxious to assert my superiority and out went that bed in the twinkling of an eye, and my men proceeded to put up mine between the two doors, and, having had a table set out for tea, I awaited the arrival of the medical officer with a quiet mind.

REST HOUSE, POTSIKROM.

Presently he arrived and we laughed together over the struggle for supremacy between our men, and pledged our future good fellowship in tea. The Chief sent me in eggs and chickens and yams as dash, the people came and looked at me, and presently the evening fell and I had my evening meal and went to bed.

And when I went to bed I repented me of having stood on my dignity. What on earth had I wanted the rest-house for? It was the last house in the village, a little apart from the rest, the great solemn forest was all around me, and I was all alone, for Grant and the men had retired with the darkness to somewhere in the village. My bed stood under a roof certainly, but I should not have dared put up the door of the rest-house for fear of making it too close, and so it meant, of course, that I was sleeping with nothing between me and that awe-inspiring forest. I do not know what I was afraid of any more than I know what I feared at Anum, but I was afraid of something intangible, born of the weird stillness and the gloom. I put a hurricane lantern at the door to scare away any wandering pigs and goats—I did not really in my heart think there would be any wild beasts—and then I proceeded to put in a most unpleasant night. First there was too much light, it fell all over my bed, and though I did not like it, I still felt a comfortable sense of safety in the light.

Then I began to itch. I twisted and turned and rolled over, and the more I moved about the more uncomfortable I became. I thought to myself, "There, it serves you right! You are always nursing the fat little black babies and now you have got some horrible disease." The thought was by no means consoling, but I was being driven so frantic that I began to think that no disease could really advance with such rapidity. Besides, all sorts of great insects were banging themselves against my mosquito curtains, so I came to the conclusion that probably the tiny sandflies were also attracted by the light and were getting through the meshes. There was nothing for it but to screw up my courage, get out of bed, and take that lantern away. I did it, crept back to bed again, listened for a little to the weird noises of the night, was relieved to find the appalling irritation showed no signs of increasing, and finally, in spite of my fears, dropped off into so sound a sleep that I was only awakened by Grant endeavouring to drive away by fair words my energetic headman, who was evidently debating whether it was not his bounden duty to clear me away, bed and all.

I told the doctor my experiences in the morning, and he confirmed my supposition that it was only sandflies and not horrible disease that had troubled my slumbers.

Very much relieved was I, for the little black babies are dear little round souls, and I should have been loath not to take them when their mothers trusted them to me. I should hesitate much before I took a baby of the peasant class in this country, but there, in the heart of Africa, it is always safe to cuddle the little, round, naked thing that has for all clothing a few beads or a charm or two tied to its hair. They are always clean and soft and round and chubby, and they do not invariably yell with terror at the white woman, though I am bound to say they often do.

MAKING POTS IN THE FOREST

We were in the heart of the forest now. There were but one or two villages and only one or two places that could be dignified by the name of clearings. At one, as big, perhaps, as a tiny London square, three or four huts had been erected, and an old woman was making pots. They were all set out in the sun to dry, and the good lady was very nervous when I wanted to take her photograph. She consented at last, and sat there shivering, in her hand a great snail shell which she used to ornament the pots. They were such a lonely little company, so cut off from all their kind, and we must have been such wondrous figures breaking in on their life and then passing on again. I gave them the last bright new pennies I had, and left them wondering.

And so we went on again through the forest, past Insuta, until, as the evening was falling, we created immense astonishment by arriving at Bechem.

Here again the rest-house was built uncomfortably, European fashion, and again my only alternative was to have my bed put up between the two doors so that I might get plenty of air. But at Bechem the town was full. It was a big town set in the midst of a great clearing, and to-day it was swarming with people, for the next day was Coronation Day, and the Chief had sent out word that all his sub-chiefs were to come in and celebrate. And here was another excitement—a white woman! How many chiefs came to see me that day I really would be afraid to say, and the Chief sent me in by way of dash a sheep, a couple of chickens, piles of plantains, yams, eggs, and all manner of native edibles. It was very amusing to stand there in the midst of the swarming people, receiving these offerings. Of course they all have to be returned with presents of value, and I was thankful they did not think me important enough to receive a cow; as it was it cost me a pound to get out of

Bechem, but my carriers were delighted for I presented them with the sheep. He was an elderly ram with long horns, and I think he was the only person who did not thoroughly enjoy the entertainment.

The Chief sent in word through his interpreter to say that the people had never seen a white woman before; there were many people here because of the Coronation, might they come and "look"? Never have I been so frankly regarded as a show. There was nothing for it but to go outside and let them look, and once more I can only hope they were satisfied. I had never seen such crowds of natives before, crowds that had not seen much of the white man and as yet were not arrayed in his cast-off clothes. All round us long Dane guns were popping off in honour of the great occasion, and tom-toms were beating half the night. When I waked next morning—I slept in the passage to get plenty of air, but I was not afraid because the rest-house was near the centre of the village—I found that at the earliest glimpse of dawn long lines of people had assembled outside my house and were patiently waiting for me to come out. I had my breakfast in the little courtyard behind the house, the people peeping through the fence of palm-poles, and when we set out on our way the Chief, in all the glory of silken robes and great umbrella, came a little way to do us honour.

Never, not even when I was married, have I been such an important person. The tom-toms beat, the umbrellas twirled, long Danes went off, horns blew, and as far as the eye could see were the villagers trailing away behind us.

The Chief escorted us for about a mile, we walking in the cool, misty morning, and then he turned, slipped his cloth from his left shoulder as a mark of respect, shook hands, wished us a prosperous journey, and bid us good-bye like the courteous gentleman he was, and we went on into the mighty forest again.

It is always cool in the early morning, and very pleasant here among the trees, so the medical officer and I walked on chatting about Bechem, when we came upon another little party of travellers, who stopped us and asked help. It was a Hausa with a couple of women, his wives in all probability, and a couple of other men, presumably his slaves. He was a tall, strong man in the prime of life, upon whose shaven head were deep lines graven by the loads he had carried. Our headman, who could speak Hausa, interpreted.

Men were following him from Nkwanta, he said, to kill him. A child had died in the town, and they said he "had put bad medicine upon it," that is, had bewitched it, and the penalty was death.

It was rather startling in this twentieth century to be brought face to face with the actors in such a tragedy, especially when we were powerless to help. We were unarmed and had with us only carriers and servants; it was the prestige of the white man that was carrying us through. The Hausa was going away from Nkwanta as fast as he possibly could, and apparently he did not want to trust himself within its bounds, even under the protection of a white man. He declined to come back with us, and what could we do? The medical officer, I think, did all that he could when he promised to report things to the Commissioner at Sunyani, and recommended the Hausa, since he would not avail himself of our protection, to get the Chiefs clerk at Bechem to write his account of the affair to Sunyani and Kumasi.

And so in the early morning we went our way, and he went his, and he disappeared into the gloom of the forest, a much troubled man. I wondered how he would ever get back to his home in the north, for there is but this one road, and that road leads through Nkwanta. He would only dare it, I think, with a large body of his own people, for who is to report to Government if a travelling Hausa should disappear?

We put in a long day that day, and in the full heat of the noontide arrived at Nkwanta, a most important place, whose Chief rules over a large tract of country. We came upon the butchers' stalls first, all kept by Hausas or Wangaras. This country, on account of the tsetse fly, will allow but few cattle to live, and these men from the north drive them down, kill them, and sell them, for the Ashantis are rich, and like to buy meat. I had hardly taken a photograph of these stalls, when from all sides I saw the people assembling, and presently the Chief appeared. He brought offerings, a sheep, fowls, eggs; yams, and plantains; but this time I pointed out that I was on a journey, and could not take the presents, as I had no means of carrying them. He was very anxious indeed we should stay for that night; said he, they were celebrating the Coronation, and there would be a big dance. I went into his house and took a photograph of the moulded clay that ornaments the walls, and a small slave-boy was proud to stand in the corner so as to give life to the picture, and I think Nkwanta was sorry we elected to go on. I was a little sorry myself afterwards, for as we passed along the forest path we met sub-chiefs going in to the Coronation ceremonies, men carried high in their hammock-chairs, followed by a motley assemblage of men and women, bearing long Danes, horns, drums, household utensils, and all the paraphernalia of a barbaric chief.

ISHANTI WOMAN AND CHILD IN THE FOREST.

And at last we came to a place where the forest was ruthlessly cleared for about a hundred feet on either side of the road, and the tropical sun poured down in all its fierceness. I did not like it. The mighty monarchs of the forest had simply been murdered and left to lie, and already Nature was busily veiling them with curtains of greenery. Why those trees had been so slaughtered I do not know. That the forest would have been better for thinning, I have no doubt, but why not leave the beautiful trees? I am sure the Germans would have done so, but the Englishman seems to have no mean. If there are too many trees he cuts them all down and makes a desert. The medical officer of course did not agree with me.

"Must get rid of the trees," said he with enthusiasm.

I looked at him. He was a young fellow, pleasant and kindly, sallowed by life in the Tropics. He wore a drab-coloured helmet, coming well down over his back, which was further protected by having a quilted spinal pad fastened down the back of his bush shirt.

"Why," I said, "do you wear so big a helmet, and a spinal pad?"

He looked at me tolerantly, as if he had always known that woman asked silly questions, and I was only confirming a preconceived idea. But he was in a way my host, so he was patient with me.

"To keep off the sun, of course," said he.

"The trees," I began; and then he felt I really was silly, for every medical man knows the proper thing is to get rid of the trees, and have some artificial form of shade. At least, that is what I gathered from his subsequent explanation. The idea is apparently to cut down all the forest trees, and when the place is bare, they can be replaced by fresh trees, planted exactly where they ought to grow. Since they are not English trees it does not matter how beautiful they are, and that they take at least two hundred and fifty years to come to perfection is a matter of small moment. So the medical officer and I disagreed, till we came to Tanosu, a little town on the Tano River.

The Chief here had just built a new rest-house, thank heaven, on the comfortable Ashanti pattern, and I was given it by the courteous medical officer, who disapproved of me on trees, while he sought shelter in the village.

The people were very curious. The Chief, who it appears is a poor man, sent the usual presents, and then the people came and looked, and looked, till after about a couple of hours of it I grew weary, and shut the doors of the courtyard. Then they applied their eyes to every crank and cranny, and I had an uneasy feeling that whatever I did unseen eyes were following me. I wanted to rejoice in the Coronation, so I asked the doctor to come to dinner and celebrate, but unfortunately my kitchen was at least a quarter of a mile away, and there were such terrible long waits between the courses that again and again I had to ask my guest if he would not go and see what had happened. We finished at last, and I wanted to drink the King's health in whisky-and-soda which was the only drink I had, but my guest was a teetotaller, so I sent for the servants, only to be informed that every one of them refrained from liquor. And as a rule I approve so highly of temperance. Only for this once did I find it rather depressing. However, we stood up and drank the King's health, and I expect the eyes that were watching us wondered what on earth we were doing. They performed on tom-toms after that, and I fell asleep in the pleasant, damp night air, to a sort of barbaric fantasia on horns and drums.

BREAKING CAMP, KETREAL

We were nearing our journey's end. Early next morning we crossed the Tano River, which is full of sacred fish, and the medical officer took my photograph in the stream, and I took his, as he crossed on his boy's shoulders, and when we crossed to the other side we found we had left every vestige of the road, the good road that had so surprised me, behind. We went along a track now, a track that wound in and out in the dense, tropical forest. Generally the trees met overhead and we marched through a tunnel, the ground beneath our feet was often a quagmire, and if we could not see the sun often, neither could we feel the rain that fell on the foliage above our heads. On either side we could see nothing but the great trunks and buttresses of the trees, and the dense undergrowth. Possibly to go for days and days through a forest like this might give a sense of oppression, but to go as I did, for but a short time, was like peeping into a new world. Never a bird or beast I saw, nothing but occasionally a long stream of driver ants, winding like a band of cut jet across the path. And so we went on and on, through the solemn forest, till at last it cleared a little. There was the sky above again, and then no forest, but on my left cornfields and the brown splash of a native town, and in front a clearing, with the rim of the forest again in the distance, and right ahead, on the top of the gently sloping rise, the European bungalows of Sunyani. I had arrived, the first white woman who had come so far off the beaten track.

ENTRANCE TO ASHANTI VILLAGE IN THE FOREST.

CHAPTER XXIV
AN OUTPOST

The white men at Sunyani—Contrast between civilisation and barbarism—The little fort—The suffrage movement—"I am as mud in the sight of my people!"—The girl who did not wish to marry the King—The heavy loads carried by the Hausas—The danger of stubbing a toe—An Ashanti welcome—The Chief's soul—The unpleasant duties of the Chief's soul—The blood of sheep versus the blood of men—A courteous lady of Odumase—The Commissioners of Ashanti—Difficulties of crossing flooded streams—One way of carrying fowls—The last night in the wilds.

At Sunyani there are usually six white men, namely a Provincial Commissioner, a medical officer—the relief had come up with me—three soldiermen, and a non-commissioned officer, and I think my sympathies are rather with that colour sergeant. The other men are all of one class, but he must be utterly alone. The houses and the men were equally delightful. I was taken into a mud-built house with a thatched roof, large and spacious. There were, of course, only holes for windows and doors, and the floors were of beaten earth, but it was most wonderfully comfortable and homelike. The Commissioner was a great gardener, my room was a bower of roses, and there were books, the newest books and magazines, everywhere. I should like to have stayed a month at Sunyani. Think of it! everything had to be carried eighty miles on men's heads, through a dense forest, across all manner of watercourses, where the white ant refused to allow a bridge to remain more than a fortnight, and yet one felt in the midst of civilisation. They told me I was brave to come there, but where was the hardship? none, none. It was all delightful. But there *was* another side. Close to the European bungalows was a little fort to which the men might retire in case of danger. They did not seem to think that they would ever be likely to require it, but there it was, and I, who had seen the old-time forts along the Coast, looked at this one with interest. It had a ditch round it, and walls of mud, and these were further strengthened by pointed stakes, bound together with barbed wire. An unpleasant place for a naked man to rush would be the little fort at Sunyani. Close against its wall so as to shelter the office, and yet outside so as not to embarrass the people, is the post and telegraph office, and so fast is civilisation coming to that outpost, that they take there for stamps, telegrams, and postal orders something like fourteen pounds a week.

I wandered round seeing everything, from the company of Waffs, exercising in the morning, to the hospital compound where the wives of the dresser and the wives of the patients were busily engaged in making fu-fu. For this is a primitive place, and here are no nursing Sisters and European comforts, and I must say the patients seem to do very well without them.

And only ten years ago, here and behind at Odumase, was the centre of the great rebellion against the white man's power; but things are moving, moving quickly. Only a week before I went up Messrs Swanzy had opened, with a black agent in charge, a store in the native town, and the day I arrived the agent brought his takings to the Commissioner for safe keeping in the treasury within the fort. It was such a tiny place, that store, simply a corrugated-iron shack, wherein were sold cotton cloths, odds and ends of cheap fancy goods, such as might be supposed to take the eye of the native, and possibly a little gin. Everything had to come on men's heads, so the wares were restricted, but the agent was well pleased with his enterprise, for that first week he had taken over £150, and this from a people who were utterly unaccustomed to buying.

BUTCHERS' SHOPS, NKWANTA.

"Things are changing, things are changing fast," said the Commissioner, and then he laughed and said that what bothered him most was the advance the suffrage movement was making. It wasn't yet militant, but he didn't know how it was going to end. The women had actually arrived at some idea of their own value to the community, and refused to marry the men their fathers had provided, if they did not happen to meet with their approval. Again and again a Chief would come to the Commissioner—a girl had declined to marry the man chosen for her, her father had appealed to the Chief, and the young lady, relying on the support of the British Government, had defied them both.

"If this woman do not marry the man I tell her to, then am I as mud in the sight of my people!" the Chief would say, flinging out protesting hands, and the Commissioner was very often as puzzled as he was.

On one occasion he came down to his court to find sitting there a good-looking girl of about seventeen, with a baby on her back. She waited patiently all through the sitting of the court, and then, when he had time to give attention to her, explained herself. She had a complaint to make. The King, or head Chief, had married her. Now the Commissioner was puzzled to know why this already much-married man had burdened himself with a wife who manifestly did not want him, and why the lady objected to a regal alliance. The King was brief and to the point. He considered himself a much injured man. The girl's parents had betrothed her to a man in her childhood, and when she grew up she did not like him, and preferring someone else, had declined to marry him. The King had been appealed to, but still she defied them, so, willy-nilly, to prevent further trouble, he had married her himself.

How that case ended I do not know. But I asked one question: "Whose is the baby?" And the baby it appeared was child to the man whom her parents and the King had rejected, so that Nature had settled the matter for them all. Whoever had her there was no getting over that baby.

Sunyani is one of the great halting places for the Hausas and Wangaras who come down from Wenchi, so on the French border and here I was introduced into great compounds, where the men who bring down cattle and horses and other goods from the north take up their abode, and rest before they start on their wearisome journey through the forest to Kumasi. I had come through in five days, but these men generally take very much longer. The Hausa carries tremendously heavy loads, so heavy that he cannot by himself lift it to his head, and therefore he always carries a forked stick, and resting his load on this, rests it also in the fork of a tree, and so slips out from underneath it. Again and again on our way up had we come across men thus resting their heavy loads. He must walk warily too, for they say so heavy is the load that the Hausa who stubs his toe breaks his neck. Slowly he goes, for time as yet is of no consequence in West Africa. A certain sum he expects to make, and whether he takes three months or six months to make it is as yet a matter of small moment to the black man, apparently, whatever his race.

MOULDING IN CHIEF OF NKWANTA'S HOUSE

After I had been all round Sunyani, and dined at the mess, and inspected the fort and the hospital, they arranged for me to go to Odumase, five miles away.

Odumase is on the extreme northern border of Ashanti, and in fact the inhabitants are not Ashanti at all, calling themselves after their own town, but it was here that the rising that overwhelmed Kumasi in 1900-1 was engineered and had its birth. Here, as a beginning, they took sixty unfortunate Krepi traders, bound them to a tree, and did them slowly to death with all manner of tortures, cutting a finger off one day, a toe the next, an arm perhaps the next, and leaving the unfortunate victims to suffer by the insects and the sun. And here, when they had taken him, they brought back the instigator of that rebellion, and showed him captive to his own people. He was no coward, whatever his sins, and he stood forth and exhorted his people to rescue him, reviling the white men, and spitting upon them. But his people were awed by the white man's troops, and they let him be taken down to Kumasi, where he was tried, and hanged, not for fighting against the British raj, but for cold-blooded murder.

So to Odumase Mr Fell took me, explaining that because I was the first white woman to go there, the people would greet me in Ashanti fashion, and I was not to be afraid.

It was well he explained. Long before we could see the town, running along the forest path came the Ashanti warriors to meet me, and they came with yells and shouts, firing off their long Danes, so that presently I could see nothing but grey smoke, and I could hear nothing much either for the yells and shouts, and blowing of horns, and beating of tom-toms. It is just as well to explain an Ashanti welcome, else it is apt to be terrifying, for had I not been told I certainly should never have realised that a lot of guns pointing at me from every conceivable angle and spouting fire and smoke, were emblems of goodwill. But they were; and then I was introduced to the chiefs, and took their photographs. And now I have an awful confession to make. I have taken so many Ashanti chiefs that I do not know t'other from which. They were all clad in the most gorgeous silken robes, woven in the country, in them all the colours of the rainbow, and they were all profusely decorated with golden ornaments. They had great rings like stars and catfish on their fingers, they had all manner of gold ornaments on their heads, round their necks, round their arms, and on their legs, and they had many symbolical staffs with gold heads carried round them. Always, of course, they sat under a great umbrella, and their attendants too wore gold ornaments. Some of the latter were known as their souls, and the Chiefs soul wore on his breast a great plate of gold. What his duties are now I do not know, I think he is King's messenger, but in the old times, which are about ten years back, his duties were more onerous. He was beloved of the Chief, and lived a luxurious life, but he could not survive his Chief. When his master died, his sun was set, and he was either killed or buried alive with him. Moreover, if the Chief had an unpleasant message to a neighbouring chief, he sent his soul to carry it, and if that chief did not like the message, and desired war, he promptly slew the messenger, put his jaw-bone in a cleft stick and sent it back. Altogether the Chiefs soul was by no means sure of a happy life, and on the whole I think must infinitely prefer the *pax Britannica*.

It takes a little time though before peace is appreciated. The last time Mr Fell had been to Nkwanta, the big town I had passed through, he found the place swimming in blood, and many stools reeking in it. It was only sheep's blood luckily, for Nkwanta had quarrelled with a sub-chief, and this was celebrating his reconciliation.

"If the white man not be here," said Nkwanta through his interpreter, "plenty men go die to-day."

"Oh, sheep are just as good," said the Provincial Commissioner.

"Well perhaps," said Nkwanta, but there was no ring of conviction in his tones.

Odumase the white men almost razed to the ground as punishment for the part it took in the great rebellion, but it is fast going up again. Many houses are built, ugly and after the white man's fashion, and many more houses are building. We passed one old man diligently making swish, that is kneading earth and water into sort of rough bricks for the walls, and I promptly took a photograph of him, for it seemed to me rather remarkable to see him working when all the rest of the place was looking at the white woman. And then I saw an old woman with shaven head and no ornaments whatever; she was thin and worn, and I was sorry for her. "No one cares for old women here," I thought, I believe mistakenly, so I called her over and bestowed on her the munificent dole of threepence. She took my hand in both hers and bowed herself almost to the ground in gratitude or thanks, and I felt that comfortable glow that comes over us when we have done a good action.

I was a fool. There are no poor in West Africa, and she was quite as great a lady as I was, only more courteous. As I left Odumase she came forward with a small girl beside her, and from that girl's head she took a large platter of most magnificent plantains, ripe and ready for eating, which she with deep obeisance laid at my feet. If I could give presents so could she, and she did it with much more dignity. Still, I flatter myself she *did* like that threepenny bit

I was very very loath to leave Sunyani. It was a place on the very outskirts of the Empire, and the highest civilisation and barbarism mingled. It must be lonely of course, intensely lonely at times, but it must be at the same time most interesting to carve a province out of a wilderness, to make roads and arrange for a trade that is growing.

They are wonderfully enthusiastic all the Commissioners in Ashanti, and when I praise German methods, I always want to exempt Ashanti, for here all the Commissioners, following in the footsteps of their Chief, seem to work together, and work with love. In the very country where roadmaking seems the most difficult, roadmaking goes on. The Commissioner at Sunyani had sent to the King of Warn telling him he wanted three hundred men to make a road to the Tano River, and the King of Warn sent word, "Certainly"; he was sending a thousand, and I left the Commissioner wondering what on earth he was to do for tools. So is civilisation coming to Ashanti, not by a great upheaval or desperate change, but by their own methods, and the wise men who rule over them, rule by means of their own chiefs. I have no words strong enough to express my admiration for those Ashanti Commissioners and the men I met there in the forest. We differed only, I think, on the subject of treefelling, and possibly had I had opportunity to learn more about things, I might have found excuses even for that.

THE MEDICAL OFFICER CROSSES THE LANO RIVER.

The rainy season was upon us, and it was time for me to go back. The medical officer, who had just been relieved, was coming down with me, and this medical officer was very sick with a poisoned hand. It was my last trek in the bush, and I should have liked to linger, but the thought of that bad hand made me go faster, for I would not keep him from help longer than I could help. So we retraced our steps exactly, doing in four days what I had taken five to do on the way up, and this was the more remarkable because now it rained. It rained heavens hard, and the little streams that our men had carried us through quite easily on the way up, were now great, rushing rivers that sometimes we negotiated with a canoe, and sometimes laboriously got over with the aid of a log. It really is no joke crossing a flooded African stream on a slimy log. I took a picture of one, with the patient Wangara crossing. Then my men carried me in my hammock to the log, and with some little difficulty I got out of that hammock on to it. I had to scramble to my feet, and the man beside me made me understand that I had better not fall over, as on the other side the water was deep enough to drown me. I walked very gingerly, because the water beneath looked unpleasantly muddy, up that tree-trunk, scrambled somehow round the root and down the other branch, till at last I got into water shallow enough to allow of my being transferred to my hammock and carried to dry land, there to sit and watch my goods and chattels coming across the same way. I felt a wretch too, for it had taken close on twenty men, more or less, to get me across without injury, and yet here were a company of Wangaras or Hausas, and the patient women had loads on their heads and babies on their backs. No one worried about them.

For perhaps the first time in my life I was more than content with that station in life into which it had pleased my God to call me. I do not think I could wish my worst enemy a harder fate than to be a Wangara woman on trek, unless perhaps I was extra bitter, and wished him to taste life as an African fowl. That must be truly a cruel existence. He scratches for a living, and every man's hand is against him. I used to feel sometimes as if I were aiding and abetting, for I received on this journey so many dashes of fowls that neither I nor the medical officer could possibly eat them all, and so our servants came in for them. More than once I have come across Grant sitting resting by the roadside with a couple of unfortunate fowls tied to his toes. In Grant's position I should have been anything but happy, but he did not seem to mind, and as I never saw the procession *en route*, I was left in doubt as to whether he carried them, or insisted on their walking after him. I saw that he had rice for them, and told him to give them water, but I dare say he did not trouble.

A BREAK IN THE FOREST BEYOND THE TANO RIVER.

The last night out, my last night in the bush I fear me for many a long day, we stopped at a village called Fu-fu, and I went to the rest-house, which was built European fashion, and was on the edge of the forest, at some distance from the village.

I found my men putting up my bed in a room where all the air came through rather a small hole in the mud wall, and I objected.

"Where?" said my patient headman, who after nearly a fortnight had failed to fathom the white woman's vagaries.

There was a verandah facing the town and a verandah facing the forest, and I promptly chose the bush side as lending itself more to privacy. Very vehemently that headman protested.

"It no be fit, Ma, it no be fit. Bush close too much"; so at length I gave in, and had the bed put up on the verandah facing the town. On the other end, I decided, the medical officer and I would chop. For we had been most friendly coming down, and had had all our meals together.

Before dinner I think the whole of the women of that village had been to see me, and had eaten up the very last of my biscuits, but I did not mind, for was it not the end of the journey, and they were so interested, and so smiling, and so nice. We had dinner, and we burned up the last of the whisky to make a flare over the plum-pudding; and then the medical officer wished me good night and wended his way to his house somewhere in the town, Grant and the cook betook themselves to another hut nearer the town and barricaded the door, and then suddenly I realised that I was entirely alone on the edge of this vast, mysterious, unexplainable forest. And the headman had said "the bush no be fit." I ought to have remembered Anum Mount and Potsikrom, but I didn't. I crept into bed and once more gave myself up to the most unreasoning terror. What I expected to come out of that forest I do not know. What I should have done had anything come I'm sure I do not know, but never again do I want to spend such a night. The patter of the rain on the iron roof made me shiver, the sighing of the wind in the branches sent fingers clutching at my heart; when I dropped into a doze I waked in deadly terror, my hands and face were clammy with sweat, and I dozed and waked, and dozed and waked, till, when the dawn came breaking through the clouds at last, it seemed as if the night had stretched itself into an interminable length. And yet nothing had happened; there had been nothing to be afraid of, not even a leopard had cried, but so tired was I with my own terrors that I slept in my hammock most of the way into Kumasi.

And here my trip practically ended. I stayed a day or two longer, wandering round this great, new trading-centre, and then I took train to Sekondi, stayed once more with my kind friend, Miss Oram, the nursing Sister there, gathered together my goods and chattels, and on a day when it was raining as if never again could the sun shine, I went down in the transport officer's hammock for the last time; for the last time went through the surf, and reached the deck of the *Dakar*, bound for England.

OFFICIAL BUNGALOWS, SUNYANI.

CHAPTER XXV
THE LAND OF OPPORTUNITIES

The enormous wealth of West Africa—The waste—The need of some settled scheme—Competitive examination for the West-African Civil Service—The men who come after the pioneers—One industry set against another—The climate—The need of women—The dark peoples we govern—The isolation of the cultivated black man—The missionaries—The Roman Catholics—The Basel missionaries—West Africa the country of raw material—An answer to the question, "What shall I do with my son?"—The fascination of Africa.

And so I have visited 'the land I had dreamed about as a little child in far-away Australia. But no, I have never been to that land. It is a wonderful country that lies with the long, long thoughts of childhood, with the desires of youth, with the hopes that are in the heart of the bride when she draws the curtain on her marriage morning. Beautiful hopes, beautiful desires, never to be fulfilled. We know, as we grow older, that some of our longings will never be granted exactly in the way we have expected them to be granted, but that does not mean that good things will not come to us, though not in the guise in which we have looked for them. Therefore, though I have never visited Carlo's country, and never can visit it, still I have seen a very goodly land, a land flowing with milk and honey, a land worthy of a high place in the possessions of any nation, and yet, I think, a land that has been grievously misjudged.

Why does no one speak of the enormous wealth of West Africa? When America was but a faint dream of the adventurous voyager, when Australia was not on the maps, the west coast of Africa was exploited by the nations growing in civilisation for her wealth of gold, and slaves, and ivory, and the wealth that was there in those long-ago days is there to-day. There is gold as of yore, gold for the working; slaves, but we recognise the rights of man now and use them only as cheap labour; and there is surely raw material and vegetable products that should bring food and wealth to the struggling millions of the older world. The African peasant is passing rich on threepence a day, and within reach of his hand grow rubber and palm oil, groundnuts and cotton, cocoa and hemp, and cocoa-nuts and all manner of tropical fruits. These things, I know, appertain to other lands, but here they are simply flung out with a tropical lavishness, and till this century I doubt if they have been counted of any particular value. If the English colonies of West Africa were cultivated by men with knowledge and patience, bringing to the work but a fiftieth of the thought and attention that is given to such matters in France, the return would be simply amazing. I have seen 25 per cent, of an ignorant peasant community's cocoa harvest wasted because there were no roads; I have seen cocoa-nut plantations useless, "because the place isn't suitable," when in all probability some parasite was killing the palms. I have seen lives and money lost in a futile endeavour to teach the native to grow cotton, when the climate and conditions cried out that cocoa was the proper product to be encouraged.

THE FORT, SUNYANI.

What the portion of West Africa I know well wants is to be worked on some settled scheme, a scheme made by some far-seeing mind that shall embrace, not the conditions of five years hence, but of fifty years hence; the man who works there should be laying the foundations of a plan that shall come to fruition in the time of our children's children, that should be still in sound working order in their grandchildren's time. The wheat of the Canadian harvest-field may bring riches in a year, the wool of Australia's plains wealth in two or three, but the trees of the African forest have taken hundreds of years to their growth, and, when they are grown, are like no other trees in the world. With them none may compare. So may these tropical dependencies of England be when rightly used, they shall come to their full growth. But we must remember they are tropical dependencies. The ordinary Englishman, it seems to me, is apt to expect to gather apples from a cocoa-nut palm, potatoes from a groundnut vine, and to rail because he cannot find those apples and potatoes. He will never find them, and the man who expects them is the man in the wrong place.

I hope some day soon to find there is a competitive examination for positions in the West-African Civil Service. Does any man grumble who has won a place in the Indian Civil Service? I think not. A competitive examination may not be the ideal way of choosing your political staff, but as yet we have evolved none better. The man who passes high in a competitive examination must at least have the qualities of industry and self-denial, and who will deny that these are good qualities to bring to the governing of a subject people?

It is curious to watch English methods of colonisation, and whether we will or no we must sit in judgment upon them. The first men who go out are sometimes good, sometimes bad, but all have this saving grace—that strong spirit of adventure, that dash and go which made England a colonising nation and mistress of the seas. It would be like asking a great cricketer to play tiddly-winks to ask one of the men who fought for Ashanti to take part in a competitive examination. They have competed and passed in a far sterner school. But the men who follow in the footsteps of the pioneers are sometimes made of different stuff. They are often the restless, discontented ones of the nation, men who complain of the land they leave, complain of the land they come to, find no good in West Africa, seek for no good, exaggerate its drawbacks, are glad to regard themselves as martyrs and to give the country an evil name. Such men, I think, a competitive examination would weed out.

There must be continuity of service. That is a foregone conclusion. At present England thinks so little of the land that is hers that she puts a man in a place but for a year, and the political officer has no chance of learning the conditions and needs of the people over whom he rules; he is a rolling stone perpetually moving on. Then it is the height of folly to set one industry against another. All should surely, in a new country, be worked for the common good. For instance, there is a railway running between Kumasi and Sekondi, a Government railway, and behind Kumasi lies a vast extent of country unexplored and unexploited, with hardly a road in it. One would have thought that it would simply be wisdom and for the good of the whole community that the railway which is Government property should be used for the opening up of the country behind. Such is the plan in Canada; such is the practice in Australia. But in West Africa Government holds different views. Ashanti wants to build a road to the Northern Territories, a road such as the Germans have made all over Togo, but Government, instead of using the railway to further that project, charge such exorbitant freight on the road material, that the road-making has come to a standstill. It is typical of the country. Each department is pitted against the other, instead of one and all working for the good of the whole. The great mind that shall be at liberty to plan, that I fear sometimes lest the Germans and French have found, has yet to come.

WOMEN MAKING FU-FU.

There are many prejudices to break down, and first and foremost is the prejudice against the climate. Now I am not going to say that West Africa is a health resort, though I went there ill and came away in the rudest health. Still I do recognise that a tropical climate is hard for a European, more especially, perhaps, for people of these northern isles, to dwell in. A man cannot afford to burn the candle at both ends there, and if he would keep well he must of necessity live in all soberness and temperance. He does not always do that, but at present, whatever his illness is due to, it is always set down to the climate, and he is always sure of a full measure of pity.

Once I stayed for a short time next to a hospital, and the Europeans in the little town were much exercised because that hospital was so full. At last it occurred to me to ask what was the matter with the patients. I was not told what was the matter with them, but I found that the only one for whom anyone had much pity was the gentleman who had D.T. But even the worst of them you may be sure would have full measure of pity in England. "Poor fellow, that awful climate!"

Doctors tell me fever is rife, and I feel they must know more about it than I do, but it has been discovered in England that a life in the open air is an almost certain preventive of phthisis, and I cannot help thinking that *a sane and sober life in the open air day and night* would be a more certain preventive against fever than all the quinine and mosquito-proof rooms that were ever dreamt of. Observe, I say, a sane and sober life; and a sane and sober life means most emphatically that a man does not rush at his work and live habitually at high pressure. For this is a temptation that the better-class of man is peculiarly liable to in West Africa. "Let us succeed, let us get on, and let us get home"; and who, in the present conditions, can blame him for such sentiments. They are such as do any man credit, but they very often, in a hot climate more especially, spell destruction as surely as the wild dissipation of the reckless man who does not care. And there is only one cure for that— the cure the French and Germans are providing. The women must be encouraged to go out. Every woman who goes and stays makes it easier for the woman who follows in her footsteps, and I can see no reason why a woman should not stand the climate of West Africa as well as she does that of India. Women are the crying need; quiet, brave, sensible women who are not daunted because the black cook spoils the soup, or the black laundryman ruins the tablecloth, who will take an intelligent view of life, and will make what is so much needed—a home for their husbands. I know there are men who say that Africa is no place for a woman. I have met them again and again. Some of those men I respected very much; some I put in quite another category. The first evidently regarded a wife as a precious plaything, not as a creature who was helpmeet and friend, whose greatest joy must be to keep her marriage vows and share her husband's life for good or ill, whose life must of necessity be incomplete unless she were allowed to keep those marriage vows. The other sort, I am afraid, like the freedom that the absence of white women gives them, a freedom that is certainly not for the ultimate welfare of a colony, for the mingling of the European and the daughter of Ham should be unthinkable. It is good for neither people.

And here we come to the great difficulty of a tropical dependency, the question that as yet is unanswered and unanswerable. What of the dark peoples we govern? They are a peasant people with a peasant people's faults and a peasant people's charm, but what of their future? The native untouched by the white man has a dignity and a charm that there is no denying; it seems a great pity he cannot be kept in that condition. The man on the first rung of civilisation has points about him, and on the whole one cannot help liking him, but the man who has gathered the rudiments of an education, as presented to men in an English school on the Coast, is, to my mind, about as disagreeable a specimen of humanity as it is possible to meet anywhere. He has lost the charming courtesy of the untutored savage, and replaced it by a horrible veneer of civilisation that is blatant and pompous; and it is only because I have met such men as Dr Blyden and Mr Olympia that I am prepared to admit that education can do something beyond spoiling a good thing. Between black and white there is that great, unbridgeable gulf fixed, and no man may cross it. The black men who attain to the higher plane are as yet so few and scattered that each must lead a life of utter intolerable loneliness, men centuries before their time, men burdened with knowledge like Galileo, men who must suffer like Galileo, for none may understand them, and the white man stands and must stand—it is inevitable—too far off even for sympathy.

All honour to those men who go before the pioneers; but for them, as far as we can see, is only bitterness.

The curious thing is that most people who have visited West Africa or any other tropical dependency will recognise these facts, and yet England continues to pour into Africa a continuous stream of missionaries. Why? For years Christianity has been taught on the Coast, and it is now a well-recognised fact that on the Coast dishonesty and vice are to be found, while the man from the interior is at least honest, healthy, and free from vice. I am not saying that religion as taught by the missionary has taught vice, but I am declaring emphatically that it has failed to keep the negro from it. Why encourage missionaries? As civilisation advances the native must be taught. Very well, let him pay for his own teaching, he will value it a great deal more; or, since the merchants want clerks and the white rulers want artisans, let them pay for the native to be taught. But very, very strongly do I feel, when I look at the comfortable, well-fed native of West Africa and the wastrel of the English streets, that the English who subscribe to missions are taking the bread from the children's table and throwing it to the dogs.

CHIEF OF ODUMASE.

Hundreds and thousands of people are ready to give to missions, but I am very sure not a fraction of them have the very faintest conception of what they are giving to. Their idea is that they are giving to the poor heathen who are sunk in the deepest misery. Now there is not in all the length and breadth of Africa, I will venture to swear, one-quarter of the unutterable misery and vice you may see any day in the streets of London or any great city of the British Isles. There is not a tribe that has not its own system of morals and sees that they are carried out; there is not the possibility of a man, woman, or child dying of starvation in all West Africa while there is any food among the community. Can we say that of any town in England? What then are we trying to teach the native? Christianity. But surely a man's god is only such as his mind can appreciate; a high-class mind has a high-class god, a kindly mind a kindly god, and an evil mind an evil god. No matter whether we call that god Christ, or by any other name, he will have the attributes the mind that conceives him gives him; wherefore why worry?

Of course I know that a large number of people feel that religion comes from without and not from within, and a larger number still say as long as a mission is industrial it is a good thing, and to both of these I can only point out the streets and alleys and tenement houses of the towns of England. It seems to me the most appalling presumption on the part of any nation with such ghastly festering sores at its own heart to try and impose on any other people a code of morals, a system of ethics, a religion, if you will, until its own body is sweet and clean. An industrial mission is doubtless a good thing, but until there are no men clamouring for the post of sandwich-men in London, no women catering to a shameful traffic in Piccadilly, I think we should keep the money for our industrial missions at home.

Let us look the thing straight in the face. They talk of human sacrifices. Are there no human sacrifices in our own midst? We lie if we say there are none. Every day we who pride ourselves upon having been a Christian nation for the last thousand years condemn little children to a life of utter hopelessness, to a life the very thought of which, in connection with our own children, would make us hide our faces in shuddering horror. So if any man is appealed to to give to missions, I would have him look round and see that everyone in his immediate neighbourhood is beyond the need of help, that there are no ghastly creatures at his own gate that the heathen he is trying to convert would scorn to have at his side. Believe me, if Christianity is to justify itself there is not yet one crumb to spare from the children's table for the dogs that lie outside.

For the individual missionary I have—in many cases, I must have—a great respect. The trouble to my mind is that Christianity presented in so many guises must be a little confusing to the heathen. There are the Roman Catholics. They are pawns in the great game played by Rome; no individual counts. They have given themselves to the missionary service to teach the heathen, and they stay until they die or until they are too sick to be of further use in the land. Of course they are helpful, any life that is oblivious of self and is utterly devoted to others must needs be helpful, and they have my deepest respect, because never, never have I been called upon to sympathise with a Roman Catholic father or sister. They have given their lives, no man can do more, and all I can say is, I would prefer they gave it to the civilising of the submerged folks of their own nations than to civilising the black man.

ASHANTI WARRIORS.

Then at the other end of the social scale are the Basel Missions. They combine business and religion very satisfactorily in a thoroughly efficient German spirit, and while the missionaries attend to the souls of the heathen and set up schools to teach them not only to read and write, but various useful trades as well, the Basel Mission Factories do a tremendous trade in all the necessaries of life. These Basel missionaries are most kindly, worthy people, and to their kindness I owe much. Occasionally I have come across a man of wide reading and with clever, observant eyes, but as a rule they are chosen from the lower middle classes among the Swiss and Germans; very often the missionary spirit runs in the families, and it passes on from father to son, from mother to daughter. These people, too, come out if not for life, like the Roman Catholics, at least for long periods of years. It is generally believed on the Coast, and I have never heard it contradicted, that when a man attains a certain standing he is allowed to marry, even though he is not due for a holiday in Europe. They have at headquarters photographs of all the eligible maidens in training for the mission field, and the candidate for matrimony may choose his wife, and she is duly forwarded to him, for the heads of the Basel Missions, like me, believe in matrimony for Africa. And most excellent wives do these Basel missionary women make. They bear their children here in West Africa where no English woman thinks she can stay more than six months, and their homes are truly homes in the best sense of the word. If example is good for the heathen, then he has it in the Basel Missions. Another thing, they must make the most excellent nucleus for German interests, for no one who has been in a Basel Mission Station or Factory can but respect these men and women and little children who make a home and a garden in the wilderness. And what I have said about the Basel Missions applies to the Bremen Missions, except that these are more pronouncedly German. But better women may I never hope to meet in this wide world than those in the Bremen Missions. And in between these two extremes are missionaries of every class and description. Against the individuals I have nothing to say, save and except this—I want to discount the admiration given to the "poor missionary." They are good men I doubt not, but they are earning a living just as I who write am earning a living, or you who read, and to my mind they are earning a living in the halo of sanctity very much more comfortably than the struggling doctor or the poor curate in an East-End parish. Whatever their troubles, they have never the bitterness of seeing the ghastly want that they cannot relieve, and if they do not live in England, they have always the joy of making a home in a new country, and that is a joy that those who talk so glibly about exile do not seem to realise.

MAKING SWISH, ODUMASE.

"But we must have the negroes taught reading and writing and trades," said a man to me once when we were discussing the missionary question; and I agree it is necessary, but I do not see why I am to regard the teacher as on a higher plane than he who teaches the same in England. And as for the religion that is taught, the only comment I have to make upon it is that no man that ever I heard of would take a mission boy or a Christian for a servant when he could get a decent heathen. Finally, considering the amount of destitution and terrible want in the streets of England, if I had my way I would put a heavy tax on all money contributed for the conversion of the heathen. Before it was allowed to go out of the country I would if I could take heavy toll, and with that toll give the luckless children of my own colour a start in life in the Colonies.

Finally, West Africa is the country of raw material. It should be England's duty so to work that country that it be complementary to England, the great manufacturing land. The peasant of the Gold Coast burning the bush to make his cocoa plantations is absolutely necessary to the girl fixing the labels on the finished product; her very livelihood depends upon him. The nearer these two are brought together in a commercial sense the better for both, and what we say of cocoa we may say of palm oil and groundnuts and other vegetable fats, of rubber, of hemp, of gold, of tin. This country which produces with tropical luxuriance should be, if properly worked, a source of immense wealth to the nation that possesses it.

And as we rise in the social scale, think of the openings this country, thickly populated, well cultivated, flourishing, would offer for the young men of the middle classes seeking a career. A political service like the Civil Service of India, officered by men who have won places there by strenuous work and high endeavour, who are proud of the positions they have won, and a busy mercantile community, serving side by side with these political officers, would go some way to answering the question on the lips of the middle-class father, "What shall I do with my son?" The work of women is widening every day, and I, who honestly believe that an ordinary woman may go where an ordinary man can, may with profit take up work even as a man may do, see scope for the women of the future there too, not only as wives and helpmeets to the men, but as heads of independent enterprises of their own.

I have finished my book, ended the task that I have set myself to do, and I hope I have been able to convey to my readers some of the fascination that Africa has always held for those who have once visited her shores. But hitherto it has been the fascination of the mistress, never of the wife. She held out no lure, for she was no courtesan. A man came to her in his eager youth asking, praying that she would give him that which should make all life good; and she trusted and opened her arms. What she had to give she gave freely, generously; there was no stint, no lack. And he took. Her charm he counted as a matter of course, her tenderness was his due, her passion was for his pleasure; but the fascination he barely admitted could not keep him. Though she had given all she had no rights, and when other desires called he left her, left her with words of pity that were an injury, of regret that were an insult.

CROSSING THE OFIN RIVER IN FLOOD.

But all this is changing. Africa holds. The man who has once known Africa longs for her. In the sordid city streets he remembers the might and loneliness of her forests, by the rippling brook he remembers the wide rivers rushing tumultuous to the sea, in the night when the rain is on the roof plashing drearily he remembers the gorgeous tropical nights, the sky of velvet far away, the stars like points of gold, the warm moonlight that with its deeper shadows made a fairer world. Even the languor and the heat he longs for, the white foam of the surf on the yellow sand of the beaches, the thick jungle growth densely matted, rankly luxuriant, pulsating with the irrepressible life of the Tropics. All other places are tame. The fascination that he has denied comes back calling to him in after years. Thus "the whirligig of time brings in his revenges." This mistress he will have none of has spoiled him for all else. And here the analogy fails. Africa holds, and the man whom she holds may yield to the fascination not only without shame, but with pride. Before her lies a great future; to the man who knows how to use her gifts she offers wealth and prosperity. To be won easily? Well, no. These gifts lie there as certainly as there is a sky above us, as that the sun will rise to-morrow, but there lie difficulties in the way, obstacles to be overcome. Africa offers the opportunities—success is for the

"One who never turned his back but marched breast forward,

Never doubted clouds would break,

Never dreamed though right were worsted wrong would

triumph,

Held we fall to rise, are baffled to fight better,

Sleep to wake.

Now at noonday in the bustle of man's work-time

Greet the unseen with a cheer!

Bid him forward, breast and back as either should be,

'Strive and thrive!' cry 'Speed—fight on—'"
